CONTENTS

Introduction   *v*

Exam preparation and technique   *vi*

Sample answer sheet   *viii*

PRACTICE PAPERS

Practice Paper 1   1

Practice Paper 2   33

Practice Paper 3   63

Practice Paper 4   95

Practice Paper 5   127

ANSWERS AND TEACHING NOTES

Practice Paper 1   161

Practice Paper 2   176

Practice Paper 3   190

Practice Paper 4   205

Practice Paper 5   221

Index   *238*

ACKNOWLEDGEMENTS

PasTest would like to thank the BMJ Publishing Group for their kind permission to reproduce extracts from the following articles:

'Randomised Controlled trial of specialist nurse intervention in heart failure.' *British Medical Journal* 2001; 323:715–718

'An observational study comparing quality of care in walk-in centres with general practice and NHS direct using standardised patients.' *British Medical Journal* 2002;324:1556–1559

'Randomised trial of acupuncture compared with conventional massage and "sham" laser acupuncture for treatment of chronic neck pain.' *British Medical Journal* 2001; 322:1574

'Antidepressant drugs and generic counselling for treatment of major depression in primary care: randomised trial with patient preference arm.' *British Medical Journal* 2001;322:772

'Reliability of N-terminal pro-brain natriuretic peptide assay in diagnosis of heart failure: cohort study in representative and high risk community populations' *British Medical Journal* 2002;321:1498–1453

'Excess mortality in a population with diabetes and the impact of material deprivation: longitudinal, population based study.' *British Medical Journal* 2001;1389–1393

PasTest would also like to thank the British Journal of General Practice for their kind permission to reproduce extracts from the following articles:

'A pilot study of pulmonary rehabilitation in primary care.' *British Journal of General Practice* 2002;52:567–568

'Blood Pressure control in treated hypertensive patients: clinical performance of general practitioners.' *British Journal of General Practice* 2001;51:9–14

MRCGP
PRACTICE PAPERS
THIRD EDITION

Edited and Compiled by

Peter Ellis
MA MMedEd MRCGP

Medical and Educational Advisor, London
Previously General Practitioner, Trainer,
Course Organiser and Examiner
Royal College of General Practitioners

Robert Daniels
MA MRCGP

General Practitioner, Townsend House Medical Centre
Seaton, Devon

PASTEST
Dedicated to your success

© 2003 PasTest Ltd
Egerton Court
Parkgate Estate
Knutsford, Cheshire
Telephone: 01565 752 000

Third edition 2003
Reprinted 2004

ISBN 1 901198 66 9

A catalogue record for this book is available from the British Library.

The information contained within this book was obtained by the authors from reliable sources. However, while every effort has been made to ensure its accuracy, no responsibility for loss, damage or injury occasioned to any person acting or refraining from action as a result of information contained herein can be accepted by the publisher or the authors.

PasTest Revision Books and Intensive Courses

PasTest has been established in the field of postgraduate medical education since 1972, providing revision books and intensive study courses for doctors preparing for their professional examinations. Books and courses are available for the following specialties:

MRCGP, MRCP Part 1 and Part 2, MRCPCH Part 1 and Part 2, MRCS, MRCOG, DRCOG, MRCPsych, DCH, FRCA and PLAB

For further details contact:

PasTest, Freepost, Knutsford, Cheshire WA16 7BR
Tel: 01565 752 000   Fax: 01565 650 264
Email: enquiries@pastest.co.uk   Web site: www. pastest.co.uk

Typeset by Saxon Graphics Ltd, Derby
Printed and bound in Europe by The Alden Group
Photographs: Nigel A Stollery GP Kibworth, Leicestershire and Clinical Assistant in Dermatology, Leicester Royal Infirmary

INTRODUCTION

The membership examination of the Royal College of General Practitioners is a constantly changing process, and in the past it has contained Multiple Choice Question papers, Modified Essay Question papers, Traditional Essay Questions and Practice Topic Questions.

The MRCGP Examination is now a modular examination consisting of four modules.

1. Paper 1 (Written Paper) – the examiner-marked paper
2. Paper 2 (Multiple Choice Paper) – the machine-marked paper
3. An assessment of consulting skills
4. Oral examination

To be successful in the MRCGP examination candidates must pass all four modules. There is a credit accumulation system and the modules can be taken together or at different sessions and can be taken in any order. This book is about the machine-marked written paper or Paper 2 which is available twice a year.

The machine-marked paper is designed to test knowledge and application of that knowledge by candidates. The paper may contain Extended Matching Questions (EMQ), Single Best Answer Questions (SBA), Multiple Best Answer Questions (MBA) and Summary Completion Questions. The paper lasts for three hours, and the usual number of items is about 180–200. All answers are recorded by candidates on sheets which can be machine-marked.

There is no negative marking for any of the question types in the machine-marked written Module. There is therefore no point in leaving a question blank. It pays to guess! Questions are machine-scored on a basis of +1 mark for a correct answer to an item and 0 for a wrong or missed response.

This book contains 5 practice papers. The items are laid out in the same format as the MRCGP examination. We have, however, added check boxes alongside each item to facilitate a system of self-assessment for those who wish to evaluate their knowledge upon completion of each practice paper.

I wish to express great thanks to PasTest for their help with the production of this book.

Peter Ellis, 2002

EXAM PREPARATION AND TECHNIQUE

In trying to pass any examination it helps to plan an effective revision programme that concentrates on the elements that are being examined and not the areas which the exam cannot or does not test.

There are certain basic principles which are relevant to each part of the MRCGP exam.

- **Read relevant literature**
  Remember that this is an examination of British general practice. You will gain far more from reading a book about General Practice than from reading about a specific subject in a textbook.

- **Ask yourself WHY?**
  The exam asks you to appraise critically what you are doing. After every consultation ask yourself about the outcome: did you feel happy about it, do you think the patient was satisfied with your management? If not, why not, and how could you have managed the situation better? After every article you read, ask yourself why the article was written, whether it was relevant, what the main points were that the author was trying to get across, and were there better ways of achieving the same result. Be critical in a constructive way about your work and your reading.

- **Form an alliance with other candidates**
  By meeting on a regular basis you can stimulate one another to be more critical. You can also divide the onerous task of ploughing through journals between the group and become very much more knowledgeable very quickly. Finally, by talking to colleagues you will retain more factual knowledge and also be able to clarify your ideas and opinions more clearly.

There are also specific techniques that will help you to prepare for the machine-marked paper. You can improve your score in machine-marked examinations by doing tests. Candidates who do not improve their scores are using practice papers in the wrong way. What normally happens is that a candidate will spend a lot of time reading textbooks and then do a practice examination. It is far better to do an examination first, and then spend a lot of time reading around the answers and extending your knowledge in this way. Even with good teaching notes you still need to read around the topic.

There are only a limited number of areas relevant to general practice on which machine-marked questions can be set. By doing a number of practice examinations in this way you can substantially increase your knowledge base and thus increase your overall score.

ON EXAMINATION DAY

By the time the day of the examination arrives you will certainly have invested a good deal of money, and probably a lot of time and effort in the exam. It is important that you do not let yourself down by making silly mistakes. Again there are certain basic rules for approaching each part of the MRCGP Examination.

- **Do not be tired**
  This may sound simple but if you have nights on call in the three to four days before the examination, then swap them. Try to keep your workload to a minimum. If you arrive tired you will not cope well with several hours of written work.

- **Arrive in time**
  Every year, for both the written and oral examinations, candidates under-estimate the time it will take them to get to the examination venue. They arrive distressed and anxious and under these circumstances can never do themselves justice.

- **Key into the task**
  By arriving in plenty of time, you have the chance to prepare mentally for the examination. Reading a current journal quietly just before going into the exam will start your brain thinking about general practice and current issues. When you sit down to start working on the papers you will already be in the right frame of mind and this will save you valuable time.

- **Read the instructions**
  No matter how well you think you know the rules, always read the instructions at the beginning. There should be no major, unexpected changes from previous years, but just in case there are, this is time well spent.

The majority of candidates will not be short of time in the machine-marked paper, but the following special techniques should help.

- Read the whole paper before you answer anything. This allows a lot of sub-conscious recall to happen before you start to mark your answers.
- Read every word in the stem and in each item. It is very easy to make simple mistakes by thinking that you read something that was not actually there.
- Mark the answer sheet carefully. Do not get the answer responses out of sequence. If you do have to alter a response rub it out well and mark the new response clearly. The answer sheets are marked by machine and an inadequately rubbed out answer could be interpreted as your true response.
- Answer every item. Remember there is NO negative marking and thus marks may be gained by guessing.

Finally, enjoy your study and enjoy using this book. Good luck with the Examination!

Royal College of General Practitioners

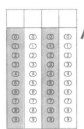

A

Name:

- Use pencil only • Make heavy marks that fill the lozenge completely
- Write your four-digit candidate number in the top row of the box to the right **AND** fill in the appropriate lozenge below each number
- Give **ONE** answer only for each question unless otherwise directed on your question paper

Design number 80301/A

Practice Paper 1

Total time allowed is three hours. Indicate your answers clearly by putting a tick or cross in the box alongside each answer or by writing the appropriate letter alongside the appropriate answer.

1 Which THREE of the following are criteria to be fulfilled in a screening programme?
- ☐ **A**   The condition must be important
- ☐ **B**   Clinical examination is not necessary
- ☐ **C**   Treatment at all stages of the disease is possible
- ☐ **D**   There is a recognisable latent or early symptomatic stage
- ☐ **E**   There must be an agreed policy on who should be screened and treated

2 A 45-year-old man presents with hearing loss. Which ONE of the following would support a diagnosis of it being noise-induced?
- ☐ **A**   A conductive deafness
- ☐ **B**   Predominantly low frequency loss
- ☐ **C**   Recruitment
- ☐ **D**   No response to a hearing aid
- ☐ **E**   Acute onset of hearing loss in one ear

SUMMARY COMPLETION QUESTION
First read the extract from the paper 'A pilot study of pulmonary rehabilitation in primary care.' BJGP 2002;52:567–568.

Methods

Patients suffering from COPD were identified by the practice doctors and nurses. Entry criteria included: history of cigarette smoking, significant disability from breathlessness, and spirometry showing FEV_1 (forced expiratory volume in one second) less than 60% of expected on more than one occasion. Patients requiring oxygen during exercise were excluded, as were those with pulse oximetry showing desaturation at rest ($SaO_2 < 90\%$).

A series of seven group meetings for between seven and nine patients were held at a community health clinic, at weekly intervals. Each session consisted of one hour of exercise and one hour on education, separated by a tea break. The rehabilitation team included a general practitioner, respiratory nurse, health visitor, counsellor and a physiotherapist.

The exercise programme consisted of group work – warm up, exercise, then relaxation, with a daily exercise routine to be done at home, based mainly on walking. Education focused on:

- the causes, effects and treatment of COPD, smoking cessation (doctor and respiratory nurse);
- emotional aspects of respiratory disability and thinking positively about the future (counsellor); and

- importance of diet and healthy lifestyle, benefits and carer support (health visitor).

Assessments included the shuttle-walking test[5] and questionnaires: the Chronic Respiratory Disease Questionnaire[6] (CRDQ), the Hospital Anxiety and Depression Score (HADS), and the Short Breathing Problems Questionnaire (SBPQ). Assessments were made before and after rehabilitation and at three, six and 12 months thereafter. Follow-up group meetings were held every one to two months, providing a social function and maintaining motivation for exercise and independence.

Results
Approximately 30 patients were identified who met the entry criteria. Fourteen patients were recruited, one left the area, the remaining 13 completed the programme and the 12-month follow-up. The main reasons given by invited patients for not taking part were: co-morbidity, intercurrent illness, other commitments and, in one case, anxiety. There were eight women and six men, age range = 50 to 81 years. The mean FEV_1 was 1.05 litres, range = 0.7 to 1.9, the mean FEV_1 % of expected value was 43.4%, range = 24% to 63%, indicating a severity of airflow obstruction comparable to those seen in hospital rehabilitation programmes.

The programme was well received by patients and staff. A questionnaire indicated a high level of satisfaction at the end of rehabilitation, all patients rating the overall programme as good or very good. Patients were very enthusiastic: 'This is the highlight of my week, it is so depressing being told there is nothing that can be done. This programme has shown me different and most of it I can do for myself'. There was a mean 50-metre improvement in shuttle-walking test after the programme, an increase of 37% (95% confidence interval [CI] = 0 to 74), but this returned to baseline over the next 12 months. Sustained improvements were found in health status measures. The CRDQ showed marked improvements: the mean total score rose by 20 points (an increase of 47% [95% CI = 16 to 78]), the minimum clinically important difference is 11 points. The mean HADS also improved: anxiety by 7% (95% CI = −32 to 18); depression by 13% (95% CI = −36 to 11) and the SBPQ fell by 10% (95% CI =−30 to 9).

The costs of running the programme were estimated at £1410 (£113.07 per completed patient), set-up costs including equipment and training were £1391.35. Total rehabilitation costs were £220.10 per patient. Analysis of use of primary and secondary care services and drug prescribing was performed for 12 months before and 12 months after rehabilitation. No important differences were found, although there was reduction in GP visits after the programme (13 before and two after).

Now read the critique below.
The authors of this study attempted to show that the success of generic pulmonary rehabilitation services in secondary care could be transferred to a primary care setting. They designed a package of care and piloted it in

general practice. This methodology allows us to gauge
(3)_____ whether the programme is acceptable to patients,
and whether it is effective, but does not allow us to assess
(4)_____ efficacy, since there is no control group.

While the results seem at first reading to be fairly promising, there are in
some respects more questions than answers. Is the intervention
(5)_____ effective in COPD or does it work better in some
patients than others? Chronic obstructive pulmonary disease encompasses
many **(6)**_____ clinical presentations and there is much
variability between patients. In particular patients may be divided into
(7)_____ responders and non-responders, and those with
an element of bronchial reversibility. Clearly these patients are likely to
respond in different ways and these may confound the outcomes.

The intervention involved a package of care, and this multidisciplinary
approach introduces multiple **(8)**_____; attention from
physiotherapists and supervised exercise every two months with exercises at
home would be expected to bring improvements in walking in anyone,
regardless of comorbidity. Seeing a GP in a **(9)**_____ rather
than a **(10)**_____ clinical setting may have focused
attention on otherwise neglected areas of management, such as use of
steroids or bronchodilators, which may have had a
(11)_____ influence on many of the outcomes tested.

The data supporting the cost-effectiveness are questionable. The
intervention involved running two courses of seven two-hour sessions. The
costs are estimated at a total of £1410 to run the programme and £1301.35
in training and equipment. The cost in terms of GP time alone could
conservatively be estimated at £1260, based on an hourly locum rate of £45.
The costs for the respiratory nurse, health visitor, counsellor and
physiotherapist would be expected to at least double this.

To summarise, this pilot study suggests that the benefits of secondary care
pulmonary rehabilitation may well be transferable to primary care. However,
before committing resources to this at the expense of other facets of
respiratory care, further studies should be undertaken to determine
comparative **(12)**_____ with usual care and between
different patient subgroups.

*From the following list, select the most appropriate response for each of the
numbered gaps in the critique.*

A   beta 2 antagonist
B   bias
C   comparative
D   confounders
E   deleterious
F   dichotomous
G   efficacy
H   efficiency

I heterogeneous
J homogenous
K independent
L negative
M positive
N primary
O proactive
P qualitatively
Q quantitatively
R reactive
S steroid
T universally

13 A practice leaflet must include which ONE of the following items of information in order to comply with the 1990 contract?

☐ **A** The age or date of birth of the doctors
☐ **B** The date of first registration of the practice nurse
☐ **C** The fees the practice charges for reports and certificates
☐ **D** Whether the practice is computerised
☐ **E** The means by which disabled patients may gain access to the building

THEME: LITERATURE

The following books and papers have been written concerning general practice:

A *What Sort of Doctor?* by a working party of the RCGP
B *The Exceptional Potential in Each Primary Care Consultation* by Stott and Davis
C *Doctors Talking to Patients* by Byrne and Long
D *The Doctor, his Patient and the Illness* by Michael Balint
E *The Inner Consultation* by Roger Neighbour
F *The Consultation: An Approach to Learning and Teaching* by Pendleton et al.

Match the statements below to the most appropriate book or paper listed above

14 Coined the phrase 'doctor as a drug ' to show the therapeutic effect of doctors as people themselves ☐

15 Suggested that a sharing style can address patients' ideas about their illness so they will be satisfied and comply with treatment ☐

16 Discussed housekeeping, meaning dealing with feelings left by one consultation ☐

17 Looked at doctors' accessibility and premises ☐

18 A study of audio-taped consultations ☐

19 Noted differing consultation styles varying from 'doctor-centred' to 'patient-centred' ☐

20 A patient presents at 32 weeks' gestation with a primary attack of genital herpes. Which ONE of the following statements is true?
- ☐ **A** Transplacental spread of the virus is rare
- ☐ **B** Cyclovir orally has been shown to be teratogenic
- ☐ **C** If herpes lesions are present at the onset of labour, caesarean section is indicated
- ☐ **D** Pregnant women are more resistant to herpes than non-pregnant women
- ☐ **E** Recurrent herpes carries the same risk to the fetus as a primary infection

21 Select TWO statements about phimosis in childhood:
- ☐ **A** By 6 months of age approximately 50% of boys have a retractable foreskin
- ☐ **B** Circumcision is associated with a higher complication rate than other childhood operative procedures
- ☐ **C** The inability to clean under the foreskin is associated with the development of cancer of the penis in adulthood
- ☐ **D** If untreated has been shown to lead to problems with sexual function in later life

22 A 14-year-old girl presents with symptoms of an eating disorder. Which ONE of the following would support that diagnosis?
- ☐ **A** Loss of pubic hair
- ☐ **B** Primary amenorrhoea
- ☐ **C** Raised LH levels
- ☐ **D** Raised ESR
- ☐ **E** Low cortisol levels

23 Select TWO statements concerning the epidemiology of chronic bronchitis:
- ☐ **A** Northern Ireland has the highest mortality rate for chronic bronchitis in the world
- ☐ **B** Less than 15% of males between 40–60 years have been shown to have evidence of chronic bronchitis
- ☐ **C** Chronic bronchitis accounts for more lost time from work than any other illness
- ☐ **D** The disease is more prevalent in rural than in urban areas

24 A child attends for the third time with a five week history of cough without malaise which has not responded to symptomatic remedies. Select the best statement about its situation:
- ☐ **A**   Chest X-ray is essential
- ☐ **B**   A trial of bronchodilators is indicated
- ☐ **C**   This is a typical presentation of pertussis
- ☐ **D**   Inhaled foreign bodies present in this way
- ☐ **E**   A trial of antibiotics is indicated

25 Select TWO statements about tinnitus:
- ☐ **A**   It is typically associated with conductive deafness
- ☐ **B**   It is associated with gout
- ☐ **C**   It has been shown to be due to a carotid bruit in some cases
- ☐ **D**   Treatment of associated depression is rarely helpful
- ☐ **E**   Cochlear nerve section is associated with a worsening of the noise

THEME: HYPERTENSION

Important hypertension trials include:
A   MRC Mild Hypertension Trial
B   European Working Party on Hypertension in the Elderly
C   Veterans Administration Co-operative Study
D   Hypertension Detection and Follow-up Program, USA
E   Systolic Hypertension in Elderly Program (SHEP) Co-operative Group
F   Australian National Board Hypertension Study

Match the following statements to the appropriate study:

26   Double-blind trial using hydrochlorothiazide, triamterene and placebo; only 840 patients recruited   ☐

27   Low-dose diuretics, beta blockers and reserpine   ☐

28   Double-blind trial in a group of people who were selected for compliance with a treatment regime   ☐

29   Single-blind trial between bendrofluazide, propranolol and placebo; showed 1 CVA saved per 850 patient treatment years   ☐

30   Used bendrofluazide in doses much larger than now used; those doses may exacerbate other risk factors   ☐

31 In research about shiftworkers, which ONE of the following has been shown?

☐ **A**   The majority of shiftworkers dislike nightwork

☐ **B**   They have an increased incidence of industrial accidents

☐ **C**   They have an increased cardiovascular mortality

☐ **D**   They have an increased incidence of peptic ulceration

☐ **E**   There is an increase in feelings of paranoia

32 Which ONE of these statements describes questionnaire design?

☐ **A**   Open and closed questions are best not combined in one questionnaire

☐ **B**   If a questionnaire is valid, then patients generally give the same answers if they complete it a second time

☐ **C**   Comprehensibility indicates that almost all areas in a subject have been addressed

☐ **D**   A Likert scale is often used to assess attitudes

☐ **E**   Open questions are easy to analyse

33 Select ONE statement about subarachnoid haemorrhage in the over 65-year-old patient:

☐ **A**   Only accounts for approximately 5% of all cases

☐ **B**   Is typically due to a ruptured atherosclerotic blood vessel

☐ **C**   Characteristically presents with headache

☐ **D**   Has a decreased mortality in comparison with younger patients

☐ **E**   Has a worse prognosis in hypertensive patients

34 A 1-year-old boy presents with an episode of unconsciousness during an episode of crying. Which ONE of the following would not support a diagnosis of breath-holding attack?

☐ **A**   Recovery within one minute

☐ **B**   Upturned eyes during the attack

☐ **C**   Drowsiness after the attack

☐ **D**   Extended tonic posture during the attack

☐ **E**   Cyanosis

35 A 45-year-old male presents with a history of long term alcohol abuse. Which TWO of the following would be true if he had alcoholic cirrhosis?

☐ **A**   Absence of jaundice excludes the diagnosis

☐ **B**   Spider naevi are rare

☐ **C**   Pain over the liver is a frequent finding

☐ **D**   Testicular atrophy is common

☐ **E**   Prognosis is unaffected by cessation of alcohol once cirrhosis has developed

36 Which ONE of the following statements is not true about jaundiced patients?
- ☐ **A** Non-A-non-B hepatitis can be transmitted by drinking contaminated water
- ☐ **B** Hepatitis B is associated with the development of hepatocellular carcinoma
- ☐ **C** Acute cholangitis carries a mortality rate of about 40%
- ☐ **D** Hepatitis A typically produces a carrier state following the acute infection

37 Select ONE item about dithranol:
- ☐ **A** Is indicated for rapidly spreading psoriatic lesions
- ☐ **B** In prolonged usage is associated with an increase in the incidence of skin malignancies
- ☐ **C** 'Short contact' therapy has been shown to be less effective than conventional treatment
- ☐ **D** Is contraindicated if potent steroids have been used in the previous 14 days

38 A patient with Alzheimer's disease is recognised to have which THREE of the following signs and symptoms?
- ☐ **A** A preference for routine
- ☐ **B** A loss of long term memory
- ☐ **C** A loss of speech in the later stages
- ☐ **D** Spatial disorientation
- ☐ **E** Ataxia

39 You see a 22-year-old man in surgery who has just been discharged from hospital having suffered a spontaneous pneumothorax. Which ONE of the following statements is true?
- ☐ **A** Spontaneous pneumothorax is a rare condition
- ☐ **B** Patients who have suffered a spontaneous pneumothorax should not fly
- ☐ **C** The commonest cause of spontaneous pneumothorax is lung biopsy
- ☐ **D** The recurrence rate is 1:4 after a single episode
- ☐ **E** Is most common in middle-aged women

40 Mr Jones, a 45-year-old sales rep, comes to see you for the results of recent blood tests taken when he was feeling tired. The only abnormality is in the liver function tests:

Albumin	42	(32–45)
Total Bilirubin	45	(5–17)
ALT	25	(<35)
Alk Phos	75	(25–100)
GGT	16	(<50)

Which of the following is the SINGLE most likely diagnosis?
- ☐ **A** Alcoholic cirrhosis
- ☐ **B** Gallstones
- ☐ **C** Hepatitis
- ☐ **D** Gilbert's syndrome
- ☐ **E** Acute pancreatitis

41 Which THREE of the following are true of hyperthyroidism?
☐ **A** The majority of cases are due to Graves' disease
☐ **B** Toxic multinodular goitre is accompanied by raised TSH levels
☐ **C** Block-replacement regimes are the treatment of choice for toxic adenomata
☐ **D** Graves' ophthalmopathy is more prevalent in smokers
☐ **E** Post-partum thyroiditis typically has a thyrotoxic phase followed by a hypothyroid phase

THEME: DERMATOLOGY

The following words are commonly used in the description of skin conditions:
A Crust
B Scale
C Macule
D Vesicle
E Papule
F Nodule
G Bullae
H Pustule
I Urticaria

Match the descriptions below with ONE of these words

42 A blister filled with blood-stained fluid ☐

43 A skin bleb filled with clear fluid ☐

44 A lump set deeply in the skin ☐

45 A raised spot on the skin surface ☐

46 A flat spot differing in colour from surrounding skin ☐

47 Horny cells loosened from the skin surface ☐

48 Select TWO of the following comments about basal cell carcinoma:
☐ **A** It is the most common skin malignancy
☐ **B** It occurs at sites of maximum skin exposure
☐ **C** It typically starts as a small ulcer
☐ **D** Crusting of the lesion indicates another diagnosis
☐ **E** It is more common in those with freckles

49 Which TWO of the following treatments have been shown to be of benefit in the treatment of cyclical breast pain?
- ☐ **A** Pyridoxine
- ☐ **B** Diuretics
- ☐ **C** Tamoxifen
- ☐ **D** Gamolenic acid
- ☐ **E** Hormone replacement therapy

50 A 23-year-old patient presents with disturbed behaviour. Which TWO of the following are diagnostic of schizophrenia?
- ☐ **A** Paranoid delusions
- ☐ **B** Thoughts being inserted into the patient's mind
- ☐ **C** Voices in the third person commenting on the patient's actions
- ☐ **D** Visual hallucinations
- ☐ **E** Ideas of reference

THEME: DEPRESSION

Treatments used in depression include:
- **A** Amitriptyline
- **B** Carbamazepine
- **C** Lofepramine
- **D** Lithium
- **E** Phenelzine
- **F** Fluvoxamine

Match the appropriate treatment to the following statements

51 Patients are instructed not to eat cheese, pickled herring or broad bean pods ☐

52 Used in bipolar disease and epilepsy ☐

53 A selective serotonin re-uptake inhibitor ☐

54 A tricyclic drug with sedative properties ☐

55 Thyroid function should be monitored during treatment ☐

56 One of the less sedative tricyclic antidepressants ☐

57 Is usually given in a dose of 140 mg daily, in a split dose ☐

58 Select TWO statements concerning emergency contraception:

☐ **A** An intrauterine contraceptive device must be inserted within three days of coitus in order to be effective

☐ **B** Insertion of an intrauterine contraceptive device has been shown to be more effective than hormonal methods

☐ **C** Failed hormonal contraception is an indication for termination of pregnancy on the grounds of teratogenic risk

☐ **D** Established breast feeding is a contraindication to hormonal postcoital contraception

☐ **E** Surveys have shown that approximately 50% of women are unaware of postcoital methods of contraception

59 Select THREE statements concerning the literature about general practice consultations:

☐ **A** Balint looked at doctors' personalities

☐ **B** Pendleton suggests that the most important information is given as the patient is leaving

☐ **C** Neighbour describes 'safety-netting' to deal with feelings left over by one consultation before starting another

☐ **D** Patient satisfaction is improved by longer consultations

☐ **E** Eric Berne described 'doctor-centred' and 'patient-centred' consultations

☐ **F** Pendleton suggests a task of choosing appropriate action for each problem presented

60 Select TWO of the following statements concerning osteoarthritis:

☐ **A** It shows a familial tendency

☐ **B** It is more common in overweight people

☐ **C** The picture of radiological damage correlates closely with the clinical condition

☐ **D** If a diagnosis of early osteoarthritis is made, joint exercise should be severely restricted

☐ **E** It is most common in the hips

61 Select TWO statements about solvent abuse:

☐ **A** It is typically an activity of females rather than males

☐ **B** Deaths are associated with the presence of aerosol propellants (freons)

☐ **C** Persistent cerebellar signs are suggestive of prolonged use

☐ **D** Very few abusers will stop within six months of starting the habit

☐ **E** The occurrence of visual hallucinations would suggest other psychopathology

62 Which ONE of the following is not a risk factor for increased mortality in an elderly patient with a chest infection?

☐ **A** Co-existing atrial fibrillation

☐ **B** A very low white cell count

☐ **C** Hypotension

☐ **D** Recent influenza vaccine

☐ **E** Confusion

63 Select THREE statements of use when considering gastric and duodenal ulceration:

- ☐ **A** Night pain is more common with duodenal ulcers
- ☐ **B** A gastric ulcer is more likely to bleed
- ☐ **C** *Helicobacter pylori* is found in over 90% of patients with duodenal ulcer
- ☐ **D** A positive family history is common for both sites
- ☐ **E** A recent survey has shown that of patients over 40 years of age presenting with dyspepsia for the first time the majority will have a malignancy

64 Select THREE statements about carcinoma of the bladder:

- ☐ **A** Typically presents with haematuria
- ☐ **B** Incidence is increasing in women
- ☐ **C** Is associated with cigarette smoking
- ☐ **D** If superficial, the majority will not recur within five years if treated by cystodiathermy
- ☐ **E** Is associated with previous abuse of alcohol

65 Which TWO of the following features would suggest a cerebral infarct rather than a cerebral haemorrhage?

- ☐ **A** Bilateral extensor plantar responses
- ☐ **B** A previous transient ischaemic attack
- ☐ **C** Co-existing cardiac disease
- ☐ **D** Consciousness impaired hours after the onset of the event
- ☐ **E** Abrupt onset accompanied by vomiting

66 Which THREE of the following are at an increased risk of chronic open-angled glaucoma?

- ☐ **A** Extremely long-sighted patients
- ☐ **B** Diabetics
- ☐ **C** Relatives of patients with glaucoma
- ☐ **D** Patients over 65 years of age
- ☐ **E** Those with astigmatism

67 Select TWO of the following statements about General Practitioners:

- ☐ **A** They are not responsible for any errors made by their practice nurse
- ☐ **B** They are responsible for care of their patients on surgery premises
- ☐ **C** They are not obliged to order any drug (that does not appear on the black list) for the treatment of a patient on a NHS prescription form
- ☐ **D** They are responsible for errors made by a spouse when answering the telephone
- ☐ **E** They have complaints made against them most often because of failure to refer to hospital

68 A 25-year-old patient presents with a history of heavy periods. which THREE of the following statements are correct?

- ☐ **A**   Approximately half the patients who complain of heavy periods have a measurably normal menstrual loss
- ☐ **B**   Dysfunctional uterine bleeding is usually caused by fibroids
- ☐ **C**   Mefenamic acid reduces bleeding by an average of 25%
- ☐ **D**   Dilatation and curettage is indicated in all patients
- ☐ **E**   Endometrial ablation can be performed using laser treatment

69 A patient visiting this country from Australia is involved in a road traffic accident. Immediate and follow-up care is necessary. Which THREE of the following statements are true?

- ☐ **A**   Immediate and necessary care is provided by the NHS free of charge
- ☐ **B**   All follow-up care is private
- ☐ **C**   All prescriptions issued must be private
- ☐ **D**   Domiciliary nursing is provided on the same basis as to UK residents
- ☐ **E**   A fee can be charged for attending the patient at the road traffic accident

70 Constitutional delay in puberty is associated with which TWO of the following?

- ☐ **A**   Boys are more often affected than girls
- ☐ **B**   Bone age on X-ray examination corresponds to chronological age
- ☐ **C**   Gonadotrophins are typically raised
- ☐ **D**   A family history of delayed puberty or menarche

71 Select THREE of the following statements, appropriate when considering breast feeding:

- ☐ **A**   The duration of early feeds should be limited
- ☐ **B**   Both breasts must be used at each feed
- ☐ **C**   Poor positioning of the baby is the most common cause of nipple pain
- ☐ **D**   Terminating feeding prematurely from one breast will decrease the nutritional value of the feed
- ☐ **E**   Late onset sore nipples are typically due to thrush
- ☐ **F**   Breast feeding is associated with an increase in the incidence of breast cancer in later life

THEME: STUDIES

Studies of populations and diseases can be:
A   Descriptive
B   Clinical trial
C   Case-control
D   Correlation
E   Meta-analysis

Match the studies below to ONE of the above types of study

72   The use of thalidomide is compared between patients who have had abnormal babies and those who have had healthy babies

73   The occurrence of lung cancer in a group of patients is compared with smoking status in that group

74   The prevalence of ischaemic heart disease is studied in a population that is randomly assigned to receive antioxidants or an inert substance

75   A survey to determine the prevalence of migraine in a population

76   The results of several investigations of exposure to radiation and the risk of leukaemia are combined to reach a conclusion

77 **When considering statistical bias in a scientific paper, which TWO of the following statements are true?**
☐ A   Retrospective studies are generally less open to bias than prospective studies
☐ B   Subjective results are less prone to bias than objective studies
☐ C   Standardisation increases bias
☐ D   Stratified sampling causes more bias than random sampling
☐ E   Control groups are essential to decrease bias
☐ F   Random numbers are preferable to regular samples

78 **Which THREE of the following factors would suggest an increased risk of suicide in depressed patients?**
☐ A   Co-existing problems of alcohol abuse
☐ B   History of aggressive behaviour
☐ C   Co-existing chronic physical illness
☐ D   Living in a rural environment
☐ E   Married status

79 Select THREE of the following statements concerning patients with backache:
- ☐ **A** A specific diagnosis is usually possible
- ☐ **B** 10% of patients can be expected to have a recurrence of pain within the next 4 years
- ☐ **C** About 5 million days are lost from work each year because of back pain
- ☐ **D** About 1 in 5 of all new orthopaedic referrals from GPs are for patients with back pain
- ☐ **E** History and examination are more important than investigations in management decisions in back pain
- ☐ **F** About 90% of patients with mechanical back pain will recover within 6 weeks

80 An adult patient who is otherwise well complains of hair loss all over the scalp. Select THREE of the following as possible causes:
- ☐ **A** Iron deficiency
- ☐ **B** Scalp ringworm
- ☐ **C** Anticoagulant therapy
- ☐ **D** Alopecia areata
- ☐ **E** Trichotillomania

81 Concerning ectopic pregnancy, select TWO of the following statements:
- ☐ **A** The frequency is increasing in the UK
- ☐ **B** Ectopic pregnancies secrete lower levels of HCG (human chorionic gonadotrophin) than a corresponding uterine gestation
- ☐ **C** Ultrasound alone is diagnostic in the majority of cases
- ☐ **D** There is a positive association with the presence of an IUCD in the uterine cavity
- ☐ **E** The death rate is increasing in the UK

82 Select TWO of the following statements about pompholyx:
- ☐ **A** Is a contact dermatitis
- ☐ **B** Characteristically occurs on the soles of the feet and the palms of the hands
- ☐ **C** Is unresponsive to topical steroids
- ☐ **D** Is associated with atopic conditions
- ☐ **E** Is typically itchy

83 Select TWO statements about ovarian cancer:
- ☐ **A** It is more common in multiparous women
- ☐ **B** There is an increased incidence if a first degree relative has had the disease
- ☐ **C** The overall five-year survival is greater than 50%
- ☐ **D** The majority of patients present with abnormal vaginal bleeding
- ☐ **E** Protection afforded by the combined oral contraceptive is proportional to the duration of usage

84 Select TWO statements concerning faecal occult blood testing:
- ☐ **A** It fulfils Wilson's criteria for a screening test
- ☐ **B** In screening programmes the majority of positive stool samples are false positives
- ☐ **C** With a three-day test the sensitivity for colonic carcinoma is over 90%
- ☐ **D** The test is more sensitive for caecal tumours than for sigmoid tumours
- ☐ **E** Banana ingestion has been shown to cause false positives

85 Select TWO statements about diabetic retinopathy:
- ☐ **A** It typically starts in the peripheral retina
- ☐ **B** It is the most common cause of blindness in those under 65 years of age
- ☐ **C** It does not usually respond to laser treatment
- ☐ **D** Micro-aneurysms are a feature of background retinopathy
- ☐ **E** New vessel formation can occur on the conjunctiva

86 Select TWO statements about pseudomembranous colitis:
- ☐ **A** It is typically associated with previous antibiotic therapy
- ☐ **B** Yersinia is the most commonly isolated organism
- ☐ **C** Treatment with metronidazole has been shown to be effective
- ☐ **D** The passing of fresh blood in the stools is a characteristic feature
- ☐ **E** It is associated with an eosinophilia in the peripheral blood film

THEME: LIPID-LOWERING DRUGS

Lipid-lowering drugs include:
- **A** Cholestyramine
- **B** Simvastatin
- **C** Bezafibrate
- **D** Nicotinic acid
- **E** Clofibrate
- **F** Probucol

Match the statements below to ONE of these drugs

87 An HMG CoA reductase inhibitor ☐

88 There has been considerable experience of its use in children ☐

89 Predisposes to gallstones by increasing biliary cholesterol excretion ☐

90 Can cause sleep disturbance ☐

91 Can cause flushing which may be severe ☐

92 An anion exchange resin which acts by binding bile acids, preventing their reabsorption ☐

93 Select THREE statements regarding Dupuytren's contracture.
- ☐ **A** Is typically painful
- ☐ **B** Most commonly affects the ring finger
- ☐ **C** Is associated with epilepsy
- ☐ **D** Is typically seen in white men
- ☐ **E** Is characteristically unilateral

94 Select THREE risk factors which increase the likelihood of congenital dislocation of the hip:
- ☐ **A** Delivery by caesarean section
- ☐ **B** Being first born
- ☐ **C** Being male
- ☐ **D** Having a positive family history
- ☐ **E** The left hip

95 Select TWO statements about heartsink patients:
- ☐ **A** The majority are women
- ☐ **B** They typically present with a single problem
- ☐ **C** They have higher referral rates than the average population
- ☐ **D** The average General Practitioner is able to identify more than 50 such patients on his list
- ☐ **E** They have significantly more social problems than the average population

96 Select THREE items that are associated with sickle cell disease:
- ☐ **A** Priapism
- ☐ **B** Impaired fertility in women
- ☐ **C** An increased incidence of stroke
- ☐ **D** Gallstones in the majority of patients
- ☐ **E** An enlarged spleen after the first decade of life

97 Psoriatic arthropathy is associated with which ONE of the following features:
- ☐ **A** A preceding history of skin lesions in the majority of patients
- ☐ **B** Non-involvement of the distal interphalangeal joints
- ☐ **C** Subcutaneous nodules
- ☐ **D** The presence of eye lesions in the majority of patients
- ☐ **E** The development of some evidence of joint involvement in the majority of patients with psoriasis

THEME: INFECTIOUS DISEASES

Infectious diseases include:
A   Scarlet fever
B   Chickenpox
C   Measles
D   Rubella
E   Infectious mononucleosis

Match the appropriate disease to the following

98   Has an incubation period of 4–6 weeks

99   Has a very short incubation period, an interval of 1–2 days between disease onset and appearance of rash, but a long infectivity period

100   90% of adults are immune, but the disease can be serious in adults who smoke, and pregnant women in the first trimester and at delivery

101   Notifiable on clinical diagnosis; the rash is accompanied by conjunctivitis and fever

102   All pregnant women with suspected disease should be investigated serologically. Seronegative health staff are immunised

103   **Select THREE items about symptoms due to a carcinoma of the colon at the time of presentation:**
☐ A   Pain occurs in the majority of patients with a right-sided lesion
☐ B   A palpable mass is present in the majority of those with a lesion in the left colon
☐ C   Change in bowel habit is present with the majority of rectal lesions
☐ D   The majority of right-sided lesions bleed
☐ E   The majority of rectal lesions bleed

104   **Select THREE statements concerning the period after bereavement:**
☐ A   Grieving is abnormal if it lasts for more than 6 weeks
☐ B   Morbidity and mortality are raised for 2–3 years
☐ C   20% of widowers die within the first year of bereavement
☐ D   Women are affected by post-bereavement mortality more than men
☐ E   Shock and blunted emotion is commonly the initial reaction

105 Select TWO items about febrile convulsions:
- ☐ **A** Have a prevalence of 2–5%
- ☐ **B** Are typically associated with fevers due to bacterial infections
- ☐ **C** Post-ictally are typically associated with transient neurological deficits
- ☐ **D** In a 3-year-old child who fails to respond to 5 mg rectal diazepam, the dose cannot be repeated for one hour
- ☐ **E** Have a stronger family history than idiopathic epilepsy

106 Which ONE of the following is not true of lipid-lowering drugs?
- ☐ **A** Cholestyramine is allowed in pregnancy and breast feeding
- ☐ **B** Simvastatin is associated with sleep disturbance
- ☐ **C** The flushing induced by nicotinic acid is typically improved by low-dose aspirin
- ☐ **D** Regular monitoring of liver function tests is necessary on treatment with bezafibrate
- ☐ **E** None of the available agents is licensed for use in children

THEME: VISUAL LOSS

Causes of visual loss, presenting to General Practitioners, include:
- **A** Migraine
- **B** Central retinal vein occlusion
- **C** Senile macular degeneration
- **D** Optic neuritis
- **E** Retinal detachment
- **F** Vitreous haemorrhage

Choose the most appropriate of these causes for the following scenarios

107 A 55-year-old woman wakes with blurred vision and develops a visual loss over the next few hours; ophthalmoscopy shows extensive retinal haemorrhages throughout the fundus ☐

108 A 71-year-old retired publican develops a progressive loss of central vision with difficulty reading, but he has relatively preserved vision in the peripheral fields ☐

109 A 44-year-old laboratory technician, who is very myopic, develops a rapidly progressive visual loss in part of the visual field; she describes the progression of sight loss as 'like a curtain' across her visual field ☐

110 A 25-year-old housewife developed gradual loss of vision with mostly intact peripheral vision; the visual loss recovers but she mentions fairly intense eye pain which she describes as between her eye and her ear ☐

111 A 42-year-old doctor has a sudden loss of vision with nausea; she makes a complete recovery within hours but mentions visual distortion and headache before the vision was lost ☐

THEME: SOCIAL CLASS

The Registrar General has six divisions of social class

A   1
B   2
C   3N
D   3M
E   4
F   5

Which social class is appropriate for the following

112 A teacher ☐

113 A labourer ☐

114 A secretary ☐

115 An electrician ☐

116 One-third of the population is in this social class ☐

117 A junior hospital doctor ☐

118 Read the following statements regarding screening. Which THREE are correct?
☐ **A**   Screening for prostate cancer using PSA testing satisfies Wilson's criteria
☐ **B**   The positive predictive value of a test may be different in different populations
☐ **C**   Screening may cause significant psychological morbidity in healthy people
☐ **D**   Screening involves selecting patients for testing whom you believe may have the disease
☐ **E**   Screening for a specific condition need not be repeated if negative
☐ **F**   The condition being screened for must be an important public health problem

THEME: MENTAL HEALTH ACT

The following are some sections of the Mental Health Act 1983

A   Section 2
B   Section 3
C   Section 4
D   Section 7
E   Section 136

continues ...

Which section applies to the following situations?

119   Used for assessment of a patient for a maximum period of 28 days ☐

120   Used for compulsory treatment of a patient with an established diagnosis ☐

121   Used for a maximum period of six months ☐

122   Used in relation to guardianship ☐

123   Used only in an emergency ☐

124   Used by the police ☐

THEME: CHILD DEVELOPMENT

A   6 months
B   9 months
C   12 months
D   18 months
E   24 months

Children are seen at all ages in general practice. Certain skills are acquired by definite ages and there may be concern if these skills are not present. From the above list of ages, select the most appropriate age to indicate when the skills listed below will be acquired

125   The child can build a 3–4 cube tower ☐

126   The child can join 3 words making a simple sentence ☐

127   The child has developed definite person preference ☐

128   The child walks with one hand held ☐

129   The child says 10–12 words with meaning ☐

130   The child tolerates children playing alongside ☐

THEME: BENEFITS

Welfare benefits received by patients include:
A   Attendance Allowance
B   Severe Disablement Allowance
C   Disability Living Allowance
D   Incapacity Benefit
E   Industrial Injury Disablement Benefit
F   Exceptionally Severe Disablement Allowance

Match the following statements with the appropriate benefit

131   A benefit to someone now 65 years old who needs help washing and dressing and toileting during the day only

132   A tax-free, non-means tested benefit payable to people under the age of 65 years

133   A benefit payable to people who are 80% or more disabled and are incapable of any work

134   A benefit paid to people over 65 years of age who require personal care or supervision during both the day and the night

135   This benefit may be paid to people between 3 and 65 years of age who are unable to walk

THEME: PARAESTHESIA AND WEAKNESS

Paraesthesia and weakness in the lower limbs may be caused by:
A   Meralgia paraesthesiae
B   Lateral popliteal nerve lesion
C   Peripheral neuropathy
D   Lumbar disc lesion
E   Subacute combined degeneration of the cord F tabes dorsalis
F   Multiple sclerosis

Match the most appropriate diagnosis to the following clinical scenarios

136   A 39-year-old bricklayer notices numbness of the outer border of his
left foot with 'weakness' of his foot; examination reveals foot drop

137   A 42-year-old gardener complains of pain and pins and needles down
the back of his left thigh and the lateral aspect of his left leg and foot

138   A 58-year-old unemployed man complains of shooting, sudden pain in
his legs; he has an unsteady gait; at examination it is noted that his
pupils are not responsive to light

139   A 48-year-old teacher complains of tight bands around her limbs; at
examination she feels an 'electric shock' sensation down her legs when
her neck is flexed

140   A 49-year-old policewoman complains of tingling on the outside aspect
of her thigh; this can occur on sitting but seems worse on standing,
though it disappears when she lies down

141   A 54-year-old historian, who has little medical history other than a
gastrectomy in his twenties, presents with a numbness in his legs;
examination reveals a 'stocking' sensory loss with extensor plantar
responses.

142   **Select TWO of the following about the management of non-insulin-
dependent diabetes mellitus:**
☐   A   Metformin is associated with weight gain
☐   B   Sulphonylureas become less effective with time
☐   C   Tight blood sugar control is the goal of treatment in the elderly
☐   D   The majority of newly diagnosed patients will show clinical evidence of
retinopathy
☐   E   The diet for overweight patients should contain approximately half the
total calories as carbohydrate

143 Choose the TWO appropriate statements about the investigation of a patient for ischaemic heart disease:

☐ **A** ST segment changes on a resting ECG indicate myocardial ischaemia

☐ **B** On exercise, testing the degree of ST depression at a given workload is of diagnostic relevance

☐ **C** Exercise testing associated with a fall in blood pressure is of good prognostic significance

☐ **D** 24-hour ambulatory monitoring shows a ratio of painless to painful ischaemia of 4:1

☐ **E** Coronary angiography has significant morbidity in 5% of patients

THEME: DYSPEPSIA

Drugs used in patients with dyspepsia include:

A Omeprazole
B Ranitidine
C Misoprostol
D Magnesium trisilicate
E Aluminium hydroxide
F Cisapride
G Metoclopramide

Match the following statements to the most commonly responsible drug

144 Can cause diarrhoea ☐

145 Can cause post-menopausal bleeding ☐

146 Can cause constipation ☐

147 Can cause galactorrhoea and gynaecomastia ☐

148 Can cause confusional state ☐

149 Can be responsible for a photosensitivity reaction ☐

150 Which ONE of the following is not true about glue ear?

☐ **A** A peak incidence at approximately 7 years of age

☐ **B** An increased incidence of tympanosclerosis after grommet insertion

☐ **C** An increased incidence in winter and spring

☐ **D** An increased incidence in the children of smokers

☐ **E** Spontaneous resolution within 12 months in over 90% of children

THEME: NORMAL DISTRIBUTION

The words below relate to a set of values in a normal distribution:
A   Mode
B   Median
C   Standard deviation
D   Mean

Match the appropriate word to the descriptions below

151   The middle number when the values are all placed in arithmetical order ☐

152   The most frequently occurring value ☐

153   The square root of the variance ☐

154   A measure of the distribution of the values around the arithmetic
average ☐

**155   At her 8-week-check a new mother tells you that she does not wish her
daughter to have the DTP (diphtheria, pertussis and tetanus combined)
vaccine, since she had a severe reaction as a child and was told that any
future offspring would be at risk of a similar reaction. Which THREE of the
following are true contraindications to vaccination:**
☐ **A**   Family history of any adverse reactions following immunisation
☐ **B**   Eczema
☐ **C**   Stable neurological conditions such as cerebral palsy or Down's syndrome
☐ **D**   Treatment with inhaled or topical steroids
☐ **E**   Family history of convulsions
☐ **F**   Use of oral polio vaccine in immunosuppressed children
☐ **G**   Child's mother is pregnant
☐ **H**   The use of BCG in HIV positive children
☐ **I**   Patients who are within 6 months of a bone marrow transplant

THEME: SCREENING

A screening test carried out in a study in general practice on child development gave the following results:

	Screening test positive	Screening test negative
Problem present	74	23
Problem absent	25	258

Options available

A	74/99	D	23/281	G	258/281	J	23
B	74/97	E	25/283	H	258/283	K	25
C	23/97	F	25/283	I	74	L	258

Select the appropriate option

156 Positive predictive value

157 Negative predictive value

158 Specificity

159 Sensitivity

160 False negative

THEME: ANAEMIA

On a blood film, anaemia can be divided into three types:
A   Microcytic
B   Macrocytic
C   Normocytic

Match the conditions below with the appropriate type of anaemia

161 Thalassaemia

162 Chronic renal failure

163 Pernicious anaemia

164 Alcoholism

165 Menorrhagia in a pre-menopausal woman

166 Malignancy

THEME: LESIONS IN THE MOUTH

Lesions in the mouth can be due to a number of causes, including:
A   Lichen planus
B   Measles
C   Syphilis
D   Erythema multiforme
E   Hand, foot and mouth disease
F   Monilia
G   Behçet's disease

Match the following scenarios with the most appropriate cause

167   Erosive lesions are seen in the mouth. They have a hard base. A flat
papule, purplish in colour but with white streaks, is seen at the left wrist ☐

168   Ulcers are seen in the mouth looking like 'snail tracks', which are
painless ☐

169   Recurrent oral ulceration is accompanied by arthritis and iritis in a
22-year-old man ☐

170   Painful ulcers are seen in the mouth of a 23-year-old student. He
mentions a sore throat and recent spots on his buttocks ☐

171   Koplik's spots are diagnostic ☐

SUMMARY COMPLETION QUESTION

*First read the extract from the results section of the paper 'Randomised controlled trial
of specialist nurse intervention in heart failure' BMJ 2001;323:715–718.*

We screened 801 patients thought to have heart failure on admission. Of the
361 who were eligible for the study and survived to have echocardiography,
177 (49%) had left ventricular systolic dysfunction. Of these, 165 gave consent
and were randomised, 81 to the usual care group and 84 to the nurse
intervention group (fig 1). Table 1 shows their clinical characteristics.

Table 1. Clinical characteristics of patients randomised to usual care or nurse intervention. Values are numbers (percentages) unless stated otherwise

	Usual care (n=81)	Nurse intervention (n=84)
Mean (SD) age (years)	75.6 (7.9)	74.4 (8.6)
Male	41 (51)	54 (64)
Living alone	38 (47)	37 (44)
Social services required	28 (35)	28 (33)
Other medical problems:		
Angina	40 (49)	38 (45)
Past myocardial infarction	41 (51)	46 (55)
Diabetes mellitus	15 (19)	15 (18)
Chronic lung disease	18 (22)	23 (27)
Hypertension	42 (52)	36 (43)
Atrial fibrillation	24 (30)	29 (35)
Valve disease	12 (15)	15 (18)
Past admission for chronic heart failure	36 (44)	27 (32)
New York Heart Association class at admission:		
II	16 (20)	19 (23)
III	33 (42)	28 (34)
IV	30 (38)	36 (43)
Degree of left ventricular systolic dysfunction:		
Mild	10 (13)	18 (22)
Moderate	42 (53)	31 (38)
Severe	28 (35)	32 (40)
Renal function at admission:		
Median (interquartile range) plasma urea (mmol/l)	9.7 (6.5–13.9)	8.1 (6.0–10.3)
Median (interquartile range) plasma creatinine (µmol/l)	116 (90–168)	108 (84–132)
Mean (SD) blood pressure at discharge (mm Hg):		
Systolic	126.1 (21.4)	116.0 (19.5)
Diastolic	70.1 (12.0)	68.4 (10.2)

By discharge, more patients in the intervention group than the usual care group had started an angiotensin converting enzyme inhibitor and stopped a calcium channel blocker (table 2). Length of hospital stay (median, interquartile range) was shorter in the intervention group (median 8.0 (interquartile range 4–10) days v 9.0 (7–12) days in usual care group). The median (interquartile range) time until death or end of study was 365 (277–365) days in the usual care group and 365 (273–365) days in the intervention group.

Table 2. Drug treatment on admission and at hospital discharge in usual care and nurse intervention groups

	Usual care		Nurse intervention	
	Admission (n=81)	Discharge (n=74)	Admission (n=84)	Discharge (n=81)
No (%) taking drug				
Loop diuretic	55 (69)	68 (92)	53 (63)	76 (94)
Thiazide diuretic	5 (6)	4 (5)	8 (10)	5 (6)
ACE inhibitor	41 (51)	53 (72)	35 (42)	65 (80)
Digoxin	15 (19)	31 (42)	16 (19)	35 (43)
β-blocker	10 (12)	5 (7)	11 (13)	2 (2)
Oral or transdermal nitrate	22 (28)	26 (35)	19 (23)	21 (26)
Calcium channel blocker	22 (28)	17 (23)	15 (18)	8 (10)
Median (interquartile range) dose (mg):				
Furosemide (frusemide) equivalent*	80 (40–120)	80 (40–120)	80 (40–120)	80 (65–120)
Enalapril equivalent†	10 (10–20)	10 (10–20)	15 (10–20)	20 (6.3–20)
Digoxin	0.125 (0.125–0.1875)	0.125 (0.125–0.1875)	0.125 (0.125–0.1875)	0.125 (0.125–0.25)
Median (interquartile range) No of drugs	5 (3–7)	6 (4.8–8)	4 (3–6)	5 (4.7)

ACE=angiotensin converting enzyme.
*Based on patients taking loop diuretics.
†Based on patients taking angiotensin converting enzyme inhibitor. Data available for 35 of usual care group and 33 of intervention group at admission and for 45 and 60 respectively at discharge.

Table 3 summarises the clinical results. Death rates were similar in the two groups, with 31% and 30% dying in the usual care and nurse intervention groups, respectively. For our primary end point (all cause death or admission with chronic heart failure) fewer patients had events in the nurse intervention group than in the usual care group (31 v 43; hazard ratio = 0.61, 95% confidence interval 0.38 to 0.96). Figure 2 shows the Kaplan–Meier curve.

Death or readmission from all causes was reduced by 28% (0.72, 0.49 to 1.04) in the nurse intervention group compared with usual care (table 3). The risk of admission to hospital for worsening heart failure was reduced by 62% (0.38, 0.19 to 0.76) in the intervention group.

When we took the number of readmissions for each patient into account, the differences between the treatment groups were greater (table 3). The number of admissions/patient/month was 0.174 in the usual care group and 0.124 in the intervention group (rate ratio 0.71, 95% confidence interval 0.54 to 0.94) for all cause admissions; the corresponding rates for admission for heart failure were 0.069 and 0.027 (0.40, 0.23 to 0.71).

Table 3. Clinical events in usual care and nurse intervention groups

	Usual care (n = 81)	Nurse intervention (n = 84)	Effect of nurse intervention relative to usual care (95% CI)	P value
No (%) of deaths				
Before discharge	6 (7)	1 (1)	—	0.061
Total	25 (31)	25 (30)	0.93 (0.54 to 1.63)*	0.81
No (%) of patients readmitted				
All causes	49 (60)	47 (56)	0.80 (0.53 to 1.19)*	0.27
Worsening heart failure	26 (32)	12 (14)	0.38 (0.19 to 0.76)*	0.0044
No (%) of deaths or readmissions				
All causes	61 (75)	52 (62)	0.72 (0.49 to 1.04)*	0.075
Heart failure	43 (53)	31 (37)	0.61 (0.38 to 0.96)*	0.033
No of readmissions (No/patient/month)				
All causes	114 (0.174)	86 (0.124)	0.71 (0.54 to 0.94)†	0.018
Worsening heart failure	45 (0.069)	19 (0.027)	0.40 (0.23 to 0.71)†	0.0004
Mean (SD) No of days in hospital				
All causes	16.7 (24.1)	10.3 (19.0)	0.65 (0.40 to 1.06)‡	0.081
Worsening heart failure	7.46 (16.6)	3.43 (12.2)	0.60 (0.41 to 0.88)‡	0.0051

All causes refers to unplanned and planned admissions
* Hazard ratio
† Rate ratio
‡ Confidence interval for difference in mean $\log_e$ (duration of hospital stay +1) retransformed to a ratio scale

Now look at the following critique of the results.

The results suggest that a reasonable number of patients were (**172**)_____ to each group, with prior screening by echocardiography ruling out (**173**)_____ of patients who do not have heart failure, which may bias the results. Comparison of the patients randomised to each arm of the trial show that the (**174**)_____ group had a higher percentage of patients who had been previously admitted with heart failure. This may bias the results relating to the endpoint of readmission. The (**175**)_____ group however had more patients with grade IV failure and severe left ventricular dysfunction, which will bias the results against the intervention.

Table 3 shows that for numbers of deaths, the (**176**)_____ were wide and the p value was (**177**)_____ , suggesting (**178**)_____ statistical significance. The endpoint of readmission shows a (**179**)_____ effect for worsening heart failure but a (**180**)_____ effect for all cause admissions.

The numbers of readmissions were not significantly different between the groups, this could be because the reduced numbers of readmissions with worsening heart failure are offset by increased admissions with other causes e.g. side effects from anti-failure medication.

The wide confidence intervals throughout suggest that (**181**)_____ studies may narrow these giving significant results, although these may also show a lack of effect.

For each of the numbered gaps in the critique, choose one word from the following list which best completes the sentence.

A > 0.05
B <0.05
C allocated
D confidence intervals
E definite
F exclusion
G forest plot
H inclusion
I indefinite
J intervention
K lack of
L larger
M mean
N median
O values
P non-significant
Q randomised
R significant
S smaller
T usual care

Practice Paper 2

Total time allowed is three hours. Indicate your answers clearly by putting a tick or cross in the box alongside each answer or by writing the appropriate letter alongside the appropriate answer.

1 Arterial leg ulceration is associated with THREE of the following:
☐ **A** Pain
☐ **B** Pigmentation
☐ **C** Induration and oedema of the gaiter area
☐ **D** Typically sited on the foot
☐ **E** Punched out appearance

2 Which ONE of the following is not associated with the second trimester of pregnancy?
☐ **A** Cardiac output which is about 40% above the non-pregnant state
☐ **B** Enhanced absorption of dietary iron
☐ **C** Increased gastric acid secretion
☐ **D** Delay in gastric emptying
☐ **E** Increased introversion

SUMMARY COMPLETION QUESTION
First read the extract from 'An observational study comparing quality of care in walk-in centres with general practice and NHS Direct using standardised patients.' BMJ 2002;324:1556–1559.

Participants and methods

Recruitment of clinical sites
We approached sites in three geographical areas, in and around Bristol, Birmingham, and London. We invited general practices involved in research or teaching to participate, and we approached walk-in centres and NHS Direct sites on the basis of their geography. Twenty out of 25 (80%) walk-in centres, 11 out of 12 (92%) NHS Direct sites, and 24 out of 62 (39%) practices agreed to participate: we included the first 20 practices to respond.

Selection of clinical scenarios
We chose five clinical scenarios, largely to represent problems likely to be presented by patients to walk-in centres (box 2). The scenario on postcoital contraception was intended to assess management of a common, straightforward problem, the scenario on chest pain to assess ability to exclude a potentially serious diagnosis and reassure accordingly, and the scenario on sinusitis to assess issues around antibiotic prescribing. The scenario on headache was devised to assess ability to explore psychosocial issues, and the scenario on asthma to assess the history taking on drugs and awareness of the side effects of the drugs.

Box 1: Service models for the three primary care settings

Walk-in centres
These offer assessment, advice, and treatment for minor illness and injuries. Most consultations are with nurses who use care protocols and clinical assessment software. The average consultation length is 14 minutes.[1]

General practice
Most consultations are with doctors who do not routinely use care protocols. The average consultation length is 9 minutes.[2]

NHS Direct
This is a telephone advice service. Consultations are with nurses, who use clinical assessment software similar to that used in NHS walk-in centres. The average consultation length is 14 minutes.[3]

Box 2: Clinical scenarios portrayed by standardised patients

1 A 23-year-old woman requesting postcoital contraception
2 A 30-year-old man with musculoskeletal chest pain
3 A 35-year-old woman with symptoms of sinusitis suggesting a bacterial cause
4 A 27-year-old man with tension headache and underlying depression
5 A 30-year-old man with worsening asthma caused by over the counter ibuprofen

---

Derivation of assessment criteria
We assessed clinical care against prospectively determined standards. We constructed lists of essential criteria for the adequate management of each scenario by a stepwise procedure, based on the Delphi process.

Standardised patient consultations
Standardised patients are people trained to portray a clinical scenario for teaching or research purposes. Five role players, each portraying one scenario, worked in each locality. Each role player visited a particular walk-in centre or general practice once, but owing to the smaller number of sites for NHS Direct, contacted one NHS Direct site up to three times. Overall, 305 contacts were planned, 100 in walk-in centres, 100 in practices, and 105 with NHS

Direct. Consultations took place from July to September 2001. The accuracy of portrayal of standardised patients, the reliability of assessment by standardised patients, and the validity of standardised patients is given on bmj.com

Analysis
For each consultation we calculated a score representing the proportion of essential criteria fulfilled for all items and separately for the three subgroups of items (history taking, examination, and diagnosis, advice, and treatment). We calculated the means of the all item and subgroup scores for each of the three primary care settings, with 95% confidence intervals calculated with design weighted survey estimators. We then undertook estimation of differences between mean scores for the three settings by using multivariable regression models (see bmj.com).

Now look at the following critique of the study.
This study sets out to compare the 'quality of care' given by the three access points for primary care. This approach relies on the presentation of a problem being **(3)**_____ . It is unclear from the methodology what steps were taken to ensure **(4)**_____ .
Further potential sources of bias lie in the **(5)**_____
process. This was done by approaching practices involved in research or teaching. Clearly these may not be representative of mainstream general practice. Furthermore, the individuals being studied will know that they are being observed, which will influence behaviour, the
(6)_____ . A more rigorous approach would be an anonymous presentation to surgeries chosen randomly without prior warning. This would prevent practitioners altering their actions in the knowledge they are being observed.

Another potential source of bias is the clinical scenario used. Were these invented or based on real case histories? Theoretical histories may well be more clinically clear-cut than real life and thus more amenable to computer aided diagnosis, biasing the study towards the Walk-in Centre and NHS Direct. What steps were taken to ensure **(7)**_____ and consistency of presentation? Without this information, the results must be viewed as potentially biased.

What were the **(8)**_____ and how were they chosen? They may have been chosen to be more suitable for NHS direct or Walk-in centre e.g. not missing vital diagnoses, rather than giving a cure which would be the aim of a GP consultation. Not knowing the outcomes makes it difficult to assess the relevance and **(9)**_____ to mainstream general practice.

To summarise, the trial methodology as presented is potentially biased in the areas of **(10)**_____, **(11)**_____ and **(12)**_____ and as such the results need to be viewed with caution.

From the list below, select the answer which best fits the gaps in the critique.

A applicability
B bias
C consistency
D 'Coriolanus effect'
E endpoints
F 'Hawthorne effect'
G honesty
H intervention
I outcome
J planning
K randomisation
L recruitment
M recruitment
N standardised
O standardisation
P statistical
Q subjects
R type 2
S validity
T variance

13 Babies who are small for their gestational age are not at risk of which ONE of the following:

☐ A Intraventricular haemorrhage
☐ B Convulsions in later life
☐ C Remaining small
☐ D Learning difficulties
☐ E Diabetes in later life

14 In differentiating between migraine and tension headache, which TWO of the following would support a diagnosis of tension headache?

☐ A A hatband distribution of pain
☐ B Tender spots on the scalp during the headache
☐ C Flushing at the onset of the headache
☐ D A watery eye during the period of the headache
☐ E Facial pain occurring during an attack of headache

15 Select ONE statement about the Mental Health Act (England and Wales) 1983:

☐ A Section 3 is for a minimum period of 6 months
☐ B Section 4 requires one medical recommendation by a doctor who has seen the patient within 12 hours of application
☐ C Detention under sections 2, 3 and 4 must be in the interests of the patient's own health or safety
☐ D Section 3 is renewable
☐ E The Mental Health Act forms can only be completed in the patient's home or in hospital

16 Which ONE of the following is NOT a common cause of accidents in people over 65 years?

☐ **A** Falls
☐ **B** Poisoning
☐ **C** Road traffic accidents
☐ **D** Fire

THEME: SCREENING

The results of a screening test in general practice looking for asthma were as follows:

	Screening test positive	Screening test negative
Asthma present	221	49
Asthma not present	74	156

Options available

A	49/270	**B**	49/205
C	221/270	**D**	221/295
E	74/230	**F**	74/295
G	156/205	**H**	156/230
I	221	**J**	49
K	74	**L**	156

Select the appropriate option

17 Specificity ☐

18 Sensitivity ☐

19 Positive predictive value ☐

20 Negative predictive value ☐

21 False negative ☐

22 Which TWO of the following would suggest a diagnosis of non-ulcer dyspepsia?

☐ **A** Morning retching
☐ **B** Night pain
☐ **C** Antacid relief
☐ **D** Inconsistent relationship between symptoms and food ingestion

23 Lasers are not used for the treatment of which ONE of the following ophthalmological conditions?

- ☐ **A**   Amaurosis fugax
- ☐ **B**   Acute glaucoma
- ☐ **C**   Senile macular degeneration
- ☐ **D**   Diabetic background retinopathy
- ☐ **E**   Myopia

24 Pulmonary fibrosis does NOT result following administration of which ONE drug named below?

- ☐ **A**   Methotrexate
- ☐ **B**   Erythromycin
- ☐ **C**   Nitrofurantoin
- ☐ **D**   Amiodarone
- ☐ **E**   Busulphan

25 Which ONE of the following expenses is directly reimbursed by the FHSA?

- ☐ **A**   Rent on premises
- ☐ **B**   Repairs to premises
- ☐ **C**   Lighting and heating costs
- ☐ **D**   Dressings and drugs for use in the surgery
- ☐ **E**   Insurance premium on the surgery premises

26 When considering drug abuse which THREE of the following are true?

- ☐ **A**   The majority of opiate abusers will still be addicted 7 years after starting the habit
- ☐ **B**   Methadone liquid can be injected intravenously
- ☐ **C**   10–20% of opiate users will die from drug-related causes
- ☐ **D**   Cocaine abuse is associated with underprivileged groups in society
- ☐ **E**   Amphetamine abuse is associated with paranoid psychosis
- ☐ **F**   The majority of people who abuse cannabis progress to 'harder' drugs

27 Under the terms of service of a General Practitioner's contract, he/she is NOT allowed to accept a fee from a patient on the practice list for which ONE of the following?

- ☐ **A**   Ear piercing
- ☐ **B**   Initial treatment following a road traffic accident
- ☐ **C**   Seat belt exemption certificates
- ☐ **D**   Signing a form for the Disability Living Allowance
- ☐ **E**   Writing a letter in support of a patient's housing application

28 Which ONE of the following is true of normal pressure hydrocephalus?
- [ ] **A**   Cognitive impairment occurs after the onset of gait disturbance
- [ ] **B**   A parkinsonian gait is the typical abnormality when walking
- [ ] **C**   Urinary incontinence can be present in the absence of disturbance of gait or mental function
- [ ] **D**   Lumbar puncture is contraindicated
- [ ] **E**   Less than 25% of patients improve after a ventricular shunt operation

29 Which ONE of the following does not apply under the Access to Medical Reports Act 1988?
- [ ] **A**   The doctor supplying the report must receive a copy of the patient's consent
- [ ] **B**   The doctor has the right to refuse to amend a report even if requested to do so by the patient
- [ ] **C**   The patient has the right to view the report for up to one year after it has been sent to the insurance company or employer
- [ ] **D**   The doctor can charge a fee if the patient requests a copy of the report
- [ ] **E**   The doctor has the right to refuse to divulge all or part of the report to a patient

30 Upon employing a new member of staff a General Practitioner should be aware that they immediately have which TWO of the following statutory employment rights?
- [ ] **A**   To receive an itemised pay statement
- [ ] **B**   To have paid time off for antenatal care
- [ ] **C**   To be given a minimum period of notice of termination of employment
- [ ] **D**   To receive payment for absence due to pregnancy
- [ ] **E**   To receive a written statement of reasons for dismissal

31 Which ONE of the following does not apply to jet lag?
- [ ] **A**   Due to an upset in circadian rhythm
- [ ] **B**   Less marked when going towards USA from UK
- [ ] **C**   Helped by sleeping on the plane
- [ ] **D**   Helped by maintaining a good non-alcoholic fluid intake
- [ ] **E**   Of about 24 hours' duration

32 Select ONE statement about following up patients with breast cancer:
- [ ] **A**   Fixed regimes of long term follow-up (5 year) by hospital have been shown to lead to a more favourable outcome
- [ ] **B**   Treatment with tamoxifen has been shown to improve prognosis in post-menopausal patients
- [ ] **C**   The incidence of cancer in the opposite breast is no greater than the incidence of breast cancer for women as a whole
- [ ] **D**   Hormone manipulation has a greater response rate than chemotherapy in the management of advanced disease

33 Department of Health recommendations for influenza vaccination do NOT include adults and children in which ONE of the following groups?
- ☐ **A** Health care workers
- ☐ **B** Patients in residential homes
- ☐ **C** Patients with diabetes mellitus
- ☐ **D** Patients with leukaemia
- ☐ **E** Patients in heart failure

34 Select ONE statement about maternity medical services:
- ☐ **A** Must be provided by a doctor on the obstetric list
- ☐ **B** Are payable as for a full term gestation, for a live delivery occurring before 28 weeks' gestation
- ☐ **C** Are payable for a patient who requests and subsequently receives a therapeutic abortion from the outset of the pregnancy
- ☐ **D** The complete fee is only payable if the GP is present at the time of delivery
- ☐ **E** Fee for post-natal visits is payable for visits done up to 28 days' post-confinement

35 Select THREE items about Kawasaki's disease:
- ☐ **A** It is most often seen in children over 5 years old
- ☐ **B** There is an acute febrile illness
- ☐ **C** There is a fatality of about 5 per 100 cases
- ☐ **D** Coronary artery aneurysms are a sequel in about 5–10% of cases
- ☐ **E** There is often reddening which spares the palms and soles
- ☐ **F** Fever lasting more than 5 days and swelling of cervical lymph nodes is often seen

36 Choose TWO statements about terminal care:
- ☐ **A** The majority of people die at home
- ☐ **B** The majority of patients with pain have more than one type of pain
- ☐ **C** Over 90% of patient pain can be controlled with drugs
- ☐ **D** With severe pain, intramuscular analgesics are more effective than the equivalent dose administered by the oral route
- ☐ **E** Portable syringe devices need to have the syringe changed at approximately 6-hour intervals

37 Select TWO items about Bell's palsy:
- ☐ **A** The majority of patients will make a recovery within 3 weeks
- ☐ **B** Brain stem lesions will cause loss of taste
- ☐ **C** Oral steroids have been shown to be effective
- ☐ **D** Lacrimation is unaffected
- ☐ **E** Repeat attacks resolve more readily than the initial attack

38 Select THREE items concerning warts:

☐ **A** The majority of patients with warts develop immunity within 2 years
☐ **B** Salicylic acid preparations should be applied for 3 months or more
☐ **C** Topical podophyllum must be left on the wart without washing for 24 hours
☐ **D** Cryotherapy with liquid nitrogen typically scars
☐ **E** Podophyllum is teratogenic

THEME: PARAESTHESIA

Causes of numbness and paraesthesia in the upper limbs include:

A   Carpal tunnel syndrome
B   Ulnar nerve lesion
C   Peripheral neuropathy
D   Cervical spondylosis
E   Multiple sclerosis
F   Syringomyelia
G   Cortical lesions

Match the following clinical scenarios to the most appropriate diagnosis

39 A 43-year-old teacher has pain and tingling in her right hand; she describes this as mainly affecting her index and middle fingers and it is worse at night ☐

40 A 46-year-old electrician has numbness of his right hand and lower arm; examination reveals a 'glove' type sensory loss with distal weakness and some wasting ☐

41 A 44-year-old plumber has tingling in his right hand and arm; some neck stiffness is noted on examination ☐

42 A 39-year-old housewife complains of 'electric shock' type feeling worse on neck movements, especially flexion; she also mentions 'tight bands' around the upper limbs and ribs ☐

43 A 41-year-old accountant has tingling in his left little finger; examination reveals slight wasting of the small muscles of the left hand ☐

44 A 38-year-old carpenter has noticed that he injured his left hand under his little finger but did not feel the injury; examination reveals loss of pain and temperature sensation in the hand and arm, with slight weakness ☐

45 You are consulted by the parents of an apparently healthy child who refuses to sleep at night. Which ONE of the following is not true?

☐ **A**   At 3 months the average child has approximately four episodes of nocturnal wakefulness

☐ **B**   At 6 months the majority of children have 15 hours of sleep during the night

☐ **C**   A regular night time routine has been shown to solve the majority of sleep problems

☐ **D**   Children with persistent sleep disturbance have an increased incidence of other behavioural problems

☐ **E**   A child who persistently cries at night should be left no longer than 5 minutes

46 THREE of the following drugs used in the treatment of rheumatoid arthritis have the side-effects stated:

☐ **A**   Gold injections cause exfoliative dermatitis

☐ **B**   Penicillamine is associated with azoospermia

☐ **C**   Methotrexate has been implicated in hepatic fibrosis

☐ **D**   Sulphasalazine is associated with thrombocytopenia

☐ **E**   Chloroquine produces retinal damage

47 Choose TWO items concerning the majority of patients with Down's syndrome:

☐ **A**   Have an IQ of between 20 and 50

☐ **B**   Die before they reach 50 years of age

☐ **C**   Have a congenital heart disorder

☐ **D**   Have a behaviour disorder

☐ **E**   Develop hypothyroidism

48 Select TWO items about subarachnoid haemorrhage:

☐ **A**   The majority of patients will die without warning

☐ **B**   The peak age range is in the under 35-year-olds

☐ **C**   There is a familial tendency

☐ **D**   The majority of patients who have surgery achieve their previous quality of life

☐ **E**   The risk of epilepsy is increased following a haemorrhage

49 Select THREE items about puerperal depressive illness:

☐ **A**   Has been shown to occur in 10% of pregnancies

☐ **B**   Is more common in single parents

☐ **C**   Is associated with lack of 'bonding'

☐ **D**   Is associated with a previous psychiatric history

☐ **E**   Has been shown to be associated with a decreased level of progestogen 6 weeks post-delivery

50 Select TWO items about carcinoma of the cervix:
- ☐ **A** It has an association with human papilloma virus infection
- ☐ **B** The majority of patients survive fewer than 5 years
- ☐ **C** Smoking has been shown to increase the risks of contracting the disease
- ☐ **D** Cytology has been shown to be reliable in identifying frank carcinoma
- ☐ **E** The peak incidence occurs between 30 and 40 years of age

51 Select THREE items about flat feet (pes planus)
- ☐ **A** Symptoms fail to correlate with the degree of structural alteration
- ☐ **B** The majority of children age 2 years have the condition
- ☐ **C** Painful mobile flat feet are an indication for corrective surgery
- ☐ **D** They are typically associated with painful night cramps
- ☐ **E** If familial typically respond to corrective measures

52 Select TWO of the following statements about eardrums with a central perforation:
- ☐ **A** They typically produce a mucoid discharge
- ☐ **B** They are associated with the production of cholesteatoma
- ☐ **C** Repair is possible via a tympanoplasty
- ☐ **D** Urgent referral to an ENT surgeon is indicated

53 Select TWO items concerning weight:
- ☐ **A** A patient with a body mass index of just greater than 20 is only slightly overweight
- ☐ **B** Body mass index is measured by the weight in kilograms divided by the square of the height in centimetres
- ☐ **C** GPs are more successful than others in helping patients reduce weight
- ☐ **D** Exercises increase the basal metabolic rate for several hours
- ☐ **E** Weight-watching groups use strategies like fines, prizes and the example of others

54 Select FOUR of the following dyspepsia treatments that are noted for the linked side-effects:
- ☐ **A** Aluminium salts cause diarrhoea
- ☐ **B** Cisapride is typically associated with acute dyskinesia in young adults
- ☐ **C** Misoprostol is associated with intermenstrual bleeding
- ☐ **D** Metoclopramide is associated with elevated prolactin levels
- ☐ **E** H2 receptor antagonists are associated with confusion in the elderly
- ☐ **F** Omeprazole is associated with photosensitivity reactions

55 When advising patients about to undergo air travel, select TWO of the following items:

☐ **A** People with a vital capacity less than 50% of the mean predicted for them, should not fly

☐ **B** There is no increase in fit frequency of epileptics

☐ **C** Diabetics on oral hypoglycaemic agents will need to decrease their dosage if undertaking a prolonged eastbound flight

☐ **D** Motion sickness on aircraft shows a tendency to increase with age

☐ **E** Recent eye surgery is a contraindication to flying

56 Which ONE of the following is true of hand, foot and mouth disease?

☐ **A** A sore throat is characteristic

☐ **B** Typically the spots are itchy

☐ **C** Spots appearing on the buttocks would exclude the diagnosis

☐ **D** It has an incubation period of approximately 21 days

☐ **E** It typically responds to oral penicillin

THEME: LITERATURE

The following books have been written about general practice:

A *Games People Play* by Eric Berne

B *Six Minutes for the Patient* by Balint and Norell

C *Culture, Health and Illness* by Cecil Helmen

D *The Consultation: An Approach to Learning and Teaching* by Pendleton et al.

E *The Inner Consultation* by Roger Neighbour

F *The Doctor, His Patient and The Illness* by Michael Balint

Match the following statements to the most appropriate book listed above

57 Describes a consultation model with five check points, including connecting ☐

58 Describes 'apostolic function' ☐

59 Looked at parent, adult and child behaviour ☐

60 Defined seven communication tasks, including defining the reasons for the patient's attendance ☐

61 Discusses illness behaviour with patients trying to answer questions like 'why me, why now?' ☐

62 Describes the 'flash' ☐

63 Which THREE of the following would support a diagnosis of irritable bowel syndrome?

- ☐ **A** Nocturnal diarrhoea
- ☐ **B** Absence of pain
- ☐ **C** Associated menstrual disturbance
- ☐ **D** Abdominal pain worsening on defaecation
- ☐ **E** Onset associated with a proven gastrointestinal infection

64 Your practice is reviewing its protocol for antenatal care. Research has shown which TWO of the following?

- ☐ **A** Routine ultrasound reduces the incidence of induction for alleged post-maturity
- ☐ **B** Anti-smoking education reduces the incidence of low birth weight babies
- ☐ **C** Measuring fundal heights routinely decreases peri-natal mortality
- ☐ **D** Routine antenatal care detects the majority of small for gestational age babies
- ☐ **E** Routine kick charts have been shown to reduce the chances of perinatal death

65 Choose ONE statement about breast lumps:

- ☐ **A** Cysts are more prevalent in post-menopausal women
- ☐ **B** Cysts should not be aspirated by General Practitioners
- ☐ **C** The majority of solitary breast cysts will recur within 2 years of initial aspiration
- ☐ **D** Patients with breast cysts have an increased risk of developing breast cancer
- ☐ **E** Lumpy breasts which are cyclically painful have been shown to respond to oil of evening primrose

66 Select TWO high-risk groups for diabetes:

- ☐ **A** Women with gestational diabetes
- ☐ **B** Women who have had low birth weight babies
- ☐ **C** Men and women with a family history of late onset diabetes
- ☐ **D** People with a history of anorexia
- ☐ **E** People with repeated urinary tract infections

67 Atrial fibrillation typically is a presenting feature of which TWO of the following?

- ☐ **A** Rheumatic fever
- ☐ **B** Sarcoidosis
- ☐ **C** Thyrotoxicosis
- ☐ **D** Alcoholic cardiomyopathy
- ☐ **E** Reiter's syndrome

THEME: MENTAL HEALTH ACT

In the Mental Health Act 1983 the following sections are of importance:
A   Section 2
B   Section 3
C   Section 4
D   Section 7
E   Section 12
F   Section 136

Match the statements below with the appropriate section from those above

68   Appropriate for detention of a patient who is acting in a bizarre way and warrants compulsory assessment   ☐

69   Appropriate for emergency detention of a patient by a single medical practitioner   ☐

70   Can be used by police when they need to detain someone who they believe is suffering from mental illness   ☐

71   Appropriate for guardianship   ☐

72   Appropriate for detention of a schizophrenic patient who refuses treatment and is a danger to other people   ☐

73   Is used to approve doctors recognised as having special expertise in mental health   ☐

74 Select TWO of the following about deliberate self-harm:
☐ A   About a quarter of patients will repeat one or more acts of non-fatal harm within one year
☐ B   Provision of intensive psychiatric and social help has been shown to significantly reduce the rate of repetition
☐ C   The provision of 'hotlines' (e.g. Samaritans) has significantly reduced the incidence of deliberate self-harm
☐ D   The majority of patients admitted to a general hospital following an episode of self-harm require transfer to a psychiatric unit
☐ E   The risk of a successful suicidal attempt within the next year is approximately 2%

75 Select THREE items about polycythaemia vera:
- ☐ **A** Splenomegaly is typical
- ☐ **B** It is associated with gout
- ☐ **C** Intractable itching would cast doubt on the diagnosis
- ☐ **D** The majority eventually develop acute leukaemia
- ☐ **E** Radiotherapy treatment decreases the chance of developing leukaemia

76 The differential diagnosis of sudden loss of vision should include which TWO of the following?
- ☐ **A** Migraine
- ☐ **B** Central retinal vein occlusion
- ☐ **C** Senile macular degeneration
- ☐ **D** Optic neuritis
- ☐ **E** Toxic optic neuropathy

77 Select ONE statement about child surveillance in general practice:
- ☐ **A** A child must register separately with a GP for child surveillance
- ☐ **B** Child health clinics attract a health promotion clinic payment from the FHSA
- ☐ **C** Child surveillance payments include an allowance for giving childhood immunisations
- ☐ **D** All GPs are eligible for inclusion in the Child Health Surveillance List
- ☐ **E** Once a child is accepted onto the child surveillance list of a GP, that GP must perform all the developmental assessment

78 THREE of the following have been shown to be associated with an increased incidence of recurrent miscarriage:
- ☐ **A** Systemic lupus erythematosus (SLE)
- ☐ **B** Raised levels of luteinising hormone
- ☐ **C** Diabetes mellitus
- ☐ **D** Thyroid disease
- ☐ **E** Parental chromosomal abnormalities

79 Select THREE statements concerning acute bronchiolitis:
- ☐ **A** Respiratory syncytial virus (RSV) is the most commonly isolated organism
- ☐ **B** It typically affects infants in the first year of life
- ☐ **C** It typically causes stridor
- ☐ **D** It shows a seasonal pattern
- ☐ **E** Complete laryngeal obstruction is possible on examination of the throat

THEME: STUDIES

Studies in general practice include those which are either:
A   Cohort study
B   Case-control

Choose the appropriate type for the following descriptions

80   Population-based ☐

81   More potential for bias ☐

82   Long term follow-up is usually required ☐

83   The incidence rate of a disease can be calculated ☐

84   Relatively easy to conduct ☐

85   Relatively inexpensive to conduct ☐

86   Relatively time-consuming to conduct ☐

87 Select THREE items about prescribing topical steroids:
☐ **A**   Absorption is enhanced by inclusion of urea in the preparation
☐ **B**   A single application to the arm of a 70 kg adult male will use approximately 4 g of preparation
☐ **C**   If used continuously they increase hair growth
☐ **D**   Ointments are indicated for most steroid-responsive conditions
☐ **E**   Depigmentation has been shown to occur at the site of prolonged usage

88 THREE of the following are true when considering periods:
☐ **A**   The average age of onset in the UK is approximately 11 years of age
☐ **B**   The average age at which patients have their last period is 50 years of age in the UK
☐ **C**   The earlier periods start the later they finish
☐ **D**   If the onset of periods is delayed beyond 16 years of age referral for investigation is indicated
☐ **E**   Estimation of LH and FSH levels is a reliable method of determining if a patient is post-menopausal

89 Select THREE of the following statements about dry eyes:
- ☐ **A** Are a cause of epiphora
- ☐ **B** Are worse in warm weather
- ☐ **C** Are associated with sarcoidosis
- ☐ **D** Sjögren's test is diagnostic
- ☐ **E** Are associated with entropion

90 Select THREE items about undescended testes:
- ☐ **A** No testis descends spontaneously after 1 year of age
- ☐ **B** All testes should be in the scrotum by 5 years of age
- ☐ **C** A unilateral undescended testis found after 16 years of age should be excised
- ☐ **D** Orchidopexy has been shown to decrease the chances of fertility
- ☐ **E** Hernial sacs are present in a minority of boys at the time of orchidopexy

91 Select TWO statements about the organisation of care for those with gout:
- ☐ **A** Allopurinol is contraindicated in the presence of renal calculi
- ☐ **B** The majority of patients with gout will have co-existing hypertension
- ☐ **C** Lipid levels are higher in those with gout than in the general population
- ☐ **D** Alcohol decreases the renal urate clearance
- ☐ **E** The majority of those with gout will have a positive family history

92 Select TWO items about the management of upper gastrointestinal bleeding:
- ☐ **A** The majority of patients will require surgery
- ☐ **B** H2 antagonists have been shown to stop initial bleeds
- ☐ **C** The mortality rate is about 10%
- ☐ **D** Gastric ulcers are more likely to bleed than duodenal ulcers
- ☐ **E** Urgent endoscopic assessment at the time of hospital admission has been shown to decrease mortality

93 Significant interactions have been shown to occur between THREE of the following drug combinations if given concurrently:
- ☐ **A** Terfenadine and erythromycin
- ☐ **B** Ciprofloxacin and theophylline
- ☐ **C** Cimetidine and warfarin
- ☐ **D** Omeprazole and alginate preparations
- ☐ **E** Allopurinol and captopril

94 An elderly patient presents with symptoms of dementia. Which ONE of the following would suggest Alzheimer's disease rather than a depressive cause?
- ☐ **A** Recent onset of symptoms
- ☐ **B** The patient continually complaining of memory loss
- ☐ **C** Mental ability worsening in the evening
- ☐ **D** 'Don't know' as a response to many questions
- ☐ **E** A previous history of depressive illness

95 Select THREE of these items about alcohol abuse:

☐ **A** Can be detected by the CRATE questionnaire
☐ **B** Can be detected by the MAST questionnaire
☐ **C** Gives increased risk of carcinoma of the oesophagus
☐ **D** Is a low risk in fishermen
☐ **E** Is a high risk in single males over 40 years of age

96 From the following list of statements regarding fitness to drive, indicate the THREE correct answers:

☐ **A** Following a stroke, provided a satisfactory recovery is made, driving may resume after 1 month for category 1 licence holders
☐ **B** Newly diagnosed insulin treated diabetics may hold a category 2 (HGV) licence as long as they have good control and have yearly reviews.
☐ **C** Following a pacemaker insertion the holders of category 1 (car) licences should not drive for 1 week
☐ **D** Following a first epileptic seizure, 6 months off driving is mandatory for category 1 licence holders
☐ **E** Patients with monocular vision may hold a category 1 licence as long as they satisfy the basic acuity requirements and have adapted to their disability
☐ **F** Colour blindness precludes either category licence
☐ **G** Following myocardial infarction patients are automatically barred from driving for 3 months

THEME: LIPID TRIALS

In trials on lipids the following are well-known:

A WOSCOPS
B Scandinavian Simvastatin Survival Study (4S)
C ASPIRE Steering Group
D Cholesterol and Recurrent Events Study (CARE)

Which comments relate to which study?

97 Many survivors of myocardial infarcts have not had their blood lipids measured ☐

98 Patients without known coronary disease have their risk of cardiovascular disease reduced by statins if the cholesterol level is above 6 mmol/l ☐

99 Studied survivors of myocardial infarcts with mildly elevated cholesterol levels and used pravastatin therapy ☐

100 Studied patients with known coronary disease and showed that treatment with a statin produced a 30% drop in total mortality ☐

101 **Sleeping tablets are commonly prescribed in general practice. From the list below pick the TWO correct statements:**

☐ **A** Temazepam is a controlled drug and hence prescriptions must be written by hand

☐ **B** Zopiclone may cause a metallic taste

☐ **C** Withdrawal effects on ceasing benzodiazepine use typically occur in the first 48 hours

☐ **D** Zopiclone is not a benzodiazepine and hence is safe for long term use.

☐ **E** Tolerance to benzodiazepines may develop within 72 hours of continuous use.

102 **You see a 34-year-old female patient in surgery for the first time. She complains of poor sleep, tearfulness, anhedonia, loss of appetite and poor concentration over the last 6 months. She is not suicidal and says that her symptoms started after the death of her mother. Which of the following would be appropriate initial treatments for her? (select THREE)**

☐ **A** Referral for consideration of electroconvulsive therapy

☐ **B** St John's wort

☐ **C** Propranolol

☐ **D** Cognitive behavioural therapy

☐ **E** Melleril

☐ **F** Fluoxetine

☐ **G** Lithium

☐ **H** Carbamazepine

103 **For the following conditions, indicate which ones are transmitted as single gene traits (THREE correct):**

☐ **A** Transposition of the great vessels

☐ **B** Phenylketonuria

☐ **C** Spherocytosis

☐ **D** Atherosclerosis

☐ **E** Ankylosing spondylitis

☐ **F** Nephrogenic diabetes insipidus

☐ **G** Pellagra

☐ **H** Asthma

104 **Choose ONE item that relates to episiotomy:**

☐ **A** Studies have shown that a wait of 1 hour for stitching is associated with significant infection

☐ **B** Episiotomy has been shown to prevent development of rectocele

☐ **C** Episiotomy rates are higher for home confinements

☐ **D** Tearing of the perineum does not occur once episiotomy has been performed

☐ **E** Apgar scores of babies born to mothers who have had an episiotomy have been shown to be higher than those without

105 Which of the following descriptions of medical research are correct? (THREE answers)

☐ **A** Randomised controlled trials are free from bias and hence are the ideal research tool

☐ **B** Richard Doll's study of British doctor's smoking is an example of a cohort study.

☐ **C** Case-control studies are prone to recall bias

☐ **D** Where confidence intervals cross the line of no effect, it may be concluded that there is no association or effect

☐ **E** The positive predictive value of a test depends on the incidence of the condition in the community being studied.

☐ **F** Meta-analysis involves combining all the trials on a subject area to increase the validity of the result

☐ **G** Qualitative research has no place in clinical medicine

THEME: EPILEPSY

The following drugs are used in the control of epilepsy:

A Primidone
B Sodium valproate
C Vigabatrin
D Phenytoin
E Carbamazepine
F Clonazepam

Match the statements to the appropriate drugs

106 Is converted to phenobarbitone ☐

107 Is also used increasingly in recurrent depressive illness but can cause visual disturbance, especially double vision ☐

108 Is highly protein bound, making interpretation of blood tests difficult ☐

109 May give false positive urine test for ketones ☐

110 Can cause gingival hypertrophy and tenderness, and may lower plasma calcium ☐

THEME: CORONARY HEART DISEASE

The following look at the risk of coronary heart disease:
A   British Regional Heart Study
B   Framingham Heart Study
C   North Karalia Project
D   Oxcheck Study
E   WHO European Collaborative Trial
F   Dundee Risk Score
G   Shaper Score
H   Seven Countries Study

Which of these is appropriate to the following?

111   Looks at relative risk of having a heart attack over the next 5 years ☐

112   Showed that differences in the consumption of saturated fats is an important factor in determining the population risk for coronary heart disease ☐

113   Looks at the absolute risk of having a heart attack over the next 5 years ☐

114   Assessed risk factors in a middle-aged group in the USA and studied fatal and non-fatal coronary events ☐

115   Offered health checks to adult population of GP practices with selective screening of cholesterol levels ☐

116   Was set up because of high morality rate from coronary events in Finland ☐

117   Recruited patients from British general practice and linked risk factors with fatal and non-fatal coronary events ☐

THEME: STATISTICS

The following terms are used in medical statistics:
A   Correlation
B   Predictive value
C   Incidence
D   Confounding
E   Confidence

Match the statements below with the most appropriate term

118   Depends on the prevalence of disease in the population studied ☐

119   Occurrence of new cases in a population in a period of time ☐

120   Needs to be eliminated in a good study ☐

121   Depends on sensitivity and specificity of the test ☐

122   Occurs when a variable changes in a direct way with another variable ☐

THEME: PRESCRIBING

Various schemes and bodies exist to improve prescribing in general practice, such as:
A   The PACT Scheme
B   Medical Audit Advisory Group
C   National Medicines Resource Centre
D   Prescribing Unit, Leeds University General Practice Department
E   Prescribing Adviser
F   Prescribing Allocation Group

Match the following statements with ONE of the above

123   Investigates the range of prescribing ☐

124   Produces quarterly prescribing reports for GPs ☐

125   Centrally funded; produces monthly bulletins ☐

126   Monitors indicative prescribing ☐

127   Advises NHS Executive on allocation of drug budgets to regions and practices ☐

THEME: PROFESSIONS

People professionally associated with general practice include:
A Health visitors
B Practice managers
C Community nurses
D Practice nurses
E Social workers

Match these statements to the most appropriate person

128 Usually employed by the health authority, can give practical and psychological support to patients and families, but spend most time in practical tasks ☐

129 Employed usually by the health authority and have some statutory duties ☐

130 Are usually employed by general practice principals, are often experienced nurses and may have family planning training ☐

131 Often have a large role in the hiring and training of staff

THEME: MISUSE OF DRUGS

The Misuse of Drugs Regulations 1985 categorises five groups of drugs:
A Schedule 1
B Schedule 2
C Schedule 3
D Schedule 4
E Schedule 5

To which schedule do the following drugs belong?

132 Diamorphine ☐

133 Diethylpropion ☐

134 Diazepam ☐

135 Amylobarbitone ☐

136 Cannabis ☐

THEME: BENEFITS

Welfare benefits include:
A Family Credit
B Child Benefit
C Income Support
D Invalid Care Allowance
E Social Fund Benefits
F Widow's payment

Which of the above relate to the following

137 Means tested benefit payable to someone working fewer than 16 hours per week on low income ☐

138 Means tested benefit payable to someone with children who is working more than 16 hours per week on low income ☐

139 Payable to someone who is unable to work because they are looking after a disabled person ☐

140 Payable to meet exceptional expenses such as funeral expenses ☐

141 A tax-free payment to someone with a child under 16 years of age ☐

THEME: DEVELOPMENTAL MILESTONES

Children reach significant developmental milestones at certain ages:
A 6 months
B 9 months
C 12 months
D 18 months
E 24 months

At what age would most children be able to do the following

142 Walk with one hand held or unsupported ☐

143 Jump using both feet ☐

144 Build a tower of 6–7 blocks ☐

145 Transfer a cube from one hand to another ☐

continued ...

146 Crawl on their tummy ☐

147 Say at least one word with meaning ☐

148 Manage a spoon well ☐

THEME: IMMUNISATIONS

The following immunisations are given for foreign travel:
A Yellow fever
B Tetanus
C Polio
D Hepatitis A
E Typhoid

Match the following statements with the immunisations

149 Given 3 yearly; adverse reactions more common after repeated injections and more marked over 35 years of age ☐

150 Given 10 yearly but not given under 9 months of age ☐

151 Given 5–10 yearly and would be suitable for travellers to northern Europe ☐

152 A live vaccine which can rarely cause paralysis in recipients or contacts ☐

153 Testing for antibodies may be worthwhile in travellers over 50 years of age ☐

154 Select ONE statement concerning indicative prescribing budgets:
☐ **A** They are only allocated to fundholding practices
☐ **B** If a practice underspends its budget, amounts saved can be added to future years' budgets
☐ **C** Practice formularies are compulsory
☐ **D** If a practice overspends, its budget remuneration can be withheld by the FHSA
☐ **E** Patients on 'expensive' medication are not included in the budget

THEME: SWELLINGS IN THE NECK AREA

Swellings in the neck may be due to:
A   Enlarged salivary gland
B   Branchial cyst
C   Dermoid cyst
D   Thyroglossal cyst
E   Sebaceous cyst

Match ONE of these to the following statements

155 May contain hair; arises along the lines of embryological development ☐

156 Filled with keratin; has a punctum ☐

157 Occurs in midline; moves on swallowing ☐

158 Remnant of second pharyngeal pouch ☐

159 Can occur with a notifiable infectious disease ☐

160 A swelling in the neck that moves with the protrusion of the tongue ☐

161 Select ONE statement about lesions on the ear:
☐ **A**   Squamous cell carcinoma typically appears on the helix
☐ **B**   Tophi appear on the earlobe
☐ **C**   Chilblains of the ear never itch
☐ **D**   Psoriasis typically occurs all over the ear
☐ **E**   Kerato-acanthoma do not appear on the ear

SUMMARY COMPLETION QUESTION

Read the extract below from 'Randomised trial of acupuncture compared with conventional massage and "sham" laser acupuncture for treatment of chronic neck pain.' BMJ 2001;322:1574.

Methods
Study design
The study was a randomised, placebo and alternative treatment controlled clinical trial performed at three outpatient departments at the universities in Munich and Würzburg, Germany, from 1996 to 1999.

Participants
Patients were consecutively preselected by the doctors of the three outpatient departments, who were informed about the inclusion and exclusion criteria. Patients who were eligible and willing to participate in the study were then

assessed by an independent examiner. This assessment included a detailed physical examination and collection of baseline data. The main inclusion criteria were that patients had had a painful restriction of cervical spine mobility for longer than one month and that they had not received any treatment in the two weeks before entering the study. Patients who had undergone surgery or those with dislocation, fracture, neurological deficits, systemic disorders, or contraindications to treatment were excluded.

Neck pain was classified according to the system of Schöps and Senn on the basis of history, characteristics of pain, manual examination, and radiological findings. Patients' conditions were defined as the myofascial pain syndrome (pain and limited mobility associated with myofascial triggerpoints), the irritation syndrome (diffuse, intense pain with difficult access for manual examination), or segmental dysfunction (segmental hypomobility revealed by manual examination and functional radiograph analysis). The diagnosis was confirmed by a second assessor. Informed consent was obtained, and the study was approved by the local ethics committees. Patients were told before randomisation that one of the three treatments might be a sham procedure.

Main outcome measures: Primary outcome measure: maximum pain related to motion (visual analogue scale) irrespective of direction of movement one week after treatment. Secondary outcome measures: range of motion (3D ultrasound real time motion analyser), pain related to movement in six directions (visual analogue scale), pressure pain threshold (pressure algometer), changes of spontaneous pain, motion related pain, global complaints (seven point scale), and quality of life (SF-36). Assessments were performed before, during, and one week and three months after treatment. Patients' beliefs in treatment were assessed.

Treatment protocols

Patients were treated five times over three weeks. Each treatment lasted 30 minutes. **Acupuncture** and sham laser **acupuncture** were performed by four experienced, licensed medical acupuncturists. Massages were performed by five experienced physiotherapists. Patients took no concomitant analgesics. Patients who rated their pain as over 20 on the visual analogue scale (0–100) or who had an inconvenient restriction of mobility at the primary study end point were referred for physiotherapy during follow up.

Acupuncture–**Acupuncture** was performed according to the rules of traditional Chinese medicine, including diagnostic palpation to identify sensitive spots. Remote and local **acupuncture** points were selected individually on the affected meridians. Relevant ear **acupuncture** points were included. In addition local myofascial triggerpoints were treated with the technique of dry needling to elicit a local twitch response of muscles. Criteria for point selection are described in detail. The most commonly used points were SI3, UB10, UB60, Liv3, GB20, GB34, TE5, and the ear point "cervical spine." Active myofascial triggerpoints were located predominantly in the musculus trapezius (nearby GB20) and levator scapulae (nearby SI14).

Massage–Patients were treated with conventional Western massage. Techniques included effleurage, petrissage, friction, tapotement, and vibration. Mode and intensity were chosen by the physiotherapist in accordance with the patient's condition and diagnosis as usual in clinical routine. Spinal manipulation and non-conventional techniques were not performed.

Placebo–Sham laser **acupuncture** was performed with a laser pen, which was inactivated by the manufacturer (Laser Pen, Seirin International, Fort Lauderdale). Only red light was emitted. Patients were not informed about the inactivation of the laser pen. To strengthen the power of this sham procedure, visual and acoustic signals common for this type of laser pen accompanied the red light emission. Criteria for selection of points were identical with those used in the **acupuncture** group, including palpation of **acupuncture** points for diagnostic reasons. Every point was treated for 2 minutes, with the pen at a distance of 0.5–1 cm from the skin.

Now look at this critique, which outlines the limitations of the study design.
The design is a prospective randomised, placebo controlled trial. This design has the benefit of random allocation but the fact that neither the subjects and practitioners are (**162**)_____ makes the subjects prone to
(**163**)_____ bias and the practitioners prone to
(**164**)_____ bias. The question of whether it is a true
(**165**)_____ trial is questionable, since the
(**166**)_____ procedure involves shining a laser at points on the skin, while the (**167**)_____ procedure involves needles being inserted. Clearly the subject will be able to tell the difference, particularly since they were forewarned that one of the procedures would be a sham procedure. A better alternative might have been needle insertion in non-acupuncture points, which would differentiate between the placebo effect and genuine acupuncture effect.

The (**168**)_____ of the data to United Kingdom general practice is unclear, since the study takes place in a
(**169**)_____ care setting with out-patient referrals. This may result in a different patient mix and a different practitioner skill mix. Furthermore, it is difficult to know whether the acupuncture treatments are standardised, and intrinsic variability between practitioners may be
(**170**)_____. Attempts to minimise other influences included asking patients not to take concomitant analgesics.

The outcome measures were clinically appropriate and used a reproducible and standardised visual analogue scale, together with a
(**171**)_____ quality of life scoring system. Follow up extended to 3 months which will demonstrate any medium term effect.

For each of the numbered gaps in the critique, choose one word from the following list which best completes the sentence.

A   allocation
B   biased
C   blinded
D   confounding
E   control
F   generalisability
G   intervention
H   masked
I   novel
J   observer
K   open
L   participant
M   placebo controlled
N   primary
O   randomised
P   reporting
Q   secondary
R   type 3
S   validated
T   validity

172   Select ONE item about lithium carbonate:

☐   **A**   Is effective in the control of schizophrenia
☐   **B**   Is available as a long-acting depot preparation
☐   **C**   Is associated with increased mortality due to renal damage
☐   **D**   Is associated with abnormalities of thyroid function
☐   **E**   Is an effective agent for rapid control of symptoms

THEME: EAR PROBLEMS

Lesions on the ear include:
A   Chilblains
B   Squamous cell carcinoma
C   Tophi
D   Psoriasis
E   Eczema
F   Kerato-acanthoma

Match the following descriptions to ONE of the above

173 Rapidly grow on the helix ☐

174 Affects the entire ear ☐

175 Affects behind and below the ears, and elsewhere on the body ☐

176 Appears on antihelix, usually ☐

177 Appears on helix and may need biopsy for diagnosis ☐

178 Painful and itchy ☐

179 Which ONE of the following drugs has not been shown to potentiate the effects of alcohol?
☐ **A** Phenytoin
☐ **B** Indomethacin
☐ **C** Atenolol
☐ **D** Chlorpheniramine
☐ **E** Monoamine oxidase inhibitors

Practice Paper 3

Total time allowed is three hours. Indicate your answers clearly by putting a tick or cross in the box alongside each answer or by writing the appropriate letter alongside the appropriate answer.

1 Select TWO items about the drug treatment of asthma with inhaler devices:

☐ **A**   The incidence of oral candidiasis is decreased by the use of spacer devices

☐ **B**   Salmeterol is indicated for p.r.n. usage

☐ **C**   Intermittent terbutaline has been shown to lead to long term worsening of asthma

☐ **D**   Steroid dosage of 600 mg daily has been shown to be associated with adrenal suppression in adults

☐ **E**   Sodium cromoglycate is of no proven value in treating acute asthmatic attacks

2 You are checking a child for squint. Which ONE of the following statements is correct?

☐ **A**   An apparently squinting eye which moves to take up fixation when the other one is covered is normal

☐ **B**   Patching the affected eye before the age of 6 will result in normal sight

☐ **C**   Squint may be a sign of retinoblastoma

☐ **D**   Surgical treatment in older children may restore sight

☐ **E**   Patching for 23 hours a day is necessary for the treatment to work

3 THREE of the following are high risk factors for osteoporosis:

☐ **A**   Late menarche

☐ **B**   Early menopause

☐ **C**   Nulliparity

☐ **D**   Alcoholism

☐ **E**   High salt consumption

SUMMARY COMPLETION QUESTION

First read the extract from the paper 'Antidepressant drugs and generic counselling for treatment of major depression in primary care: randomised trial with patient preference arm.' BMJ 2001:322;772.

Abstract

Objectives: To compare the efficacy of antidepressant drugs and **generic counselling** for treating mild to moderate depression in general practice. To determine whether the outcomes were similar for patients with randomly allocated treatment and those expressing a treatment preference.

Design: Randomised controlled trial, with patient preference arms. Follow up at 8 weeks and 12 months and abstraction of GP case notes.

Setting: 31 general practices in Trent region.

Participants: Patients aged 18–70 who met research diagnostic criteria for major depression; 103 patients were randomised and 220 patients were recruited to the preference arms.

Main outcome measures: Difference in mean Beck depression inventory score; time to remission; global outcome assessed by a psychiatrist using all data sources; and research diagnostic criteria.

Results: At 12 months there was no difference between the mean Beck scores in the randomised arms. Combining the randomised and patient preference groups, the difference in Beck scores was 0.4 (95% confidence interval -2.7 to 3.5). Patients choosing **counselling** did better than those randomised to it (mean difference in Beck score 4.6, 0.0 to 9.2). There was no difference in the psychiatrist's overall assessment of outcome between any of the groups. 221/265 (83%) of participants with a known outcome had a remission. Median time to remission was shorter in the group randomised to antidepressants than the other three groups (2 months v 3 months). 33/221 (15%) patients had a relapse.

Conclusions: **Generic counselling** seems to be as effective as antidepressant treatment for mild to moderate depressive illness, although patients receiving antidepressants may recover more quickly. General practitioners should allow patients to have their preferred treatment.

Methods

Recruitment and treatment

Full details of the methods have been published. Briefly, we invited a random sample of 410 general practices in the Trent health region to enter patients into the trial. General practitioners recruited participants and obtained informed consent. Eligible patients were those aged 18–70 years who met the research diagnostic criteria (assessed by the general practitioner using a checklist) for major depression.

We excluded patients with psychosis, suicidal tendencies, postnatal depression, a recent bereavement, or drug or alcohol misuse. The study was approved by 12 local research ethics committees.

For patients who agreed to randomisation, treatment was allocated by telephone with a randomisation strategy using blocks of four stratified by practice. Patients who refused randomisation but agreed to participate in the patient preference trial were given their choice of treatment. Treatment and follow up were identical in the randomised and patient preference groups.

We provided general practitioners with written guidelines on routine drug treatment of depression. Patients in the **counselling** arms were given six sessions by experienced counsellors, who adopted the **counselling** approach that they believed to be most suitable.

Data collection and follow up

All patients completed the Beck depression inventory and SF-36 questionnaire at enrolment. At the follow up visits eight weeks and 12 months after enrolment, the general practitioner completed a form that included the research diagnostic criteria and the patient was asked to complete a form including the Beck depression inventory and SF-36. Patients who did not keep their follow up appointments were asked to complete the forms at home.

We also abstracted information from general practitioners' case notes. This included general practitioner appointments; psychiatric and other hospital referrals; inpatient treatment; prescribed treatments (both antidepressants and other drugs); and referral to counsellors outside the study protocol.

Results

Response rates

The figure shows the numbers of patients recruited and followed up. There was no systematic difference between the proportions of patients completing the 12 month questionnaire in terms of treatment or whether they were randomised (P=0.34 for heterogeneity between the four groups). Sixty five (63%) patients in the randomised trial completed the Beck depression inventory and SF-36 at 12 months compared with 142 (65%) in the patient preference trial. The proportions of patients in each group who kept their 12 month appointment differed (P=0.01), with attendance ranging between 25% for patients choosing antidepressants and 53% for those randomised to antidepressants.

Read the critique below.

The results for this study provide interesting data; it appears at first sight that there is little difference between the mean Beck depression score at the end of 12 months in the randomised group, while in the patient preference arm there was a difference in favour of counselling. On closer inspection though, there are several areas which cast doubt on the results.

The individual interventions are **(4)**_____ . Patients were either **(5)**_____ to 'routine drug treatment' or a counselling approach that the counsellors believed 'to be most suitable'. This approach presents opportunities for both bias and **(6)**_____. The trial aims to assess 2 interventions **(7)**_____ but in fact may be testing many different varieties, e.g SSRIs, tricyclics, St John's Wort, cognitive behavioural therapy, bibliotherapy … the list is potentially endless. There is a body of evidence that suggests that these treatments all have different side-effect profiles, tolerability and efficacy differences and these will all influence **(8)**_____ in the groups. What steps were taken to exclude confounders? What steps were taken to determine if patients who had chosen counselling were self medicating with other treatments e.g. St John's Wort?

The study aims to compare the **(9)**_____ through a randomised control trial. It is clear from the data that belief in a therapy will have an effect on efficacy. Could this be acting as a **(10)**_____ in the **(11)**_____ group? Not expressing a strong preference does not mean that the patients randomised had no views about efficacy. Since there was no **(12)**_____ this may be a significant confounder.

The recruitment process excluded patients with a history of drug or alcohol abuse. This removes a large number of patients with depressive illness and it may be that the results are not generalisable to this group and this would limit the extent to which the trial data could be **(13)**_____ to everyday practice. Questions are also raised by the follow up. Less than 70% of patients had a questionnaire carried out at 12 months and less than 55% were seen at 12 months. Why did these patients fail to attend? Did they feel completely cured? Or had they all been admitted to psychiatric hospitals or committed suicide. Such a large drop out rate may have a significant influence on the results.

For each of the numbered gaps in the critique, choose the most appropriate response from the list below.

A   bias
B   blinding
C   comparable
D   confounding
E   control group
F   cure
G   drugs
H   efficacy
I   extrapolated
J   groups
K   heterogeneous
L   homogenous
M   interpreted
N   modalities
O   outcome
P   placebo
Q   preference
R   randomised
S   randomised
T   therapeutic

14 Select TWO statements concerning breast feeding:

☐ A   UK government health targets for the year 2000 include one that 75% of babies are to be breast-fed
☐ B   Mastitis is typically caused by Streptococcus
☐ C   It typically takes longer than bottle feeding
☐ D   It causes babies to be obese with the same frequency as bottle feeding
☐ E   Weaning onto cows' milk should take place at 6 months of age

THEME: BODIES ALLIED TO GENERAL PRACTICE

Local and national bodies allied to general practice and having a close impact on it include:

A   HEC
B   MAAG
C   GMC
D   PPA
E   GPC

Match the following statements with the appropriate body

15   An authority of regional status accountable to the Secretary of State; promotes training schemes for workers in the field ☐

16   Has status of Special Health Authority and has one of the biggest computer systems within the NHS ☐

17   Provides guidelines on expected standards of care and conduct ☐

18   Formerly known as GMSC; it is a committee of the BMA ☐

19   A local body established in co-operation by FHSAs and LMCs ☐

20 **When prescribing hormone replacement therapy, which ONE of the following statements is true?**
☐ **A**   Diabetes is an absolute contraindication to treatment
☐ **B**   Oestradiol implants have been shown not to improve atrophic vaginitis
☐ **C**   Breakthrough bleeding whilst on treatment can be safely ignored
☐ **D**   Unopposed oestrogen therapy has an adverse effect on lipid levels
☐ **E**   To be effective in the treatment of osteoporosis, it should be given for approximately 10 years

21 **In the management of acute ischaemic stroke in an otherwise healthy patient, which SINGLE treatment has been shown to be the most effective in reducing death and severe disability.**
☐ **A**   Aggressive treatment of hypertension in the acute phase
☐ **B**   The use of GABA agonists
☐ **C**   Thrombolysis
☐ **D**   Immediate systemic anticoagulation
☐ **E**   Stroke rehabilitation units
☐ **F**   Systemic steroids

22 Select TWO items about pulled elbow:
- ☐ **A** Affects children of pre-school age
- ☐ **B** Is caused by a fall on the outstretched hand
- ☐ **C** Requires operative reduction
- ☐ **D** X-rays show a characteristic appearance
- ☐ **E** Is more common on the left than the right

23 Which ONE of the following statements is true regarding community-acquired pneumonia?
- ☐ **A** The commonest isolated pathogens are viruses
- ☐ **B** Legionella serology is the investigation of choice if atypical pneumonia is possible
- ☐ **C** In patients with chest X-ray changes, a repeat chest X-ray on completion of the antibiotic course will confirm cure
- ☐ **D** Azithromycin is the first line antibiotic of choice due to its good side-effect profile
- ☐ **E** No pathogen is isolated in 45% of cases

24 Statistics about accidents show that which THREE of the following are true:
- ☐ **A** Road traffic accidents are the most common cause of accidents in young
- ☐ **B** Falls are the most common cause of accidents in people over 65 years
- ☐ **C** Seat belt legislation resulted in little reduction in death or serious accidents for drivers
- ☐ **D** Drowning is an unusual cause of accidents in children under 14 years
- ☐ **E** Alcohol is a significant factor in accidents occurring in young people and the elderly

25 A finding of a raised prolactin level could NOT be explained by which ONE of the following?
- ☐ **A** Hypothyroidism
- ☐ **B** Metoclopramide
- ☐ **C** Pregnancy
- ☐ **D** Bromocriptine
- ☐ **E** Acromegaly

26 THREE of the following have been shown to be ototoxic:
- ☐ **A** Quinine
- ☐ **B** Frusemide
- ☐ **C** Erythromycin
- ☐ **D** Ciprofloxacin
- ☐ **E** Nifedipine

27 A 54-year-old patient presents with her periods 'restarting' after an absence of one year. Select THREE of the following:

- ☐ **A** She should be investigated
- ☐ **B** Topical oestrogens are a probable cause
- ☐ **C** Cervical polyps do not cause symptoms at this age
- ☐ **D** Urethral caruncles do not bleed
- ☐ **E** If accompanied by discharge this increases the likelihood of carcinoma of the cervix

28 Select TWO of the following about coronary artery bypass grafting:

- ☐ **A** It does not improve the survival of those with persisting anginal pain at rest
- ☐ **B** Operative mortality is approximately 10% in the UK
- ☐ **C** Females have a higher operative risk than males
- ☐ **D** If angina is absent at one year, recurrence risk is minimal
- ☐ **E** Internal mammary artery conduits produce better results than saphenous vein grafts

29 In statements about smoking and alcohol use in the U.K. which ONE of the following is not correct?

- ☐ **A** More women smoke than men
- ☐ **B** The average male smoker consumes approximately 20 cigarettes per day
- ☐ **C** Cigarette smoking in children aged 11–15 years is falling
- ☐ **D** Patients with alcohol problems consult their GPs twice as often as the average patient
- ☐ **E** Heavy drinkers who do not smoke have an increased incidence of cancers

30 When considering post-viral fatigue syndrome, which TWO of the following apply?

- ☐ **A** Fatigue is the second most common reason to consult the doctor by the general population
- ☐ **B** Delayed fatigue developing after exertion would suggest a different diagnosis
- ☐ **C** The majority of patients have no psychopathology
- ☐ **D** Depression is the most common psychiatric disorder
- ☐ **E** Prolonged rest is the treatment of choice

31 Select THREE of the following about schizophrenia:

- ☐ **A** The onset is usually between 15 and 45 years of age
- ☐ **B** The age of onset is earlier in females
- ☐ **C** Paranoid delusions are usually diagnostic
- ☐ **D** A long duration of untreated psychosis predicts a chronic disease
- ☐ **E** Apathy is common in chronic schizophrenia

32 **Sudden infant death syndrome (SIDS) is associated with which THREE of the following?**
- ☐ **A** A difficult delivery in labour
- ☐ **B** A mother addicted to narcotic agents
- ☐ **C** A decreasing risk with greater parity
- ☐ **D** Sleeping in a prone position
- ☐ **E** Being a twin

33 **Regarding trigeminal neuralgia, which of the following is the SINGLE best initial treatment?**
- ☐ **A** Amitryptyline
- ☐ **B** Sumatriptan
- ☐ **C** Carbamazepine
- ☐ **D** Radiofrequency ablation
- ☐ **E** Baclofen

THEME: STROKE MANAGEMENT

The following are sometimes used in the management of stroke:
- **A** Warfarin
- **B** Aspirin
- **C** CT scan
- **D** MRI scan
- **E** Carotid endarterectomy

Match the following with the most appropriate from the above list

34 Used in the primary prevention of strokes when the risk appears relatively low ☐

35 Used in the primary prevention of strokes in a patient under 65 years who has had a transient ischaemic attack ☐

36 Useful when needing to separate infarction from haemorrhage ☐

37 Useful when a carotid bruit is heard on clinical examination ☐

38 Used in high-risk patients ☐

39 Useful in a 60-year-old man with atrial fibrillation but no family or personal history of stroke ☐

40 **When treating scabies with gamma benzene hexachloride (Quellada), which TWO of the following are relevant?**
- ☐ **A** The application should be preceded by a hot bath
- ☐ **B** It is contraindicated in pregnant women
- ☐ **C** Itching that fails to resolve 2 weeks after treatment is an indication for a further application
- ☐ **D** A single application left in contact with the skin has been shown to be adequate treatment
- ☐ **E** Treatment of the face is essential if all the mites are to be eradicated

41 **Select ONE statement about the alcohol withdrawal syndrome:**
- ☐ **A** The risk of developing symptoms is related to the amount of intake
- ☐ **B** Seizures typically occur within the first 12 hours after stopping drinking
- ☐ **C** Delirium tremens has a mortality in excess of 20%
- ☐ **D** Auditory hallucinations occurring after 72 hours of the last alcohol intake would signify that there was some other pathology
- ☐ **E** Withdrawal symptoms typically commence within 3–6 hours of the last drink

42 **Select TWO features about agoraphobic patients:**
- ☐ **A** Are typically female
- ☐ **B** Have a higher incidence of marital problems than the general population
- ☐ **C** Typically have a fear of fainting
- ☐ **D** If they report depersonalisation this would indicate other pathology
- ☐ **E** Show a good response to aversion therapy

43 **Select THREE characteristics of fixed drug eruptions:**
- ☐ **A** Always occur at the same site with a specific drug
- ☐ **B** Appear within 5–10 minutes of administration
- ☐ **C** Discoloration of the skin remains for several months
- ☐ **D** Have blistering in the lesions which makes the diagnosis unlikely
- ☐ **E** Have well-defined borders

44 **Select THREE of the following about the Access to Health Records Act 1990:**
- ☐ **A** Provides rights of access to computer held records only
- ☐ **B** Health visitor records are exempt
- ☐ **C** There is no right of access to notes made before November 1991
- ☐ **D** A doctor has 21 days to respond to a request for access
- ☐ **E** A fee may be charged for allowing a patient access

45 **Select ONE piece of advice given to patients about driving:**
- ☐ **A** Patients who have a pacemaker fitted should not drive
- ☐ **B** After a heart attack, patients should avoid driving for 3 months
- ☐ **C** An epileptic can only drive when he has been fit-free for 2 years
- ☐ **D** Patients experiencing a migraine headache should not drive
- ☐ **E** Patients should not drive for 4 weeks following coronary angioplasty
- ☐ **F** Patients should not drive for 12 hours following minor out-patient surgery requiring a general anaesthetic

46 THREE of the following statements are true of cardiac valve disease in the elderly:

☐ **A** Aortic stenosis is the commonest valve lesion
☐ **B** A soft murmur excludes aortic stenosis
☐ **C** Rheumatic heart disease is the cause of the majority of cases of mitral stenosis
☐ **D** Prolapsed mitral valve is the main cause of mitral regurgitation
☐ **E** The majority of patients over 70 years of age have a murmur

47 TWO of the following drugs undergo significant first-pass metabolism:

☐ **A** Salbutamol
☐ **B** Paracetamol
☐ **C** Codeine
☐ **D** Metoclopramide
☐ **E** Aciclovir

48 In the management of heart failure, which ONE of the following treatments is unlikely to be helpful:

☐ **A** Spironolactone
☐ **B** Digoxin
☐ **C** Calcium channel blockers
☐ **D** Beta blockers
☐ **E** ACE inhibitors
☐ **F** Exercise training

49 Select TWO of the following about acute suppurative otitis media:

☐ **A** Has a peak incidence at 2–3 years of age
☐ **B** Is more common in smoking households
☐ **C** Is more common in atopic individuals
☐ **D** The majority are bacterial in origin
☐ **E** Approximately 5% will develop mastoiditis

50 Concerning pulmonary embolism in pregnancy, select THREE of the following:

☐ **A** The majority of cases occur antenatally
☐ **B** Primigravidae are more at risk than belle multigravidae
☐ **C** Patients with a previous history of thromboembolism should have prophylactic treatment throughout the pregnancy
☐ **D** It is the commonest cause of maternal death in the UK
☐ **E** Those who have an instrumental delivery are at greater risk of a post-natal embolism than those who deliver normally

51 Select THREE statements about acute appendicitis:

☐ **A** Increasing dietary fibre has been shown to decrease the incidence of the condition

☐ **B** It occurs in more than 10% of the population

☐ **C** The majority of elderly patients have perforated by the time they reach surgery

☐ **D** Few children have perforated by the time they reach surgery

☐ **E** Retrocaecal appendices are associated with classic symptoms

52 Select THREE of the following about leukaemia in childhood:

☐ **A** The peak incidence is at 7–12 years of age

☐ **B** The majority are acute myeloblastic leukaemia

☐ **C** The majority of patients with acute lymphoblastic leukaemia will survive 5 years after cessation of therapy

☐ **D** Maintenance cytotoxics are usually needed for about 3 years

☐ **E** One new case will be seen every 200 years

53 Choose THREE of the following items about cancer of the colon:

☐ **A** A diet high in animal fat and low in fibre appears to be a risk factor

☐ **B** Familial adenomatous polyposis coli always leads to cancer of the colon if the patient lives to normal life span

☐ **C** Hereditary non-polyposis colorectal cancer accounts for about 15% of cases of colonic cancer

☐ **D** Familial adenomatous polyposis presents in early teenage years with loose stools and mucus

☐ **E** Faecal occult blood testing is a sensitive test for colonic cancer

54 Select ONE statement concerning impotence in men:

☐ **A** Sudden onset is more likely to be organic

☐ **B** Is more common in those with peripheral arterial disease

☐ **C** When treated with papaverine, it is given into the dorsal vein of the penis

☐ **D** An erection produced by papaverine typically lasts 12 hours

☐ **E** Vacuum condoms are available on NHS prescription

THEME: BREAST CANCER SCREENING

The following are important reports and trials about breast cancer screening:
A   Health Insurance Plan
B   Malmo Mammographic Screening Trial
C   The Nijmegen Project
D   UK Trial of Early Detection of Breast Cancer Group
E   The Forrest Report

Match the following with ONE of the above

55   Invited some women to learn breast self-examination   □

56   An early randomly controlled trial, with a one yearly screening interval, showed a 30% reduction in mortality in woman aged 40–60 years   □

57   A randomly controlled trial involving women older than 45 years showing no significant difference in mortality between screened and controlled group survival   □

58   Was used as the basis for the introduction of the UK National Breast Screening Programme   □

59   A case–control trial using one view mammography of women 35 years and older showed greater than 50% reduction of mortality   □

THEME: DIABETES

The following studies concern diabetic retinopathy:
A   The Oslo Study
B   The Pima Indians of Arizona
C   The Bedford Study
D   The Stena Study

Match the following statements to the most appropriate study

60   The most marked worsening was seen in those with worst and best control   □

61   Studied a group of whom 50% are diabetic   □

62   Patients showed slowed deterioration with subcutaneous insulin infusion   □

63 Choose THREE statements about the senile squalor syndrome (Diogenes' syndrome):

☐ **A** Typically affects married couples
☐ **B** The majority have significant psychiatric illness
☐ **C** Is significantly associated with heavy alcohol intake
☐ **D** Rapidly improves on admission to hospital
☐ **E** Patients are of above average intelligence

64 Which ONE of the following does not apply to the mumps, measles and rubella (MMR) vaccine?

☐ **A** More than 85% of 2-year-old children have been vaccinated in the UK
☐ **B** The incidence of confirmed rubella in pregnancy has more than halved since introduction of the vaccine
☐ **C** It is contraindicated in children who are HIV positive
☐ **D** Meningoencephalitis has been reported following exposure to the vaccine
☐ **E** Should be used within one hour of reconstitution

65 Choose TWO items concerning squint:

☐ **A** It is a typical presentation of retinoblastoma
☐ **B** Paralytic squints are more common in children than in adults
☐ **C** Operative treatment will correct amblyopia at the age of 8 years
☐ **D** Patching can lead to amblyopia in the 'good' eye
☐ **E** Co-operation of the child is necessary before considering referral

66 Which ONE of the following does not trigger anxiety states?

☐ **A** Monoamine oxidase inhibitors
☐ **B** Hypoglycaemia
☐ **C** Severe angina
☐ **D** Caffeine
☐ **E** Paroxysmal atrial tachycardia

THEME: SCROTAL SWELLINGS

Some causes of lumps found in the scrotum include:
A   Inguinal hernia
B   Epididymal cyst
C   Hydrocoele
D   TB of epididymis
E   Testicular tumour

Choose the most appropriate of these in the following circumstances

67   In a 32-year-old man there is a lump in the scrotum which appears hard; the testis cannot be felt but the lump transilluminates very well

68   In a 38-year-old man there is a small swelling in the scrotum; on examination the upper end of the swelling cannot be found

69   A 34-year-old presents with a swelling in his scrotum; the testes appear normal clinically but there is a lump in the scrotum which transilluminates slightly

70   A 41-year-old has noticed on self-examination a lump on one side of the scrotum; this is confirmed as being a hard thickening just separate from the testis

71 Oral contraceptives confer THREE of the following gynaecological benefits:
☐   A   Decreased incidence of cervical erosion
☐   B   Suppression of benign breast disease
☐   C   Decrease in ovarian cancer
☐   D   Decrease in endometrial cancer
☐   E   Decreased risk of carcinoma in situ of the cervix

72 A 30-year-old female patient presents with episodes of vomiting. TWO of the following would suggest a diagnosis of Addison's disease:
☐   A   Abdominal pain
☐   B   Weight loss
☐   C   Hypokalaemia
☐   D   Very low blood urea
☐   E   Hypertension

73 Select TWO items about restless legs:
- ☐ **A** Are a familial complaint
- ☐ **B** Show a tendency to worsen in the evening
- ☐ **C** Are worsened by benzodiazepine hypnotics
- ☐ **D** An association with systemic disease has not been shown
- ☐ **E** Is associated with excessive coffee ingestion

74 Choose FOUR items relating to milestones of childhood development:
- ☐ **A** By 9 months, most children are standing with support
- ☐ **B** At 6 weeks, most children are smiling and their eyes follow in the horizontal plane
- ☐ **C** At 9 months, most children can walk with one hand held
- ☐ **D** At 1 year, most children can use about 20 words with meaning
- ☐ **E** By the age of 3 years, most children are dry by day
- ☐ **F** At 3 years, children can usually walk up and down stairs alone

75 Choose TWO of the following about audit:
- ☐ **A** Is a contractual obligation for GPs
- ☐ **B** Is prescriptive
- ☐ **C** Is a passive process
- ☐ **D** Is looking for mistakes
- ☐ **E** The boundaries between audit and research are clear-cut
- ☐ **F** Is a process of education through experience

76 Choose THREE of the following about acute pyelonephritis in pregnancy:
- ☐ **A** Typically presents in the first trimester
- ☐ **B** Reoccurs in approximately one-quarter of cases
- ☐ **C** Is associated with an increased chance of pre-term labour
- ☐ **D** Is associated with fetal growth condition
- ☐ **E** Ciprofloxacin is indicated for treatment

77 Select THREE of the statements about puerperal psychosis:
- ☐ **A** Typically presents by the 6th week following delivery
- ☐ **B** Typically presents with mania, eventually becoming depressive
- ☐ **C** Is associated with an increased risk of infanticide
- ☐ **D** ECT has been shown to be of no value in treatment
- ☐ **E** Typically remits within 2–3 months

78 Adult gastrointestinal infections have been shown to have THREE of the following characteristics:
- ☐ **A** Campylobacter typically produces a febrile illness
- ☐ **B** Shigella is associated with blood in the stools
- ☐ **C** Giardia produces severe colicky pain
- ☐ **D** Salmonella without blood stream invasion lasts 3–4 days
- ☐ **E** Salmonella with blood stream invasion typically lasts 7–10 days

79 Select THREE of these items about hypertrophic cardiomyopathy:
- ☐ **A** Is an inherited disorder
- ☐ **B** Is typically a disease of old age
- ☐ **C** Characteristically presents with shortness of breath
- ☐ **D** Is an uncommon cause of sudden death in athletes
- ☐ **E** Electrocardiographic changes are typical

80 Select ONE of the following items that has been shown to reduce the incidence of dementia:
- ☐ **A** Social support of the bereaved
- ☐ **B** A well-balanced diet
- ☐ **C** Avoidance of beef
- ☐ **D** Treatment of hypertension
- ☐ **E** Over 75 screening by General Practitioners

81 Select FOUR poor predictive factors for chronic schizophrenia:
- ☐ **A** History of perinatal trauma
- ☐ **B** Insidious onset
- ☐ **C** Late onset
- ☐ **D** Higher socio-economic class
- ☐ **E** Schizoid personality trait
- ☐ **F** Family history of schizophrenia
- ☐ **G** Living in a Third World country

82 Select THREE items about corneal ulcers due to herpes simplex infection:
- ☐ **A** Recur in the majority of cases
- ☐ **B** If associated with anterior uveitis may lead to secondary glaucoma
- ☐ **C** Typically need treatment with acyclovir for more than 2 weeks
- ☐ **D** Decreases visual acuity in the majority of patients
- ☐ **E** Have a characteristic appearance on staining the cornea with fluorescein
- ☐ **F** Are typically painless

83 Select THREE items about chlamydial infection:
- ☐ **A** Typically causes a vaginitis
- ☐ **B** Is asymptomatic in the majority of women
- ☐ **C** Is the most common cause of chronic prostatitis
- ☐ **D** If discovered in pregnancy treatment should begin before delivery
- ☐ **E** Associated urethritis is typically associated with a dysuria and a negative midstream urine culture

84 Select THREE of the following about the epidemiology of backache in the United Kingdom:

☐ **A**   More than 10 million working days are lost per year
☐ **B**   The average General Practitioner sees less than 30 acute backs per year
☐ **C**   The majority recover within one month without treatment
☐ **D**   Fewer than 1 in 200 undergo surgery
☐ **E**   Strict bed rest for four weeks has been shown to reduce the overall time away from work

85 THREE of the following have been shown to trigger attacks of irritable bowel syndrome:

☐ **A**   Metronidazole
☐ **B**   Wheat bran
☐ **C**   Milk
☐ **D**   Nystatin
☐ **E**   Hypnosis

86 Nocturnal cramps have been shown to be caused by THREE of the following:

☐ **A**   Cirrhosis of the liver
☐ **B**   Venous obstruction
☐ **C**   Peripheral arterial disease
☐ **D**   L5/S1 disc compression
☐ **E**   Salbutamol administration

THEME: CHILDHOOD MILESTONES

Children's ages:
A   12 months
B   18 months
C   2 years
D   3 years
E   4 years
F   5 years

At what age would most children be able to perform the following tasks?

87   Can state age and sex

88   Can state first and last name

89   Can say 2–3 words with meaning

90   Can build a 3–4 cube tower

91   Can hop on one foot

92   Can copy a circle

93 **Active management of the third stage of labour by use of controlled cord traction and oxytocic drugs has been shown to be associated with THREE of the following:**
☐ A   A longer third stage of labour
☐ B   An increased incidence of post-partum haemorrhage
☐ C   An increased incidence of retained placenta
☐ D   An increased incidence of post-partum hypertension
☐ E   An increased incidence of post-partum vomiting

94 **Hypercalcaemia can result from which THREE of the following?**
☐ A   Malignancy
☐ B   Hypothyroidism
☐ C   Use of thiazide diuretics
☐ D   Immobilisation
☐ E   Vitamin D deficiency
☐ F   Renal dialysis

95 A baby is diagnosed as having a patent ductus arteriosus at 7 days of age. Select THREE of the following:

☐ **A** Closure typically takes place within 48 hours of birth
☐ **B** Prematurity is associated with delay in closure
☐ **C** Indomethacin has been shown to promote closure
☐ **D** Without treatment the majority of patients will die before 30 years of age
☐ **E** Infective endocarditis rarely complicates the condition

96 A 19-year-old man has come to see you for travel advice before going round the world in his gap year. He tells you he has heard that antimalarial tablets are ineffective and have lots of side-effects. Which of the following are true regarding malaria? (THREE best answers)

☐ **A** Patients who become unwell only after returning home, are unlikely to have malaria
☐ **B** There is an effective vaccine for malaria
☐ **C** Mefloquine should not be used by people with a previous history of mental illness
☐ **D** Insecticide treated nets are proven to be beneficial in preventing malaria
☐ **E** The fever in malaria always follows a swinging pattern
☐ **F** Doxycycline is effective in prophylaxis but may cause sunburn
☐ **G** People who have lived in malarial areas as children need not take antimalarials when they return
☐ **H** Malaria is never fatal

THEME: CHEST PAIN

Causes of chest pain seen in general practice include:

A   Pulmonary embolism
B   Myocardial infarction
C   Pericarditis
D   Pneumothorax
E   Oesophageal reflux
F   Related to spinal cord
G   Aortic aneurysm
H   Cardiac neurosis

Which would be the most likely diagnosis in the following patients?

97   A tall man of 22 years who experiences a tight pain and becomes very short of breath suddenly ☐

98   A rather obese 43-year-old lady experiences repeated burning pain especially on bending to put on her shoes and in the evening after dinner ☐

99   A 24-year-old female has sudden central chest pain; friends say she went 'blue' and she starts spitting up specks of blood ☐

100   A 52-year-old man has aching upper chest pain and shoulder pain which he has noticed since changing office one week ago ☐

101   A 68-year-old man describes a dull ache which suddenly became a 'tearing' feeling; this pain goes into his back and he feels cold and clammy ☐

102   A 64-year-old man experiences severe chest pain with sudden onset of sweating and difficulty breathing; he told his work colleagues he had pain in his right arm and they noticed he was very pale ☐

103   A 44-year-old man describes pain under his left nipple, and is unable to take a deep breath; he is tender in the area of pain and around the heart apex beat area ☐

104   When considering fibrinolytic drugs in myocardial infarction, which statement is correct?

☐   **A**   Streptokinase is given by i.v. bolus injection
☐   **B**   The use of aspirin is contraindicated for 12 months after use of streptokinase
☐   **C**   Fibrinolytic drugs are contraindicated in patients over 80 years of age
☐   **D**   Streptokinase can be repeated 3 months after initial use if a second infarct develops at that time
☐   **E**   A recently diagnosed duodenal ulcer is a contraindication to the use of a fibrinolytic

THEME: HEADACHES

Types of headache include:
A   Tension headache
B   Cervical nerve root irritation
C   Migraine
D   Cluster headaches
E   Sinusitis
F   Depression

Match the following statements with the most appropriate type of headache

105   A 35-year-old woman with patches of tenderness in the scalp during headaches   ☐

106   A 40-year-old man with episodes of severe headaches and a watery eye   ☐

107   A 32-year-old woman who describes her headache as a weight on the top of the head   ☐

108   A 54-year-old woman with aches and pains, poor appetite and a persistent headache   ☐

109   A 42-year-old teacher who gets flushing and pallor at the onset of her headache   ☐

110   A 46-year-old secretary who describes a throbbing headache associated with difficulty in focusing on her shorthand work   ☐

111 Which ONE of the following would not represent a developmental milestone in a normal child?

- ☐ **A**   At 6 weeks the Moro reflex is still retained
- ☐ **B**   At 7 months the majority can stand without support
- ☐ **C**   At 12 months they can say 3 words with meaning
- ☐ **D**   At 30 months the majority will be dry at night
- ☐ **E**   At 54 months the majority can dress themselves

THEME: INCOME

General practice income is derived from various sources, including:

A   Non-medical income
B   Private medical work
C   Practice allowances
D   Capitation fees
E   Item-of-service payments
F   Reimbursements

Match the following with the appropriate source

112 Solicitors' reports ☐

113 Work as a school medical officer ☐

114 Child health surveillance ☐

115 Night visit payments ☐

116 Computer systems payment ☐

117 Rural practice payment ☐

118 Lecturing on an MRCGP course ☐

THEME: THROMBOLYTIC TRIALS

Thrombolytic treatment trials and groups include:
A   GREAT group survey
B   ISIS-2
C   European Myocardial Infarct Project
D   British Heart Foundation Working Group
E   GISSI

For which of these is the following true?

119   Suggests that GPs who give thrombolytics at home should have a defibrillator available ☐

120   Double-blind trial of anistreplase against placebo in home or hospital; it showed mortality was almost 50% lower in the early treatment group in this rural study ☐

121   Compared anistreplase against placebo in different situations – showed cardiac deaths were about 15% less in pre-hospital treatment ☐

122   Compared streptokinase and aspirin usage ☐

THEME: MENTAL HEALTH ACT

The following are some sections of the 1983 Mental Health Act:
A   2
B   3
C   5
D   135
E   136

Which section applies to the following situations?

123   Gives the police right of entry into premises to remove a patient to a place of safety ☐

124   Used in an emergency situation in hospital ☐

125   Used for a maximum of 28 days ☐

126   Hospital managers must appeal on behalf of the patient on renewal if the patient does not appeal ☐

127   Allows police to remove a patient from a public place to a place of safety ☐

THEME: BENEFITS

The following are some of the many welfare benefits:
A   Severe Disablement Allowance
B   Attendance Allowance
C   Disability Living Allowance
D   Incapacity Benefit
E   Statutory Sick Pay

Which benefit relates to the following?

128 Paid to a person who requires help with mobility and is virtually unable to walk ☐

129 Paid by employers to employees for 28 weeks ☐

130 For someone incapable of any work, who has not paid any National Insurance contributions and is at least 80% disabled ☐

131 Paid to someone over 65 who requires substantial personal care or supervision ☐

132 Paid to a person under 65 who requires help with personal care day and night ☐

133 Paid at three rates to someone who continues to be unfit for any work ☐

134 A 1-year-old child with diarrhoea attends the surgery, select THREE of the following that indicate significant dehydration:
☐ A   Crying with few tears
☐ B   Visible weight loss
☐ C   Bradycardia
☐ D   Dry mouth
☐ E   Irritability

THEME: INFECTIOUS DISEASES

There is usually an interval between the onset of disease and the appearance of a rash in the following infectious diseases:

A   Rubella
B   Chickenpox
C   Scarlet fever
D   Measles
E   Typhoid

Match the following with the appropriate disease

135   A period of 7–14 days between disease onset and rash ☐

136   Usually 3–5 days between onset and appearance of rash ☐

137   A very short interval or none at all between onset and rash; the rash is characteristic with lesions of different stages ☐

138   An interval of 1–2 days; a very long infectivity period which can be dramatically shortened by appropriate treatment ☐

139   A very short or no interval between disease onset and rash; the rash is often transient and clinical diagnosis unreliable ☐

THEME: STATISTICS

In statistics the following are commonly used:

A   Standard deviation
B   Mode
C   Median
D   Mean
E   Correlation coefficient

Match the following statements with the appropriate term

140   The most commonly occurring value ☐

141   If +1, this indicates a complete direct association ☐

142   Measures the dispersion around the average value ☐

143   The middle figure when all are put in order ☐

144   The arithmetic average ☐

145 A 20-year-old patient with asthma rapidly becomes more dyspnoeic. Select THREE of the following:

- ☐ **A** The extent of rhonchi predicts the severity of the attack
- ☐ **B** Pneumothorax typically occurs in this age group
- ☐ **C** Tachycardia is a reliable predictor of severity
- ☐ **D** Peak flow levels are unreliable in judging severe disease
- ☐ **E** The majority of acute attacks develop within 24 hours of the first symptom

THEME: SCREENING

The results of a screening test looking for diabetes in a general practice study were as follows:

	Diabetes present	Diabetes not present
Screening test positive	164	57
Screening test negative	31	98

Options available:

A	164	E	164/195	I	57/155
B	57	F	164/221	J	57/122
C	31	G	31/129	K	98/129
D	98	H	31/195	L	98/155

Select the appropriate option

146 Sensitivity ☐

147 Specificity ☐

148 Positive predictive value ☐

149 Negative predictive value ☐

150 False positive ☐

151 Select ONE of the following concerning Parkinson's disease:

- ☐ **A** Tremor is the most prominent feature of parkinsonism in the elderly
- ☐ **B** It has a prevalence of approximately 1 in 1000 in the elderly
- ☐ **C** Prolonged use of levodopa is associated with 'freezing' episodes
- ☐ **D** Selegiline is only suitable for patients who no longer respond to levodopa
- ☐ **E** It does not cause cognitive impairment

THEME: ILLUSTRATIONS

Link the following illustrations to the appropriate diagnosis from the option list:

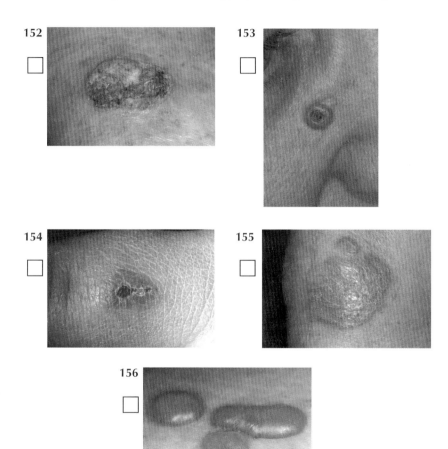

152 ☐

153 ☐

154 ☐

155 ☐

156 ☐

Diagnosis option list:

A Basal cell carcinoma
B Measles
C Pemphigoid
D Pemphigus
E Psoriasis
F Rubella
G Scabies
H Squamous cell carcinoma
I Varicella

157 A patient presents with acute onset of a painful, photophobic red eye with impairment of vision. Which THREE of the following are possible diagnoses?

- ☐ **A**   Episcleritis
- ☐ **B**   Iritis
- ☐ **C**   Keratitis
- ☐ **D**   Sub-conjunctival haemorrhage
- ☐ **E**   Glaucoma

158 The differential diagnosis of a pustular rash occurring on the palms of the hands should include which THREE of the following?

- ☐ **A**   Infected eczma
- ☐ **B**   Scabies
- ☐ **C**   Pustular psoriasis
- ☐ **D**   Ichthyosis
- ☐ **E**   Erythema multiforme

THEME: RHEUMATOID ARTHRITIS

Drugs used in the treatment of rheumatoid arthritis include:

A   Methotrexate
B   Chloroquine
C   Gold
D   Penicillamine
E   Sulphasalazine

Match the following statements with the most appropriate of these drugs

159   Can cause exfoliative dermatitis ☐

160   Can cause retinal damage ☐

161   Can cause hepatic and pulmonary fibrosis ☐

162   Oral pigmentation, similar to that in Addison's disease, may be seen ☐

163   Can be used in severe uncontrolled psoriasis ☐

164   Monthly Amsler testing by the patient may be used in long-term therapy ☐

165   Can be associated with azoospermia ☐

166   Loss of taste may occur but returns whether or not treatment is stopped ☐

167 You see a 37-year-old man in surgery who has come to discuss the results of his recent gastroscopy. This showed moderately severe gastro-oesophageal reflux. Which of the following is the SINGLE best treatment option?

☐ A   Referral to a surgeon
☐ B   Treatment with H2 receptor antagonist
☐ C   Triple therapy to eradicate *Helicobacter pylori*
☐ D   Treatment with a proton pump inhibitor
☐ E   Advice regarding weight loss
☐ F   Dietary modification

168 During the normal ovulatory cycle TWO of the following apply:

☐ A   After ovulation, cervical mucus is a watery, stretchy, transparent secretion
☐ B   During ovulation the os will admit the tip of a finger
☐ C   Basal body temperature is higher in the luteal phase
☐ D   After ovulation the cervix remains soft to the touch
☐ E   Ovulation predictor tests measure oestrogenic surge

169 From the following list select the SINGLE best treatment for stress incontinence in women?

☐ A   Oestrogen therapy in postmenopausal women
☐ B   Colposuspension
☐ C   Faradic stimulation of pelvic floor
☐ D   Anterior colporrhaphy
☐ E   Doxazosin
☐ F   Intermittent self catheterisation

SUMMARY COMPLETION QUESTION
Read the extract below from the paper 'Reliability of N-terminal pro-brain natriuretic peptide assay in diagnosis of heart failure: cohort study in representative and high risk community populations.' BMJ 2002;321:1498–1453.

Abstract
Objective: To investigate the performance of a novel assay for N-terminal pro-brain natriuretic peptide (NT-proBNP) in diagnosing heart failure in various randomly selected general and high risk community populations.
Design: Community cohort study (substudy of the echocardiographic heart of England screening study).
Main outcome measure: Sensitivity, specificity, positive and negative predictive values, likelihood ratios, and area under receiver operating characteristic curve for NT-proBNP assay in the diagnosis of heart failure.
Results: For NT-proBNP in the diagnosis of heart failure in the general population (population screen), a level of >36 pmol/l had a sensitivity of 100%, a specificity of 70%, a positive predictive value of 7%, a negative predictive value of 100%, and an area under the receiver operating characteristic curve of

0.92 (95% confidence interval 0.82 to 1.0). Similar negative predictive values were found for patients from the three other populations screened.

Methods

This is a prospective substudy of the echocardiographic heart of England screening (ECHOES) study of the prevalence of left ventricular dysfunction and heart failure.

The main study was carried out in 16 randomly selected primary care practice populations in England after stratification for age and socioeconomic status. Patients were randomly selected from each of four population cohorts, identified in each practice from computerised practice registers: randomly sampled patients from those aged 45 years and older (general population screen); patients with a clinical diagnostic label of heart failure; patients prescribed diuretic drugs; and patients at high risk of heart failure (history of myocardial infarction, angina, hypertension, or diabetes).

We conducted this substudy in the last four practices, containing the final 607 consecutively screened patients randomly selected from the four target groups (307 in the general population, 103 with an existing clinical diagnosis of heart failure, 87 taking diuretics, and 134 at high risk of heart failure, with some sampled from more than one cohort). These practices were representative of the socioeconomic spread of patients achieved by the initial stratification. All patients gave informed consent, and the study had full ethical approval.

We screened patients by history, New York Heart Association functional class, clinical examination, quality of life (SF-36 health status questionnaire), spirometry, resting 12 lead electrocardiography, and echocardiography, including Doppler studies. We diagnosed heart failure on the basis of the agreed gold standard of the European and American guideline criteria (box). Three experienced cardiovascular clinicians conducted blinded adjudication of clinical records in equivocal cases. Aetiologies for heart failure included left ventricular systolic dysfunction, atrial fibrillation, and significant valve disease. We made no attempt to define diastolic heart failure in this study.

A research fellow took blood for the peptide assay from the right antecubital fossa of consenting patients after five minutes' supine rest, into 5 ml K+EDTA tubes. Blood was kept at room temperature for up to 24 hours before transport to a local laboratory for centrifugation and freezing of plasma to 20°C. Once a week the frozen samples were collected for central storage at 70°C. Assays of NT-proBNP (Roche Diagnostics, Germany) were subsequently performed at a central independent laboratory, blinded to the results of the screening assessments. The NT-proBNP immunoassay – an enzyme linked immunosorbant assay (ELISA) – required only three operator dependent steps and total incubation of under two hours.

Now look at this critique of the abstract.

The study attempts to answer the question 'Is NT-proBNP a useful

(170)_____ tool in the investigation of heart failure?' To be clinically useful in confirming heart failure a test should have a

(171)_____ sensitivity and specificity, although it may have a low positive **(172)**_____ value, depending on disease prevalence. The study uses a cohort rather than a randomised control study and compares the intervention with the **(173)**_____ diagnostic tool, echocardiography.

The participants were screened by an accepted **(174)**_____ tool, the New York Heart Association classification, and **(175)**_____ measures of quality of life as well as standard bedside investigations. Equivocal cases were diagnosed by observers who were **(176)**_____, to minimize inclusion bias.

Blood samples were taken and analysed according to a **(177)**_____ protocol. The outcome measures were appropriate for the research question, and were clinically applicable. The high **(178)**_____ makes the test a clinically useful test for excluding heart failure, i.e a negative test suggests heart failure unlikely and echocardiogram unnecessary, while the lower **(179)**_____ suggests that the test on its own is insufficient to diagnose heart failure, since false positives may be present.

For each of the numbered gaps in the critique, choose one word from the following list which best completes the sentence.

A   blinded
B   diagnostic
C   exclusion
D   false
E   gold standard
F   high
G   inclusion
H   low
I   negative
J   objective
K   positive
L   predictive
M   prevalence
N   randomised
O   sensitivity
P   specificity
Q   standardised
R   subjective
S   therapeutic
T   cathartic
U   true
V   validated
W   variance

180 Teratogenicity has been shown to occur as follows with which THREE of the drugs listed?

☐ **A** Sodium valproate has been shown to be associated with an increased risk of spina bifida

☐ **B** Phenytoin is associated with congenital heart disease

☐ **C** Carbamazepine is associated with bone marrow depression

☐ **D** Lithium carbonate is associated with congenital heart disease

☐ **E** Heparin is associated with central nervous system defects

THEME: MOUTH ULCERS

The causes of mouth ulcers include:

A Reiter's syndrome
B Primary syphilis
C Trauma
D Lichen planus
E Aphthous ulcers
F Hand, foot and mouth disease

Match the descriptions below with ONE of the above causes

181 Associated with arthritis, iritis and genital ulcers ☐

182 Has a painless, hard base ☐

183 Small round ulcers with a red margin, often painful ☐

184 Lesions are 'cotton wool' patches or erosive ☐

185 Sore throat is an early feature. There are often spots on the buttocks ☐

186 Lesions on soles and palms, vesicular in nature, may be seen ☐

Practice Paper 4

Total time allowed is three hours. Indicate your answers clearly by putting a tick or cross in the box alongside each answer or by writing the appropriate letter alongside the appropriate answer.

SUMMARY COMPLETION QUESTION
First read the extract from the methods section of the paper 'Blood pressure control in treated hypertensive patients: clinical performance of general practitioners.' BJGP 2001;51:9–14.

Method
Study design and subjects
We conducted a cross-sectional study on 195 GPs[1] in 132 practices in The Netherlands from November 1996 to April 1997. This study served as a baseline for an intervention trial to optimize the quality of cardiovascular care. GPs in the southern half of The Netherlands were invited by letter and via bulletins to participate. The participating GPs identified hypertensive patients treated with antihypertensive medication who came for a follow-up visit. We excluded all patients aged under 18 or over 80 years.

Measurements
In 1991, the Dutch College of General Practitioners issued national guidelines for the detection and management of hypertension. We used these clinical guidelines to select key recommendations for the management of uncontrolled blood pressure in treated hypertensive patients. These guidelines are based on scientific evidence, broad consensus, and clinical experience.[2] Most Dutch GPs are familiar with the guidelines six to 12 months after publication.[3] The target for pharmacological treatment in the 1991 Dutch hypertension guidelines is a DSP of ~90 mmHg (whereas other national and international guidelines recommend <90 mmHg[3]). The selected key recommendations included four recommendations for non-pharmacological measures, one for pharmacological treatment, and one for follow-up.

A self-report form was developed to assess clinical performance of GPs with respect to the 1991 Dutch hypertension guidelines. This form included items to assess age, sex, and clinical characteristics of the patient, as well as items to assess whether specific actions were performed by the GP. The questions on patient characteristics could be answered with yes (present), no (absent), and with a question mark, (unknown); these items concerned smoking, a body mass index of 30 kg/m^2, excessive alcohol intake, and target organ damage (heart failure, stroke, or impaired renal function). The actions could be scored with yes (action performed) and no (action not performed). The DSP and the period until the next follow-up appointment could be filled in as mmHg and weeks, respectively.

Characteristics of the GPs were determined using a questionnaire filled in by one GP per practice. Data were collected on age, sex, and working hours of the GPs, type of practice (single-handed versus partnership), and list size.

The practice location was classified as urban if the number of registered addresses in that area exceeded 1500 per square kilometre.

Procedure
Each GP recorded follow-up visits of hypertensive patients during a period of two months. Research assistants visited the practices at the start of the recording period to explain the use of the self-report forms. The GPs were asked to complete the forms immediately after a follow-up visit. The GPs were not allowed to screen the patient's record after the visit; only information that the GP was aware of during the visit was to be recorded on the form. Another study showed that GPs complete these kinds of self-report forms reliably (average kappa = 0.76)

Now look at this critique, which outlines the limitations of the study design.
The study sought to find **(1)**_____ between the control of blood pressure and characteristics of the GPs who managed the care.
(2)_____ was by letter and bulletin board, although it is unclear who was invited to join the study and what percentage of those invited agreed to participate. This may mask **(3)**_____ bias e.g. invitation by email may favour computerised practices. Self-selection may encourage participation of those who feel they are good at hypertension management while discouraging those who are less proficient. Exclusion of patients over 80 years old removes those difficult patients who often have multiple pathology, i.e. **(4)**_____ bias, which may limit **(5)**_____ of results to elderly populations.
    Use of a self report form for assessment of clinical performance may introduce **(6)**_____ in several areas: participants will know they are being assessed and this will influence their behaviour; participants will be recording their own performance and this will result in **(7)**_____ bias. The use of a sentinel GP in each practice to give in formation on characteristics of the other GPs in the study may mean that this information is not truly **(8)**_____ of individuals in the study.
    The time frame for **(9)**_____ may be criticised as being too small to give a **(10)**_____ selection of cases: patients with well controlled hypertension will not be included if they are attending every three months for review, resulting in bias towards newly diagnosed or poorly controlled patients.

For each of the numbered gaps in the critique, choose one word from the following list which best completes the sentence.
A   assessment
B   associations
C   bias
D   cohort
E   demonstrates

F differences
G exclusion
H generalisability
I inclusion
J indicative
K observer
L predictive
M recruitment
N representative
O sampling
P sensitivity
Q specificity
R suggests
S typical
T valid

11 Select ONE feature about cryotherapy:

☐ A The majority of children of 5 years of age can tolerate cryotherapy
☐ B Basal cell carcinomas are unsuitable for treatment
☐ C If a 'triple response' occurs the treatment should not be used again
☐ D Local swelling means the length of application was excessive
☐ E Liquid nitrogen does not destroy viruses

12 Select THREE features about polycystic ovary syndrome:

☐ A Is detectable by ultrasound
☐ B Is associated with oligomenorrhoea
☐ C Has no increased risk of early miscarriage
☐ D Has a decreased LH/FSH ratio
☐ E Associated hirsutism responds to cyproterone acetate

13 Select ONE item about seborrhoeic eczema in infancy:

☐ A Has a peak age of onset under 3 months of age
☐ B Is typically itchy
☐ C Resolves spontaneously in the majority of children
☐ D Typically fails to respond to emollients
☐ E Characteristically involves the flexures

THEME: SOCIAL CLASS

The Registrar General has six divisions of social class, with one division subdivided:

A   1
B   2
C   3N
D   3M
E   4
F   5

Place the following in the correct division as above

14   Shopkeeper ☐

15   Lawyer ☐

16   Managing director ☐

17   Labourer ☐

18   Clerical office worker ☐

19   Teacher ☐

THEME: LEG ULCERS

Leg ulcers are usually either:
A   Ischaemic
B   Venous

Match the following statements with the appropriate type of ulcer

20   Typically painful ☐

21   Typically pigmented ☐

22   Often in those patients over 70 years of age ☐

23   Often 'punched out' in appearance ☐

24   Surrounding skin is often affected ☐

25 Following a bereavement which ONE item is correct?
- ☐ **A** Approximately 20% of widowers die in the first year
- ☐ **B** Mortality is greater for women than for men
- ☐ **C** Mortality is not greater than expected at 3 years post-bereavement

26 Select TWO items concerning atrophic vaginitis:
- ☐ **A** Initial soreness from topical treatment diminishes with continued use
- ☐ **B** Candida infection is the most common cause of associated itching
- ☐ **C** Local oestrogen therapy initially burns on application
- ☐ **D** Prolonged local oestrogen therapy needs to be supplemented with progestogen
- ☐ **E** Oestrogenic effects on the sexual partner have been reported when the spouse uses topical oestrogens

27 Select THREE items about folic acid:
- ☐ **A** It is found in green vegetables
- ☐ **B** It is absorbed in the upper small bowel
- ☐ **C** It is degraded by cooking
- ☐ **D** It will reverse the macrocytosis associated with alcoholism
- ☐ **E** Its body stores are usually adequate for 3 years

28 A 13-year-old boy attends the surgery without an adult accompanying him, he has a sore throat. Legally a General Practitioner must carry out which ONE of the following?
- ☐ **A** Examine and prescribe as appropriate
- ☐ **B** Refuse to see him unless a responsible adult is present
- ☐ **C** Write to the parent asking them to come to the surgery
- ☐ **D** Examine but not prescribe

29 Consider the following data from the 4S trial of cholesterol reduction in patients with ischaemic heart disease:

> "..in the placebo group 12% of patients died, in the simvastatin group 8% of patients died, a risk reduction of 30%"

Which SINGLE answer correctly describes this data?
- ☐ **A** The absolute risk reduction is 30%
- ☐ **B** This data suggests that 3.3 patients are needed to be treated to prevent one death
- ☐ **C** The relative risk reduction is 12%–8%, i.e. 4%
- ☐ **D** The number of patients who need to be treated with simvastatin to prevent one death is 25
- ☐ **E** The number needed to harm is the reciprocal of the absolute risk reduction

30 Select THREE items about multiple sclerosis:
- ☐ **A**   The peak age of onset is about 30 years of age
- ☐ **B**   There is no hereditary disposition
- ☐ **C**   The majority of patients have full remission after the first attack
- ☐ **D**   Specific diagnostic tests are now available
- ☐ **E**   The mean life expectancy is over 30 years after the presenting complaint

31 Regarding the treatment of hypertension with ACE inhibitors, which ONE of the following statements is true?
- ☐ **A**   They may be safely used in combination with potassium sparing diuretics
- ☐ **B**   They have no effect on diabetic control
- ☐ **C**   In the HOPE study, ramipril produced a clinically significant blood pressure reduction in the majority of patients
- ☐ **D**   Renal function must be checked before initiating treatment and at 1 week after initiation
- ☐ **E**   ACE inhibitors must be started in hospital

32 Select THREE of the following statements about cancer of the cervix uteri:
- ☐ **A**   It is the cause of death in less than 5% of all female cancer deaths
- ☐ **B**   It is almost certainly caused by human papilloma virus (HPV) type 13
- ☐ **C**   The time taken to progress from CIN I to invasive carcinoma is about 10 years
- ☐ **D**   High-risk groups include early age of first pregnancy
- ☐ **E**   People in a low socio-economic class are at high risk
- ☐ **F**   The cervical screening programme has resulted in a decreasing death rate in young women

33 Select TWO items about head lice:
- ☐ **A**   The overall incidence is declining in the UK
- ☐ **B**   Resistance to standard preparations has not emerged
- ☐ **C**   Shampoos are more effective than lotions
- ☐ **D**   Treatment with carbaryl confers a residual protective effect
- ☐ **E**   Malathion is inactivated by swimming in chlorinated water
- ☐ **F**   Nit combing is essential if the disease is to be eradicated

34 Select TWO of the following statements about Wood's light:
- ☐ **A**   Is a source of infra-red light
- ☐ **B**   Causes eczematous skin to fluoresce pink
- ☐ **C**   Causes scalp ringworm to fluoresce green
- ☐ **D**   Will detect complete loss of pigment in vitiligo
- ☐ **E**   Will help differentiate common warts from seborrhoeic warts

35 Select TWO items concerning accidents in children:
- ☐ **A**   They are the most common cause of death in the 1–15 age group
- ☐ **B**   The majority of accidental deaths occur in the home
- ☐ **C**   Every year 1:100 children will attend the doctor with an accidental injury
- ☐ **D**   Preventative education has been shown to save lives

36 Select TWO items concerning people who are registered as blind:

☐ **A** A TV licence fee is not payable

☐ **B** Parking concessions are available

☐ **C** Severe Disablement Allowance (SDA) is not appropriate for those of working age

☐ **D** Free postage is available only on items relating to the incapacity

37 Hypertensive retinopathy has TWO of the following features:

☐ **A** Cotton wool spots are a feature of grade III retinopathy

☐ **B** The changes associated with grade II retinopathy are reversible with good hypertensive control

☐ **C** Retinal haemorrhages associated with retinopathy typically interfere with vision

☐ **D** Papilloedema due to hypertension is indistinguishable from that due to raised intracranial pressure

☐ **E** Arterio-venous crossing changes indicate arteriosclerosis

38 A 63-year-old man has a high ESR. Which ONE of the following would not support a diagnosis of myeloma?

☐ **A** Hypercalcaemia

☐ **B** Osteosclerotic lesions on X-ray

☐ **C** Rouleaux on a peripheral blood film

☐ **D** Peripheral neuropathy

☐ **E** Unexplained bruising

39 Select TWO items concerning endometriosis:

☐ **A** Ectopic endometrium is found in the majority of patients who have a laparoscopy for infertility

☐ **B** Medical treatment of endometriosis has been shown to improve future fertility

☐ **C** Pain is proportional to the extent of the disease

☐ **D** Cyclical pain is typical

☐ **E** Medical treatment rarely causes an improvement within 6 months

40 Select TWO statements about the Children Act 1989:

☐ **A** Emergency Protection Orders have a maximum duration of 8 days

☐ **B** Only social workers can apply for an Emergency Protection Order on a child

☐ **C** Parental access is precluded during an Emergency Protection Order

☐ **D** Care orders and supervision orders are mutually exclusive

☐ **E** Police protection provisions allow parental responsibility to be transferred to the police

41 Pacemakers are associated with which TWO of the following?
- ☐ **A** A restriction in activity
- ☐ **B** The majority being implanted for the treatment of complete heart block
- ☐ **C** Unreliable ECG appearances in the event of a myocardial infarction
- ☐ **D** The most common cause of death post-implant being primary pacemaker failure
- ☐ **E** A lifespan of at least 5 years

42 You are consulted by the parents of a 5-year-old boy recently diagnosed as having cystic fibrosis. Select TWO of the following items:
- ☐ **A** Late diagnosis implies medical neglect
- ☐ **B** There is a 1:2 chance of subsequent children being affected
- ☐ **C** The majority of patients with this condition will die by their late teens
- ☐ **D** Affected boys are usually azoospermic
- ☐ **E** Affected adolescents have an increased incidence of glucose intolerance

THEME: IMMUNISATIONS

Immunisations given to children include:
A MMR
B DTP
C DT
D BCG
E Polio

Which of the above apply to the following statements?

43 Usually given at 12–15 months ☐

44 Often given at 2, 3 and 4 months, and then not given again ☐

45 Given usually over the age of 10 years ☐

46 Given between 3 and 5 years and then not given again ☐

47 Given only if tuberculin-negative ☐

48 Select TWO items about carpal tunnel syndrome:
- ☐ **A** Pain radiating to the shoulder excludes the diagnosis
- ☐ **B** The dominant hand is typically affected
- ☐ **C** Local steroid injections typically worsen the pain
- ☐ **D** It is associated with hypothyroidism
- ☐ **E** Thenar wasting is a characteristic feature

49 Select TWO items about acute torticollis:
- ☐ **A**   It typically occurs in the 15–30 year age group
- ☐ **B**   It indicates underlying cervical arthritic changes
- ☐ **C**   Active and passive movements are limited
- ☐ **D**   Pain typically increases in intensity throughout the day
- ☐ **E**   The neck is typically flexed towards the painful side

THEME: ACTS

The following Acts are of importance to General Practitioners:
- **A**   NHS and Community Care Act 1990
- **B**   Access to Health Records Act 1990
- **C**   Access to Medical Report Act 1988
- **D**   Data Protection Act 1984

Match the following statements with the appropriate Act

50   Allows General Practitioners to control a budget funding primary care services   ☐

51   Allows patients to see reports prepared about them for insurance companies or employers   ☐

52   Allows patients to see medical records about them   ☐

53   Allows information to be held for a specific lawful purpose   ☐

54 Select TWO items about inhaled corticosteroids:
- ☐ **A**   Nebulised steroids are less efficient than metered dose inhalers
- ☐ **B**   Adrenal suppression in adults has been shown to occur with a total daily dose of 1000 micrograms
- ☐ **C**   Larger volume spacer devices increase oropharyngeal deposition
- ☐ **D**   Inhibition of growth in children using 800 micrograms daily has been reported

55 Select THREE statements concerning urinary tract infections in children:
- ☐ **A**   The majority have no structural abnormality
- ☐ **B**   10% of children will have had an infection by the time they are 10 years of age
- ☐ **C**   The commonest abnormal finding is vesico-ureteric reflux
- ☐ **D**   Approximately half will present with non-specific symptoms under the age of 2 years
- ☐ **E**   They may present as a diarrhoeal illness

THEME: BENEFITS

The following welfare benefits are of importance:
A   Statutory Sick Pay
B   Severe Disablement Allowance
C   Invalid Care Allowance
D   Disability Living Allowance
E   Incapacity Benefit
F   Attendance Allowance

Match the following with the appropriate benefit

56   Paid to people incapable of work for at least 28 weeks who are at least 80% disabled ☐

57   Paid to people over 65 years who require considerable supervision or care during the day or night ☐

58   Paid to employees when unable to work because of a short term illness ☐

59   Paid to people who are incapable of work on medical grounds for more than 28 weeks and who have paid sufficient National Insurance contributions ☐

60   Paid to people under 65 years who are unable to walk because of a physical illness ☐

61 Select THREE items concerning research in general practice:
☐ **A**   Research protocols typically contain the curriculum vitae of the researcher
☐ **B**   Ethics committees have no interest in the source of finance for a research project
☐ **C**   All risks must be made known to the participating patients
☐ **D**   Retrospective studies from patients' records require consent from the patient concerned
☐ **E**   Structured interviews do not need specialist interviewers to obtain accurate results

62 Select THREE statements about meningococcal meningitis:
☐ **A**   Vaccine is not effective against all strains
☐ **B**   Prevalence is increasing
☐ **C**   Resistance of strains to penicillin has emerged
☐ **D**   Chloramphenicol is the chemoprophylactic agent of choice
☐ **E**   Immediate family members have a minimally increased risk of contracting the disease from an infected house member

THEME: STATISTICS

The following are words and descriptions commonly used in statistics:

A   Mode
B   Bimodal
C   Single normal distribution
D   Positively skewed
E   Equal variance, different means
F   Median
G   Mean
H   Equal means, different variance

Match the following to ONE of these words or descriptions

63      ☐

64   ☐

65   ☐

66      ☐

67 Select THREE items about bulimia nervosa:

☐   A   The majority of patients with this condition are underweight
☐   B   Drug treatment has been shown to be more effective than intensive psychological treatments
☐   C   Fetal abnormalities have been shown to be more common in those patients who have bulimia
☐   D   If associated with anorexia it carries a worse prognosis
☐   E   It is associated with diuretic abuse

68 Your practice is unsure whether to give iron supplements routinely in pregnancy. In discussing the matter THREE of the following are true:

- ☐ **A** Plasma ferritin levels accurately reflect maternal iron stores
- ☐ **B** Neonatal iron stores are acquired in the last trimester
- ☐ **C** Iron supplementation has been shown to reduce iron depletion
- ☐ **D** Iron requirements are greatest in the first trimester
- ☐ **E** Ferrous salts have a higher incidence of side-effects than the other iron salts

69 Select THREE items concerning sudden infant death syndrome (SIDS):

- ☐ **A** First-born children are at particular risk
- ☐ **B** The risk in twins is greater than in singletons
- ☐ **C** Most occur between 6 and 12 months of age
- ☐ **D** Most occur between October and March
- ☐ **E** The risk is reduced by placing the baby in a supine position to sleep
- ☐ **F** Babies born by breech delivery are at particular risk

70 Depressive disorders are typically associated with THREE of the following:

- ☐ **A** Feeling worse in the evening
- ☐ **B** An abnormal dexamethasone suppression test
- ☐ **C** Delusions of poverty
- ☐ **D** Amenorrhoea
- ☐ **E** Difficulty in falling asleep

71 Normal adolescence is characterised by THREE of the following:

- ☐ **A** The first sign of puberty in boys is testicular growth
- ☐ **B** The first sign of puberty in girls is the appearance of pubic hair
- ☐ **C** The major part of weight gain is due to deposition of fat
- ☐ **D** Girls are ahead of boys in all aspects of pubertal development
- ☐ **E** Full stature is achieved approximately 4 years after the peak growth spurt

72 Legislation on wearing seatbelts requires drivers to wear seatbelts with exception to which ONE of the following:

- ☐ **A** After recent surgery on the abdomen
- ☐ **B** When in an advanced stage of pregnancy
- ☐ **C** Whilst the driver is reversing
- ☐ **D** After recent thoracic surgery

73 Choose THREE statements about hypothermia:

- ☐ **A** Immersion in water as a cause of hypothermia increases the probability of death
- ☐ **B** Cardiac arrhythmias do not occur until the body temperature is $33°C$
- ☐ **C** Unconsciousness typically occurs below a temperature of $33°C$
- ☐ **D** Confusion is a feature of a core temperature of $34°C$
- ☐ **E** Rewarming should occur at the same rate at which a patient becomes cold

74 A 35-year-old woman with no previous medical history complains of double vision since waking. On examination she has an isolated lateral rectus palsy on one side. Which of the following is the SINGLE most likely diagnosis?
- ☐ **A** Sarcoidosis
- ☐ **B** Mononeuritis multiplex
- ☐ **C** Multiple sclerosis
- ☐ **D** Bell's palsy
- ☐ **E** Myasthenia gravis

75 Select TWO items about cataract surgery:
- ☐ **A** It is more successful if performed at a late stage
- ☐ **B** It increases the risk of retinal detachment
- ☐ **C** Thickening of the posterior capsule is a complication of extracapsular extraction
- ☐ **D** Bed rest is required for 24 hours post-operatively
- ☐ **E** Intra-ocular implants are only suitable for myopic patients

76 TWO of the following are true of angiotensin-converting enzyme inhibitors:
- ☐ **A** Drug-induced cough typically resolves if treatment is continued
- ☐ **B** They are associated with intra-uterine death
- ☐ **C** Lithium carbonate toxicity is potentiated
- ☐ **D** Hyponatraemia only occurs if they are given concurrently with diuretics
- ☐ **E** Skin rashes occur in less than 1% of patients

77 Which ONE of the following items best describes Idiopathic Thrombocytopaenic Purpura?
- ☐ **A** Patients usually have splenomegaly
- ☐ **B** In childhood, most cases resolve spontaneously
- ☐ **C** In adults, most cases follow a viral illness
- ☐ **D** The disease is characterised by extensive haemorrhage
- ☐ **E** In adults, there are no circulating antibodies

78 A 15-year-old girl presents with anterior knee pain, a diagnosis of chondromalacia patella would be supported by which THREE of the following?
- ☐ **A** Pain on pressing the patella
- ☐ **B** Pain worse on ascending stairs rather than on descending
- ☐ **C** Palpable crepitus on passive movements
- ☐ **D** A normal 'skyline' knee X-ray
- ☐ **E** Hyperextension of the knee joint by 10° or more

79 Select THREE statements about miscarriage:

☐ **A** Only 25% of women who have had three recurrent miscarriages will have a baby without any medical intervention

☐ **B** Bacterial vaginosis is a risk factor for mid-trimester miscarriage

☐ **C** A Rhesus-negative woman should be given anti-D within 72 hours of bleeding in any stage of the pregnancy

☐ **D** 40–50% of first miscarriages are due to chromosomal abnormalities

☐ **E** Between about 5% and 15% of all pregnancies end in miscarriage

80 Choose TWO statements concerning opiate addiction:

☐ **A** Doctors not licensed may prescribe methadone to a drug addict

☐ **B** A central register of opiate addicts is maintained

☐ **C** Withdrawal symptoms commence 12 hours after the last dose of methadone

☐ **D** Convulsions are associated with rapid withdrawal

81 Select ONE item about health visitors:

☐ **A** Must have a post-basic training in paediatric nursing

☐ **B** Must have a post-basic training in obstetrics

☐ **C** The majority conduct over-75 screening on behalf of General Practitioners

☐ **D** Have a statutory obligation to visit post-natally on the first day after discharge from hospital

☐ **E** Have self-employed status

82 Which ONE of the following drugs would not be responsible for an increase in the level of the serum alkaline phosphatase?

☐ **A** Nitrofurantoin

☐ **B** Phenytoin

☐ **C** Erythromycin

☐ **D** Tetracycline

☐ **E** Disulfiram

83 A patient requests a home confinement. In responding to her which TWO of the following are true?

☐ **A** Fetal monitoring of low risk cases decreases morbidity in the baby

☐ **B** A doctor need not be present at a home confinement

☐ **C** An abnormal delivery is more common in lower social classes

☐ **D** The majority of babies require some form of specialised assistance at or shortly after birth

☐ **E** A General Practitioner is under no contractual obligation to provide home care if the patient insists on a domiciliary confinement

84 Select THREE items about laparoscopic cholecystectomy:
- ☐ **A** It is only suitable for a minority of patients with gallstones
- ☐ **B** The operative time is longer
- ☐ **C** Return to work is earlier
- ☐ **D** Post-operative complications are more frequent
- ☐ **E** A nasogastric tube needs to be passed pre-operatively

85 THREE of the following are true of pre-eclampsia:
- ☐ **A** Proteinuria is an early feature
- ☐ **B** Circadian rhythm of blood pressure is reversed
- ☐ **C** 90% of normal pregnant women have oedema at term
- ☐ **D** Early control of blood pressure has been shown to retard its progression
- ☐ **E** It is associated with placental abruption

THEME: STUDIES

Statistical data in studies can be:
- **A** Quantitative
- **B** Discrete
- **C** Continuous
- **D** Qualitative

Match the following statements with the type of data (use each type of data ONCE only)

86 Like blood pressure readings, can have any value ☐

87 Like the number of people seen in a surgery, has a definite value ☐

88 Data that can be given an exact number ☐

89 Data that can be described but not counted ☐

THEME: SCREENING

The results of a screening test for a cancer are as follows:

	Disease present	Disease absent
Screening test positive	70	30
Screening test negative	10	90

Options available

A	70	F	10/100
B	30	G	70/80
C	10	H	90/100
D	90	I	30/120
E	70/100	J	90/120

Select the appropriate option

90 Sensitivity

91 Specificity

92 Positive predictive value

93 Negative predictive value

94 False positive

95 False negative

96 Select TWO statements concerning rubella:
- **A** The incubation period is 14–21 days
- **B** It is contagious
- **C** Prodromal symptoms of fever and conjunctivitis are usually present
- **D** The rash may be transient
- **E** Infection in pregnancy is serious and usually involves a florid rash

97 THREE of the following would support a diagnosis of maxillary sinusitis:
- **A** Swelling of the cheek
- **B** Pain in the teeth
- **C** Pain worse on bending
- **D** Clear nasal discharge
- **E** Tenderness over the maxillary antrum

98   THREE of the following statements are true of eye disease:
- ☐ **A**   Recurrent chalazia are associated with acne rosacea
- ☐ **B**   Blepharitis is common in patients with psoriasis
- ☐ **C**   Correction of entropion requires an operation under general anaesthetic
- ☐ **D**   Alkalis are less damaging than acids if accidentally splashed into the eye
- ☐ **E**   Kaposi's sarcoma can affect the conjunctiva

THEME: LITERATURE

The following literature discusses consultations:
A   *The Doctor, his Patient and the Illness* by M Balint
B   *Meetings Between Experts: An Approach to Sharing Ideas in Medical Consultations* by Tuckett *et al.*
C   *The Consultation: An Approach to Learning and Teaching* by Pendleton *et al.*
D   *The Inner Consultation* by R Neighbour
E   *Doctors Talking to Patients* by Byrne & Long
F   *The Doctor–Patient Relationship* by Freeling & Harris
G   *Culture, Health and Illness* by C Helman
H   *Games People Play* by E Berne

Match the following with the appropriate literature from the list above

99   Coined the phrase 'drug doctor'   ☐

100   Described consulting styles varying from 'doctor-centred' to 'patient-centred'   ☐

101   Devised consultation mapping   ☐

102   Discussed management plans and outcomes being given different priorities by different people depending on their roles and values   ☐

103   Described complex transactions between people in terms of their ego status   ☐

104   Described the 'apostolic function' of a doctor   ☐

105   Described seven communication tests, starting with defining the reason for the patient's attendance   ☐

106 Select THREE of the following items about identifying patients with psychological problems in a consultation. Research has shown General Practitioners:

☐ **A**   Detect most disorders
☐ **B**   Vary nine-fold in their diagnosis of psychological problems
☐ **C**   Who show more empathy detect more problems
☐ **D**   Who make eye contact detect more problems
☐ **E**   Who are good at dealing with interruptions to the consultation detect fewer problems

107 Absorption of TWO of the following drugs has been shown to be increased if they are given on an empty stomach:

☐ **A**   Digoxin
☐ **B**   Allopurinol
☐ **C**   Co-trimoxazole
☐ **D**   Theophylline
☐ **E**   Penicillin

108 Select TWO statements about haemorrhagic disease of the newborn:

☐ **A**   Formula milk fed babies are at particular risk
☐ **B**   Vitamin D is implicated
☐ **C**   The risk is increased if the baby's mother has been on medication for epilepsy
☐ **D**   A single dose of oral vitamin supplement is usually sufficient to prevent the disease
☐ **E**   Prematurity is a high risk

109 A recently born baby has been diagnosed as having a hemiplegia due to cerebral palsy. When counselling the parents subsequently the doctor should be aware of THREE of the following:

☐ **A**   The mean IQ is about 80
☐ **B**   The majority of children have speech problems
☐ **C**   The incidence of specific learning defects has been shown to be greater than for the general population
☐ **D**   Those with persistent hypotonia have a better prognosis than those who develop spasticity
☐ **E**   For children with an IQ greater than 70, education should be in the normal system

110 **When counselling a couple with involuntary infertility, THREE of the following are true:**
- ☐ **A** The most common reason for the problem is an abnormality of the Fallopian tubes
- ☐ **B** The majority of couples not using contraceptives will conceive within 12 months
- ☐ **C** Reconstructive tubal surgery carries an increased risk of ectopic pregnancy
- ☐ **D** The majority of women receiving clomiphene for anovulation will still not ovulate
- ☐ **E** *In vitro* fertilisation is associated with an increased incidence of fetal abnormalities

111 **Prescriptions are issued free to patients with which ONE of the following conditions?**
- ☐ **A** Rheumatoid arthritis
- ☐ **B** Chronic glaucoma
- ☐ **C** Asthma
- ☐ **D** Myxoedema
- ☐ **E** Hyperthyroidism

112 **When considering whether to give antibiotics to a patient with a sore throat, TWO of the following are true:**
- ☐ **A** Approximately 30% of throat swabs grow beta-haemolytic Streptococcus
- ☐ **B** About 20% of throat swabs grow *Haemophilus influenzae*
- ☐ **C** The decrease in the incidence of rheumatic fever commenced at the time of the introduction of antibiotics
- ☐ **D** Tonsillar exudate in an over 15-year-old is typically associated with glandular fever
- ☐ **E** Enlarged tonsillar glands are typically associated with bacterial infection

113 **Select TWO items about screening tests:**
- ☐ **A** A highly sensitive test will have a high false-negative rate
- ☐ **B** A highly specific test will have a low false-positive rate
- ☐ **C** The prevalence of a disease indicates the total number of cases that present in a population each year
- ☐ **D** The prevalence of a disease influences the predictive value of a test
- ☐ **E** The negative predictive value indicates those patients who refuse to have the screening test

114 **When advising patients about exposure to sun, TWO of the following are true:**
- ☐ **A** Solar keratoses never progress to malignancy
- ☐ **B** Solar keratoses are more common in fair-skinned people
- ☐ **C** Chronic sun exposure leads to loss of skin elasticity
- ☐ **D** Basal cell carcinoma never metastasise
- ☐ **E** Sunburn typically develops within 2 hours of exposure

115 **Owning dogs has been shown to be associated with THREE of the following:**

☐ **A** An increase in presentation of minor health problems to the General Practitioner

☐ **B** An increase in one-year survival following a myocardial infarction

☐ **C** A lower blood pressure when matched with the average population

☐ **D** Lower lipid levels when matched with the average population

☐ **E** Increase in gastrointestinal infections

THEME: MENTAL HEALTH ACT

The following sections of the Mental Health Act (1983) can be of importance:

A Section 2

B Section 3

C Section 4

D Section 5

E Section 7

F Section 12

Match the appropriate section to the following statements

116 Used to 'approve' doctors as having special expertise in psychiatric conditions ☐

117 Used in guardianship ☐

118 Used in emergency situations only, when the patient needs to be taken to hospital ☐

119 Used in emergency situations only, when the patient needs to be kept in a hospital, from where he or she wishes to leave ☐

120 Used to admit a patient with bipolar affective disorder, who is not taking medication and refuses any intervention; he or she is acting in a dangerous manner, and requires treatment ☐

121 **Below is a list of conditions and complementary treatments. Select the pairings for which there is evidence of effectiveness. (FOUR correct answers)**

☐ **A** Horse chestnut seed extract for chronic venous insufficiency
☐ **B** Melatonin as a treatment for jetlag
☐ **C** Acupuncture for smoking cessation
☐ **D** Saw palmetto extract for the treatment of benign prostatic hypertrophy
☐ **E** Acupuncture for the treatment of asthma
☐ **F** Feverfew in the prophylaxis of migraine
☐ **G** Arnica for soft tissue trauma
☐ **H** Glucosamine supplements for the treatment of osteoarthritis
☐ **I** Iridology in the diagnosis of vitamin deficiency

122 **A 30-year-old female patient presents with a febrile illness and tender red nodular lesions on the lower legs. Which ONE of the following is the most probable diagnosis?**

☐ **A** Lyme disease
☐ **B** Erysipelas
☐ **C** Erythema nodosum
☐ **D** Acanthosis nigricans
☐ **E** Kaposi's sarcoma

123 **Which ONE of the following drugs is least likely to cause thrombocytopaenia?**

☐ **A** Gold
☐ **B** Heparin
☐ **C** Quinine
☐ **D** Warfarin
☐ **E** Bendrofluazide

THEME: CHILD DEVELOPMENT

At the following ages, children have developed certain important skills:

A 6 months   **E** 3 years
B 12 months   **F** 4 years
C 18 months   **G** 5 years
D 24 months

Match the following with the appropriate age option

124 Plays with other children; able to stand on one leg briefly   ☐

125 Plays imaginatively; able to copy a circle and a cross   ☐

continues ...

126 Able to count 12 objects ☐

127 Able to give first and last name and age; able to catch a ball ☐

128 Says 10–12 words with meaning ☐

129 Builds a 3–4 cube tower ☐

130 Walks whilst holding onto furniture ☐

THEME: POLYARTHRITIS

Types of polyarthritis include
A Rheumatoid arthritis
B Osteoarthritis
C Ankylosing spondylitis
D Rheumatic fever
E Systemic lupus erythematosus
F Reiter's syndrome
G Psoriatic arthropathy

Match the following to the most appropriate type of arthritis

131 A 45-year-old lady has morning stiffness and symmetrical involvement of the joints in the hands and feet, which have been inflamed ☐

132 A 30-year-old man presents with arthritis which moves from joint to joint ☐

133 A 55-year-old man has pain in the hands, worse on movement; there are enlargements in the hands related to the distal interphalangeal joints ☐

134 A 32-year-old man with non-symmetrical swelling of the distal interphalangeal joints; he mentions pitting of his nails ☐

135 A 25-year-old man with painful, swollen knees and feet; he mentions continual back stiffness and recent pain in the eye ☐

136 A 29-year-old lady with an abrupt onset of swelling of joints in hands and feet; she thinks this is associated with exposure to the sun, which has also caused a facial rash ☐

137 A 22-year-old man who has a sudden onset of pain in knee, associated with a feeling of grit in the eyes; vesicles are noted on the soles of his feet and on the palms ☐

138 Select TWO items about stress polycythaemia:
- ☐ **A**   The PCV is typically greater than 0.55
- ☐ **B**   The total body red cell mass is raised
- ☐ **C**   It is more common in females
- ☐ **D**   It is associated with obesity
- ☐ **E**   It is associated with excessive alcohol consumption

139 You see a 1-year-old boy with a fever. Bag urine shows blood and leucocytes on dipstick and you send off a sample for microscopy and culture. He is treated empirically with trimethoprim. The result shows:

$>100 \times 10^3$ white cells

Red blood cells

Pure growth of *E. coli*

Which of the following is the SINGLE best course of initial action?
- ☐ **A**   Start a prophylactic antibiotic immediately and refer for paediatric assessment
- ☐ **B**   Refer to a surgeon for consideration of ureteric reimplantation
- ☐ **C**   Recommend regular cranberry juice
- ☐ **D**   Repeat the urine specimen since these results from a bag urine are most likely to represent contamination from skin flora
- ☐ **E**   Send urine specimens once a month and treat positive results

140 A 21-year-old man who works in a clothing store comes to see you in surgery. He describes severe anxiety symptoms which are having a significant effect on his social and work life and requests treatment. From the list below, select the SINGLE best treatment?
- ☐ **A**   Propranolol
- ☐ **B**   Diazepam
- ☐ **C**   Trifluoperazine
- ☐ **D**   Citalopram
- ☐ **E**   Phenobarbitone
- ☐ **F**   Caffeine

THEME: NUMBNESS AND PARAESTHESIA

Numbness and feelings of paraesthesia are commonly encountered in general practice. The following are possible causes:

A   Meralgia paraesthetica
B   Carpal tunnel syndrome
C   Ulnar nerve lesion
D   Lateral popliteal nerve lesion
E   Peripheral neuropathy
F   Lumbar disc lesion
G   Multiple sclerosis

Choose the most appropriate cause for the following clinical scenarios

141 A 36-year-old lecturer has intermittent recurrent symptoms in arms and legs, and describes 'shocks' when bending his neck ☐

142 A 52-year-old rather obese man has noticed sensory loss in his lower legs; examination reveals distal weakness with 'stocking' type sensory loss ☐

143 A 47-year-old lady notices tingling in her left hand which is worse at night; her index finger seems particularly affected by the tingling feeling ☐

144 A 51-year-old obese man notices tingling in the outer aspect of his thighs ☐

145 A 35-year-old man complains of back and leg pain with numbness down his left thigh ☐

THEME: HYPERTENSION TRIALS

The following are important trials in hypertension:
A   Veterans Administration Co-operative Study
B   Multiple Risk Factor Intervention Trial
C   MRC Mild Hypertension Trial
D   European Working Party on Hypertension in the Elderly
E   SYST-EUR-Trial

For which of these trials is the following true

146 Showed that one CVA was prevented by 850 patient years of treatment   ☐

147 Was carried out in a group who were highly compliant with a drug regime   ☐

148 Recruited very few patients per centre and showed that deaths from CVA were not reduced in this group over 60 years of age   ☐

149 Showed no reduction in CVAs in the treated group, but had a low incidence of CVAs in the control group   ☐

150 Used a much larger dose of bendrofluazide than would be used now   ☐

151 **A 42-year-old man presents with a depressive illness, FOUR of the following factors would support an unfavourable prognosis:**
☐ A   Loss of mother prior to 12 years of age
☐ B   Previous depressive illness
☐ C   Involvement with local charitable organisations
☐ D   Obsessional personality
☐ E   A wife housebound with multiple sclerosis
☐ F   Active social life

152 **THREE of the following are true of infective endocarditis:**
☐ A   Mitral valve prolapse is a risk factor
☐ B   The route of the infecting organism is obvious in the majority of cases
☐ C   The mortality is minimal once treatment commences
☐ D   Anaemia is an atypical finding
☐ E   The plasma viscosity is typically elevated

153 When looking at nails which are discoloured THREE of the following are true:

- ☐ **A** Penicillamine stains nails yellow
- ☐ **B** An irregular yellow area associated with a thickened nail plate is typically due to tinea infection
- ☐ **C** Familial leuconychia causes small white streaks on the nails
- ☐ **D** Yellow nail syndrome is associated with lymphoedema elsewhere in the body
- ☐ **E** Chloroquine stains nails green

154 THREE of the following would suggest an atypical grief reaction:

- ☐ **A** Onset of distress delayed until 4 weeks after the death
- ☐ **B** Open hostility to relatives
- ☐ **C** Extreme social isolation
- ☐ **D** Absence from work for 6 weeks
- ☐ **E** Non-specific suicidal ideas

155 When initiating treatment with a progestogen-only contraceptive, ONE of the following points is true:

- ☐ **A** Extra contraceptive precautions should be used if started on day 1 of the cycle
- ☐ **B** They should not be taken for 4 weeks prior to surgery
- ☐ **C** If switching from a combined oral contraceptive, they should be commenced after the 7–day break
- ☐ **D** Post-abortion they should be started on the day after the operation
- ☐ **E** They are secreted in significant amounts in breast milk

THEME: EYE PROBLEMS

Causes of red eye seen in general practice include:
A   Acute conjunctivitis
B   Acute iritis
C   Acute glaucoma
D   Episcleritis
E   Keratitis

Match the appropriate diagnosis to the clinical scenarios below

156   A 55-year-old woman with severe pain in one eye which is red; there is visual disturbance and the pupil is noted to be dilated ☐

157   A 57-year-old lady with a painful red right eye; there is visual disturbance; the pupil appears normal but there is diffuse inflammation of the conjunctiva ☐

158   A 49-year-old man has a sticky discharge from both eyes which are both red ☐

159   A 48-year-old has intense pain in his left eye with redness of the eye especially around the cornea; the pupil is seen to be constricted ☐

160   A 42-year-old man has a gritty feeling in the left eye and the lids feel sticky to him; there is slight inflammation of the left eye ☐

161   **Select THREE statements about recent weight loss of over 5% in a patient over 65 years of age:**
☐   **A**   Physical illness in the majority of cases
☐   **B**   Malignancy in approximately 20%
☐   **C**   The reason for the weight loss is usually not apparent at the initial examination
☐   **D**   Follow-up is indicated in those with no apparent pathology
☐   **E**   The majority of those without obvious pathology continue to lose weight

162   **You have a 68-year-old woman in the practice with a diagnosis of 'pernicious anaemia'. She is maintained on monthly injections of hydroxocobalamin. On reviewing her case TWO of the following are true:**
☐   **A**   A Schilling test can be performed even though B12 stores are replete
☐   **B**   Dietary deficiency is more common than autoimmune gastric atrophy
☐   **C**   Dependency upon B12 is unknown
☐   **D**   Hydroxocobalamin is usually given every 3 months
☐   **E**   Excessive administration of B12 causes harmful side-effects

THEME: ABDOMINAL PAIN

The following causes of abdominal pain are sometimes seen in general practice:
A   Biliary colic
B   Peptic ulcer
C   Appendicitis
D   Renal colic
E   Pancreatitis
F   Diverticulitis

Match the following scenarios with ONE of these causes

163 A 35-year-old accountant describes 'pain and wind' which sometimes wakes him at night, and has been intermittently present for about 3 months ☐

164 A 48-year-old man describes severe abdominal pain which appears to radiate into his back ☐

165 A 28-year-old has a 2-day history of abdominal pain with recent vomiting and raised temperature; there is tenderness in the right lower abdomen on examination ☐

166 A 51-year-old lady describes intermittent abdominal pain which she finds hard to place; her abdomen is generally tender but especially in the right upper abdomen ☐

167 A 43-year-old woman has intermittent abdominal and right-sided back pain, and has been vomiting; examination shows tenderness in the right abdomen but especially so in the right side of the back laterally ☐

168 A 66-year-old retired banker described abdominal pain over the last few months, and complains of long term constipation; examination reveals tenderness especially in the left lower abdomen ☐

THEME: THYROID DISEASE

Thyroid cancers can be:
A   Anaplastic
B   Papillary
C   Follicular

Match the following statements to the type of cancer

169 Most common thyroid cancer in the elderly ☐

170 Most common thyroid cancer in the young ☐

171 Particularly metastasises to bone ☐

172 Best prognosis ☐

THEME: HEART PROBLEMS

Tachycardia may be caused by a variety of conditions which include:
A   Anxiety
B   Anaemia
C   Fever
D   Thyrotoxicosis
E   Phaeochromocytoma
F   Carcinoid syndrome

Match the following clinical scenarios with the most appropriate cause from the above list

173 A 39-year-old female with diarrhoea and a racing regular heart beat; she is concerned about episodes of flushing and wheezing and wonders if this might be the menopause ☐

174 A 41-year-old female has a regular fast heart beat; she is tall and thin and friends say her facial appearance has altered over the last few months ☐

175 A 38-year-old female complains of palpitations along with a dull ache in the chest; she describes the need to take deep breaths as she can no longer breathe in satisfactorily ☐

176 A 32-year-old female has palpitations and notices attacks of sudden sweating; her husband says she is often pale at that time and seems to have headaches. ☐

THEME: CANCERS

A typical GP with an average list size sees new cases of cancers at varying intervals depending on the type of cancer. From the list of time intervals below, select the appropriate interval for each type of malignant tumour described:

Time intervals

A   6 months
B   12 months
C   2 years
D   5–6 years
E   10 years
F   25 years

Types of malignant tumour

177 Stomach ☐

178 Breast ☐

179 Brain ☐

180 Thyroid ☐

181 Bronchus ☐

182 Ovary ☐

THEME: LESIONS

Match the illustrated lesions with the relevant diagnosis

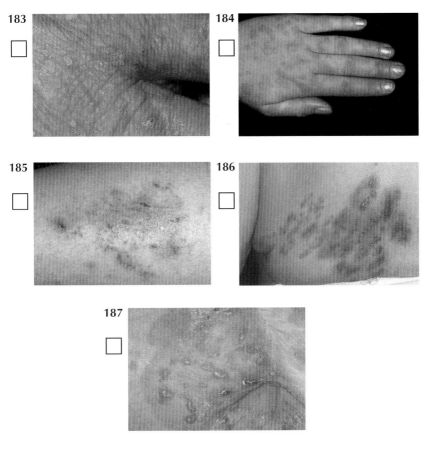

Diagnosis option list:
A   Eczema
B   Erythema multiforme
C   Herpes zoster
D   Lichen planus
E   Measles
F   Pemphigus
G   Pemphigoid
H   Psoriasis
I   Scabies

THEME: ECGs

Option list

A A
B B
C C
D D
E E
F F
G G
H J wave
I P wave
J PQ interval
K PR interval
L ST interval
M QRS complex
N R wave
O T wave
P U wave

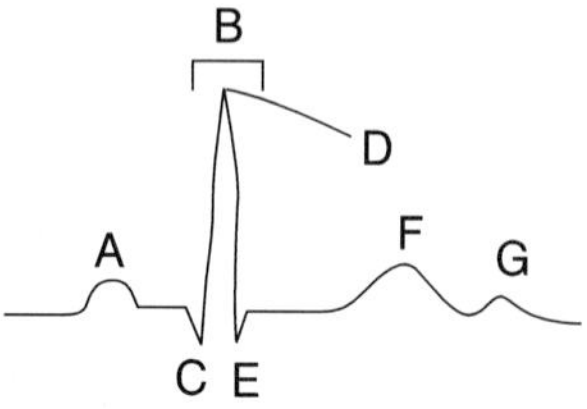

Figure 1.

Read the following information about ECGs. Fill in the spaces with the appropriate word from the option list. Each word my be used once, more than once, or not at all.

ECGs are used in the investitation and diagnosis of cardiac disorders.

The ECG is recorded on special paper, which moves through the ECG machine at 25 mm/sec. The special paper is divided into large squares each measuring 5 mm wide. The electrical activity is converted into various waveforms of the type shown in figure 1. The individual components of the waveform have standard names.

The **(188)**_____ is produced by atrial depolarisation beginning in the SA node, and is shown as letter **(189)**_____ in figure 1. The **(190)**_____ is the time between the onset of atrial depolarisation and the onset of ventricular depolarisation. It is measured from the beginning of the **(191)**_____ to the first deflection of the **(192)**_____.

The **(193)**_____ represents septal and ventricular depolarisation. This show as letter **(194)**_____ in figure 1.

The first positive deflection of ventricular depolarisation is called the **(195)**_____.

The **(196)**_____ is produced by ventricular repolarisation.

Practice Paper 5

Total time allowed is three hours. Indicate your answers clearly by putting a tick or cross in the box alongside each answer or by writing the appropriate letter alongside the appropriate answer.

1 A 2-year-old child becomes acutely ill. Which ONE of the following would not support a diagnosis of Reye's syndrome?

☐ **A** Chickenpox 10 days previously
☐ **B** Behaviour changes
☐ **C** Profuse vomiting
☐ **D** Normal liver function tests
☐ **E** Recent administration of aspirin

2 Select THREE items relevant when considering a diagnosis of diabetes mellitus:

☐ **A** Blood glucose progressively decreases with age
☐ **B** The majority of people with glycosuria have diabetes
☐ **C** Routine urine testing detects the majority of previously undiagnosed diabetics
☐ **D** A fasting blood glucose of greater than 7.2 mmol/l is diagnostic of diabetes
☐ **E** The majority of diabetics will have retinal changes at diagnosis

3 Under the theoretical model of the consultation proposed by Stott and Davies THREE of the following aspects of a consultation are considered:

☐ **A** Prevention
☐ **B** Patients' expectations
☐ **C** Management of continuing problems
☐ **D** Modification of health seeking behaviour
☐ **E** Sharing of the problem with the patient

4 A 78-year-old resident of a residential home becomes increasingly agitated. Which ONE of the following would not account for this?

☐ **A** Recent introduction of digoxin
☐ **B** Paracetamol being given for osteoarthritis
☐ **C** Temazepam as a hypnotic that has been given for the last 5 years
☐ **D** A silent myocardial infarction
☐ **E** Dehydration

THEME: STUDY TYPES

Types of study include:
A   Quantitative
B   Qualitative
C   Cross-sectional
D   Descriptive
E   Retrospective
F   Prospective
G   Case-control
H   Longitudinal
I   Intervention

Using these types only once, match the following with the most appropriate study type

5   Used to explore attitudes or beliefs; its methodology comes from social sciences

6   Involves a counting study and comes from epidemiology

7   A study looking at the consulting patterns of diabetic patients over the last 3 years

8   A study looking at patients with diabetes to see if they will develop ischaemic heart disease

9   A study of poorly controlled diabetics and well-controlled diabetics looking at the development of diabetic retinopathy

10   A study of patient satisfaction in diabetic patients

11   A study of drug use in weight control in diabetic patients

12 Select ONE item about the 'Red Book' (Statement of fees and allowances):
☐   **A**   It is a legally binding document
☐   **B**   Can only be amended by legislative change
☐   **C**   Is negotiated by the LMC on behalf of all General Practitioners

13 Choose THREE items of advice about driving heavy goods vehicles:

☐ **A**   An HGV driver should avoid driving for at least 6 months following a myocardial infarct and then may be allowed to continue if certain criteria are met

☐ **B**   An HGV driver can drive if he is free of fits for 3 years

☐ **C**   An HGV driver who develops insulin-dependent diabetes cannot continue to drive

☐ **D**   An HGV driver should stop the vehicle if he has the beginning of a migraine attack

☐ **E**   If an HGV driver has minor trauma and has an abdominal X-ray at casualty which shows an aortic aneurysm, he should be advised to avoid driving because of the aneurysm

14 Allergic conjunctivitis is associated with TWO of the following:

☐ **A**   A clear ocular discharge

☐ **B**   A reduction in visual acuity

☐ **C**   Photophobia

☐ **D**   Epiphora

☐ **E**   A need to avoid contact lenses

SUMMARY COMPLETION QUESTION

First read the extract from the methods section of the paper 'Excess mortality in a population with diabetes and the impact of maternal deprivation: longitudinal, population based study.' BMJ 2001;322:1389–1393.

Methods

The area administered by Middlesbrough and Redcar and Cleveland local authorities, referred to here as South Tees, had a population of 290 000 in 1994. This area has high unemployment, and mortality is above the national average. Migration rates in the area are low: during the study less than 3% of the cohort registered outside Tees Health Authority.

Participants

The cohort was derived from the South Tees district diabetes register and comprised all diabetic patients with an address in South Tees who were alive on 1 January 1994. The diabetes register is maintained by full time staff and contains demographic and clinical data on all people known to have diabetes. Data are collected prospectively from the adult and paediatric secondary care diabetes services, all primary care centres within the district, and the diabetes eye service. South Tees ethical committee granted approval for the study.

Analyses were undertaken for the population of people with diabetes as a whole and also for the population subdivided into type 1 and type 2 diabetes. The criteria for assigning type 1 diabetes were age 35 or less at diagnosis and receiving insulin treatment at the start of the study; the criteria for type 2 diabetes were age over 35 at diagnosis or not taking insulin.

Death registration

All participants were registered by the Office for National Statistics, and the date of death, causes of death, and underlying cause of death were obtained from death certificates for deaths occurring between 1 January 1994 and 31 December 1999 inclusive. The inconsistent inclusion of diabetes on death certificates creates problems when the underlying causes of death in groups with and without diabetes are compared. To correct for this a second underlying code for cause of death was derived in all cases where the underlying cause of death was diabetes ICD-9 (international classification of disease, ninth revision) code 250 by removing diabetes from the list of causes and recoding the underlying cause of death using ICD-9 rules. Diabetes remained the underlying cause of death if it was the only listed cause or if the immediate cause of death was a short term metabolic complication, such as hypoglycaemia or ketoacidosis.

Comparison populations

Most studies of mortality related to diabetes use whole population data as the comparator, despite the fact that these data include people with diabetes, leading to bias in the estimated effect. This bias can be considerable when the prevalence of diabetes is high or the standardised mortality ratio is large. Using local data and removing people known to have diabetes from the comparison group should minimise this bias.

The national comparison was made by using population and mortality data for England and Wales, 1994–8. The local comparison was made with the population of South Tees without known diabetes. This population was derived by removing people known to have diabetes from population figures for each year obtained from the Tees Valley Joint Strategy Unit. Mortality data were calculated by removing deaths of those known to have diabetes from the full local mortality data obtained from Office for National Statistics VS3 returns for South Tees, 1994–9, provided by Tees Health Authority. Deaths were matched by year of death, sex, five year age band, and cause of death (for cause specific analyses) and were adjusted for the decline in cohort numbers each year.

Material deprivation

Postcodes were used to allocate each participant to a 1991 census enumeration district, and a Townsend score was generated for each district as a measure of material deprivation. Participants were then grouped into fifths by their score.

Now look at this critique, which outlines the limitations of the study design.

The study aims to **(15)**_____ the mortality of patients with diabetes with that of patients without diabetes. To do so successfully the
(16)_____ i.e. mortality in diabetics and the
(17)_____ i.e. mortality in non-diabetics must be accurate.

The first stage in obtaining this information is to identify all diabetics in the area studied. This was done by identifying the **(18)**_____ from the diabetes register, which relies on notification from secondary care services in the area and from primary care. It is not clear from the methods what criteria were used to define diabetes; merely relying on clinical intuition may result in misdiagnosis and false positives and false negatives being included in the cohort. Furthermore, these patients will only represent treated diabetics, while patients with undiagnosed diabetes are not treated, and potentially contribute to the non-diabetic cohort mortality figures. A better protocol might have been to screen a cohort with **(19)**_____ diagnostic tests and allocate them according to the results. This would also reduce **(20)**_____ bias.

   (21)_____ of diabetics into type 1 and type 2 within the cohort is inaccurate, with insulin treated type 2 diabetics being **(22)**_____ in the type 1 subgroup. These are often the result of treatment failures with oral medications and may thus bias the results towards better outcomes for the **(23)**_____ subgroup.

   Death registration information for specific causes of death often relies on **(24)**_____ diagnosis, a more scientific although impractical approach would be to carry out a post mortem on every patient.

For each of the numbered gaps in the critique, choose one word from the following list which best completes the sentence.

A   case-control
B   classification
C   cohort
D   compare
E   contrast
F   denominator
G   diagnosis
H   excluded
I   exclusion
J   included
K   inclusion
L   objective
M   observer
N   numerator
O   recall
P   standardised
Q   statistical
R   subjective
S   type 1
T   type 2

THEME: DRUGS USED IN HYPERTENSION

The following drugs are used in hypertension:
A   Thiazide diuretics
B   Calcium antagonists
C   Beta blockers
D   ACE inhibitors
E   Vasodilators

Which class of drugs should not be used in the following patients

25   Patients with asthma   ☐

26   Patients with gout   ☐

27   Patients with chronic obstructive pulmonary disease   ☐

28   Patients with glucose intolerance   ☐

29   Patients with heart failure   ☐

30 When considering alcohol dependency in women, TWO of the following are true:
☐   **A**   Alcohol-dependent women are more prone to cerebral damage than alcohol-dependent men
☐   **B**   Alcoholic cirrhosis has a greater prevalence in women
☐   **C**   Affective disorders have been shown to be more common in males
☐   **D**   Vulnerability to intoxication is dependent on the stage of the menstrual cycle
☐   **E**   Typically women begin drinking heavily earlier than their male counterparts

31 Select THREE items about cervical smears:
☐   **A**   The sensitivity is about 50%
☐   **B**   The specificity is very high at about 50%
☐   **C**   The transformation zone moves into the cervical os in older women
☐   **D**   CIN is a histological diagnosis
☐   **E**   The false-negative rate may be dependent on the taker of the smear
☐   **F**   False positives rarely occur

32 Select THREE features of psoriasis:

☐ **A** Will affect approximately 2 in every 100 patients
☐ **B** Tends to leave scars
☐ **C** Typically is itchy
☐ **D** On the face can be treated safely with dithranol
☐ **E** Is typically symmetrical
☐ **F** Usually begins between the ages of 15–25 years

33 When considering a protocol for the management of epilepsy within your practice, select THREE items:

☐ **A** Patients should be referred to a neurologist after a first fit
☐ **B** If a first fit occurs after 30 years of age, idiopathic epilepsy is the probable diagnosis
☐ **C** Only a minority of epileptics have an inherited condition
☐ **D** The majority of GPs will be aware of all the epileptics on their lists
☐ **E** The majority of epileptics do not receive an annual check from either their GP or consultant

34 Select ONE item concerning hepatitis B vaccine:

☐ **A** Seroconversion is age dependent
☐ **B** The preferred site of injection for maximal absorption is the buttock
☐ **C** Hypersensitivity reactions occur in more than 5% of patients
☐ **D** Local soreness occurs in less than 10% of injections
☐ **E** The genetic recombinant vaccine also protects against hepatitis C

35 A 19-year-old student presents with bloody diarrhoea 2 weeks after completing a backpacking holiday in east Africa. THREE of the following should be included in a differential diagnosis:

☐ **A** Typhoid fever
☐ **B** Amoebic dysentery
☐ **C** Schistosomiasis
☐ **D** Lassa fever
☐ **E** Malaria

THEME: STATISTICS

A brief study of the numbers of phone calls received by different people in a general practice gave the following results:
Number received: 1, 1, 3, 5, 7, 8, 17

From the option lists choose:
Calculate
36 the mean ☐

37 the mode ☐

38 the median ☐

A 0.5
B 1
C 105
D 2
E 3
F 4
G 5
H 6
I 7
J 8
K 17

39 Select THREE items about post-traumatic stress disorder:
☐ **A** It typically commences within 1 week of the event
☐ **B** The majority of those exposed to a disaster will suffer chronic symptoms
☐ **C** Feelings of unreality occur
☐ **D** Guilt feelings are typical
☐ **E** Recovery is hindered by being pressed to talk about the event in the early stages

40 Urgent referral to an ophthalmologist is indicated for TWO of the following:
☐ **A** Episcleritis
☐ **B** Herpes zoster with visual disturbance
☐ **C** Blocked naso-lacrimal duct at 6 months of age
☐ **D** A dendritic ulcer
☐ **E** A corneal abrasion

41 Select THREE items about the care of patients in community hospitals:

☐ **A**   The majority of GPs have access to such hospitals
☐ **B**   The average age of patients in these hospitals is over 70 years
☐ **C**   The average cost of an in-patient admission is greater than for a general hospital
☐ **D**   The workload of GPs with access to community hospitals is greater
☐ **E**   The majority of patients are discharged to their own homes

42 When advising a patient about hysteroscopic endometrial ablation, THREE of the following are true:

☐ **A**   Danazol is given pre-operatively
☐ **B**   It is unsuitable in patients with previously treated CIN
☐ **C**   The healing process takes 3 months
☐ **D**   It is suitable for day case surgery
☐ **E**   Subsequent scanty bleeding would be an indication of treatment failure

43 Select THREE items about lesions of the Achilles tendon:

☐ **A**   Tendonitis is associated with a raised heel tab on the shoe
☐ **B**   Local steroid injections are associated with rupture of the tendon
☐ **C**   Complete rupture is best treated by surgery
☐ **D**   Shoe raise typically leads to shortening of the tendon if used to treat Achilles tendonitis
☐ **E**   Ultrasound treatment leads to a worsening of the pain

44 A 4-year-old boy is noted to have a cardiac murmur on routine examination. THREE of the following would indicate that it is innocent in nature:

☐ **A**   Diastolic in timing
☐ **B**   Murmur louder on deep inspiration
☐ **C**   Short duration
☐ **D**   Soft murmur
☐ **E**   A normal chest X-ray

45 Carcinoma of the bronchus is associated with exposure to which TWO of the following:

☐ **A**   Asbestos
☐ **B**   Silica dust
☐ **C**   Sulphur dioxide
☐ **D**   Aniline dyes
☐ **E**   Radon gas

46 Which ONE of the following would not support a diagnosis of Ménière's disease?

- ☐ **A** Tinnitus
- ☐ **B** A feeling of fullness in the ear
- ☐ **C** Fluctuating sensorineural hearing loss
- ☐ **D** A positive Romberg's test
- ☐ **E** Nystagmus occurring between acute attacks

47 An incidental finding of an easily palpable firm spleen is most likely due to which THREE of the following?

- ☐ **A** Glandular fever
- ☐ **B** Carcinomatosis
- ☐ **C** Chronic myeloid leukaemia
- ☐ **D** Lymphoma
- ☐ **E** Myelosclerosis

48 Select TWO items about skin lesions on soles of feet:

- ☐ **A** Pompholyx affecting the soles is non-irritant
- ☐ **B** Specific lesions on the soles occur in some cases of Reiter's syndrome
- ☐ **C** Pustular psoriasis may occur
- ☐ **D** Lichen planus lesions are characteristically seen

49 Select THREE items about carcinoma of the oesophagus:

- ☐ **A** The incidence is decreasing
- ☐ **B** Adenocarcinoma has a better prognosis than squamous carcinoma
- ☐ **C** It is associated with coeliac disease
- ☐ **D** It typically presents with weight loss
- ☐ **E** It is a complication of achalasia

50 There is no synergism between which ONE of the following pairs of drugs:

- ☐ **A** Propranolol and nifedipine
- ☐ **B** Bendrofluazide and glibenclamide
- ☐ **C** Spironolactone and frusemide
- ☐ **D** Ibuprofen and warfarin
- ☐ **E** Ethanol and chlorpheniramine

51 Select ONE item about rheumatoid arthritis:

- ☐ **A** If the rheumatoid factor is present, this is diagnostic in the elderly
- ☐ **B** Morning stiffness wears off after about 10 minutes
- ☐ **C** The metacarpophalangeal joints are rarely involved
- ☐ **D** Someone with a negative rheumatoid factor test can be reassured they do not have rheumatoid arthritis
- ☐ **E** Regular use of NSAIDs can prevent disease progression
- ☐ **F** Patients describe 'walking on pebbles'

52 When considering the psychological aspects of pain, select TWO of the following:

- ☐ **A** Approximately 25% of patients with chronic pain will show significant response to a placebo
- ☐ **B** Introverts seek pain relief sooner than extroverts
- ☐ **C** Complaints of pain are less common in the elderly
- ☐ **D** Pain perception is increased by social isolation

53 Select THREE items about diverticular disease:

- ☐ **A** Diverticula are seen more frequently in the distal colon
- ☐ **B** Non-fermentable fibre is more effective than fermentable fibre in treatment
- ☐ **C** It has an increased incidence of carcinoma of the colon
- ☐ **D** Bleeding is indicative of developing malignancy
- ☐ **E** Pneumaturia is a rare complication

THEME: MENTAL HEALTH ACT

The following are important sections of the Mental Health Act 1983 (England and Wales):

A	Section 2	**E**	Section 7
B	Section 3	**F**	Section 135
C	Section 4	**G**	Section 136
D	Section 5		

Match the appropriate section to the following statements

54 Allows for reception into guardianship ☐

55 Its purpose is compulsory admission of a patient with a mental disorder for treatment ☐

56 The purpose of this section is compulsory admission for assessment in an emergency; the patient has no right of appeal ☐

57 This allows removal of a patient by the police from a public place for medical examination ☐

58 This allows in-patients to be detained on an emergency basis ☐

59 Which ONE of the following would suggest that a patient who is HIV positive has developed 'full blown' AIDS?
- ☐ **A**   Persistent generalised lymphadenopathy
- ☐ **B**   Night sweats
- ☐ **C**   Non-Hodgkin's lymphoma
- ☐ **D**   Fatigue
- ☐ **E**   Weight loss

60 In epididymitis which TWO items are true?
- ☐ **A**   It has a peak incidence at 12–18 years of age
- ☐ **B**   Iliac fossa pain is typical
- ☐ **C**   The scrotal contents remain normal in size
- ☐ **D**   Ultrasound scanning is diagnostic
- ☐ **E**   It is associated with chlamydial infection

61 Select TWO items about immunisations:
- ☐ **A**   Cholera immunisation is important for several Third World countries
- ☐ **B**   Yellow fever vaccination is needed yearly for repeated travel
- ☐ **C**   Rabies immunisation is usually given into the gluteal muscle
- ☐ **D**   Gamma globulin should be given first in any course of immunisations before travel
- ☐ **E**   Live typhoid vaccine should be avoided if antibiotics are being taken
- ☐ **F**   Typhoid immunisation is not recommended after the age of 35 years

62 THREE of the following are true of a 'frozen shoulder':
- ☐ **A**   Recovery is usually complete
- ☐ **B**   Painful arc is typical of rotator cuff lesions
- ☐ **C**   Local tenderness bears no relationship to the site of the lesion
- ☐ **D**   Immobilisation is the treatment of choice
- ☐ **E**   The pain is typically worse during the night

63 A 50-year-old man presents with pain in the left ear, on examination the ear appears to be normal. Which ONE of the following would not account for the pain?
- ☐ **A**   Arthritis of C2–C3 level of the cervical spine
- ☐ **B**   Carcinoma of the pyriform fossa
- ☐ **C**   Impacted wisdom teeth
- ☐ **D**   Trigeminal neuralgia
- ☐ **E**   Tonsillitis

64 A young adult patient presents with dyspnoea, and a chest X-ray shows hilar lymphadenopathy. Choose THREE possible causes:

☐ **A** Streptococcal pneumonia
☐ **B** Sarcoidosis
☐ **C** Lymphoma
☐ **D** Tuberculosis
☐ **E** Pulmonary rheumatoid disease

THEME: THE RED EYE

Options:

A Acute glaucoma
B Acute iritis
C Dendritic ulcer
D Corneal abrasion
E Episcleritis
F Arc eye
G Conjunctivitis
H Subconjunctival haemorrhage
I Blepharitis

For each of the descriptions below, select the most appropriate diagnosis from the list above. Each option may be used once, more than once or not at all

Scenarios:

65 Attacks are often preceded by haloes around lights, followed by severe unilateral pain often with vomiting. On examination the cornea is hazy, and the pupil is fixed ☐

66 May cause a purulent exudate that lasts several weeks ☐

67 Acute onset of pain, photophobia, blurred vision and a small pupil with circumcorneal redness. Slit lamp examination reveals pus cells in the anterior chamber ☐

68 An occupational condition, which causes pain, epiphora, and blepharospasm. Fluorescein staining reveals pitting on the corneal surface ☐

69 Causes localised conjunctival injection with no other symptoms ☐

70 Select TWO items concerning cervical smears:
- ☐ **A** Atypia on a single occasion correlates well with the presence of CIN
- ☐ **B** The majority of florid cases of carcinoma of the cervix are diagnosed from cervical smears
- ☐ **C** If there is a history of genital warts a smear should be undertaken annually
- ☐ **D** Cervical erosions typically bleed on touch during the smear
- ☐ **E** Once fixed a cervical smear must reach the laboratory within 48 hours to allow accurate interpretation

71 TWO of the following would support a diagnosis of irritant contact dermatitis:
- ☐ **A** Severity that varies with the amount of exposure to the irritant
- ☐ **B** Rash developing 2 days after exposure
- ☐ **C** Reactivation of a rash in other sites
- ☐ **D** Positive patch tests
- ☐ **E** No previous exposure to the suspected irritant

72 Toddler diarrhoea is characterised by THREE of the following:
- ☐ **A** Typically occurs after an acute infection
- ☐ **B** Is associated with failure to thrive
- ☐ **C** Trial of a milk free diet has been shown to be beneficial
- ☐ **D** Lack of any undigested food in the stools
- ☐ **E** Response to loperamide

73 Select THREE items about benzodiazepine dependence:
- ☐ **A** The majority of patients taking a benzodiazepine regularly for 6 months or more will suffer a withdrawal reaction on stopping the drug
- ☐ **B** Dependence has been shown to occur after 3 weeks of treatment
- ☐ **C** A characteristic feature of withdrawal is loss of appetite
- ☐ **D** Auditory hallucinations would indicate other psychopathology
- ☐ **E** Beta blockers have been shown to attenuate the withdrawal symptoms

74 Select THREE items about scientific studies:
- ☐ **A** Significance levels are greater the higher the value of p
- ☐ **B** Accepting the null hypothesis means that there is significant difference
- ☐ **C** Student's t test is of use in small groups of data
- ☐ **D** Spearman's rank correlation is used for rank correlated groups of data
- ☐ **E** Standard deviation measures the variation about the mean

THEME: BENEFITS

Some important welfare benefits are:
A   Income Support
B   Family Credit
C   Incapacity Benefit
D   Child Benefit
E   Invalid Care Allowance
F   Severe Disablement Allowance
G   Disability Living Allowance
H   Attendance Allowance

Match the following with ONE of the above

75   Tax-free non-means-tested payment for anyone with a child under 16 years

76   Tax-free non-means-tested payment for people over 65 years who need help with personal care because of a physical or mental problem

77   Tax-free payment for people on low wages working more than 16 hours/week and bringing up children

78   Means-tested benefit for people working fewer than 16 hours/week and on low income

79   Payable to people incapable of any work who have paid National Insurance contributions

80   Payable to people who have given up work to look after a disabled person

THEME: SCREENING

A study was carried out in a general practice setting on a screening tool. The study gave the following results:

	Problem present	Problem absent
Screening tool positive result	82	31
Screening tool negative result	27	212

Options available

A   82/113
B   82/109
C   31/113
D   31/243
E   27/109
F   27/239
G   212/243
H   212/239
I   82
J   31
K   27
L   212
M   239
N   243

Select the appropriate option

81   Specificity

82   Positive predictive value

83   False positive

84   False negative

85   Sensitivity

86   Negative predictive value

87 TWO of the following are true of vaginal contraceptive diaphragms:
- **A**   They should be removed within 2 hours of intercourse
- **B**   The size may need to be changed if the patient's weight varies by more than 7 lb
- **C**   They can be used if utero-vaginal prolapse is present
- **D**   They need to be renewed annually
- **E**   They can be used if the patient is allergic to rubber

88 Select ONE item about applying for an order under the Mental Health Act:

- ☐ **A** The nearest relative must be a first-degree relative
- ☐ **B** The majority of admissions under the Act from general practitioners are made under Section 4
- ☐ **C** Doctors are at greater legal risk from failing to use the Act than from over-zealous use
- ☐ **D** Psychiatric community nurses can make an application for admission
- ☐ **E** Sexual deviancy, in itself, is a justification for compulsory admission

89 Select THREE items about the symptomatic treatment of vomiting:

- ☐ **A** Hyoscine is available as a skin patch
- ☐ **B** Domperidone is licensed as an injection
- ☐ **C** Cinnarizine is available without a prescription
- ☐ **D** Prochlorperazine is associated with postural hypotension
- ☐ **E** Chlorpromazine is as effective as prochlorperazine

90 Choose THREE statements about febrile convulsions:

- ☐ **A** Typically occur in the second year of life
- ☐ **B** Are commoner in social class V
- ☐ **C** Are more common in boys rather than girls
- ☐ **D** With complex fits lasting longer than 15 minutes have been shown to be associated with epilepsy in later life
- ☐ **E** Show a familial incidence

91 Select THREE items concerning varicose veins:

- ☐ **A** Sclerotherapy cures less than 10% over a 5-year period
- ☐ **B** Ligation of the long saphenous vein is more complex than the short saphenous vein
- ☐ **C** After multiple avulsions compression is necessary for about 1 week
- ☐ **D** Walking distances should be commenced on the day of surgery
- ☐ **E** The average patient with uncomplicated surgery for veins in one leg will require 6 weeks away from work

92 During pregnancy, TWO of the following chronic diseases typically deteriorate:

- ☐ **A** Epilepsy
- ☐ **B** Migraine
- ☐ **C** Multiple sclerosis
- ☐ **D** Asthma
- ☐ **E** Sickle cell disease

93   THREE of the following statements are true about eye drops:
☐ **A**   Fluorescein stains soft contact lenses
☐ **B**   Pilocarpine causes pupillary dilatation
☐ **C**   Oxybuprocaine causes stinging when installed into a normal eye
☐ **D**   Tropicamide anaesthetises the cornea
☐ **E**   Adrenaline produces local irritation

THEME: VOLUNTARY BODIES

The following are well-known voluntary bodies:
A   NSPCC
B   Marie Curie Memorial Foundation
C   Turning Point
D   The Samaritans
E   ASH
F   Terrence Higgins Trust
G   Relate
H   Cruse

Which voluntary body would most appropriately deal with these problems?

94   Marriage guidance   ☐

95   AIDS   ☐

96   Smoking   ☐

97   Child abuse   ☐

98   Cancer   ☐

99   Drug abuse   ☐

100 Bereavement in the widowed   ☐

101   Select THREE items about the Guillain–Barr, syndrome:
- ☐ **A**   There is typically an antecedent 'viral' infection
- ☐ **B**   Sensory symptoms predominate over motor symptoms
- ☐ **C**   It typically develops insidiously
- ☐ **D**   The majority of cases recover
- ☐ **E**   The central nervous system is typically spared

102   Select THREE statements concerning diabetic pregnancies:
- ☐ **A**   Congenital abnormalities are more common
- ☐ **B**   Pre-term labour is decreased in frequency
- ☐ **C**   Uncomplicated pregnancies are usually induced at 40 weeks' gestation
- ☐ **D**   Neonatal jaundice is decreased in the offspring
- ☐ **E**   Epidural analgesia is contraindicated in diabetics

103   A 6-year-old boy presents with a limp and pain in the hip. Which ONE of the following differential diagnoses would not normally be considered?
- ☐ **A**   Tuberculosis of the hip
- ☐ **B**   Perthes' disease
- ☐ **C**   Slipped upper femoral epiphysis
- ☐ **D**   Septic arthritis
- ☐ **E**   Non-accidental injury

THEME: PROSTATE PROBLEMS

The following drugs are sometimes used in patients with benign prostatic hyperplasia:
A   Tamsulosin
B   Finasteride
C   Prazosin
D   Indoramin

Match the following statements with the most appropriate drug:

104   Inhibits 5α-reductase resulting in shrinkage of prostatic glandular tissue   ☐

105   Is a selective alpha-blocker initially given in a dose of 500 micrograms twice daily   ☐

106   Is an agent which is more selective than other α1–blockers; said to act on α1A-receptors   ☐

107 In considering the diagnosis of erythema multiforme, select TWO of these items:

☐ **A** It typically occurs without any discernible precipitating cause
☐ **B** The rash is not characteristic
☐ **C** If mucous membranes are involved, carries a worse prognosis
☐ **D** Recurrent episodes are extremely rare
☐ **E** It typically resolves after approximately 10 days

THEME: INFECTIOUS DISEASES

Infectious diseases, at some time of importance to general practitioners, include:

A *Haemophilus influenzae* type B infections
B Measles
C Smallpox
D Chickenpox
E Influenza

Match the following with the appropriate disease

108 Immunisation against this was introduced in 1992 and is now given to children ☐

109 Antigenic shift occurs ☐

110 90% of adults are immune to this infection despite no routine immunisation programme ☐

111 Antigenic drift occurs in this ☐

112 Subacute sclerosing panencephalitis is a rare late complication ☐

113 This has been eradicated and vaccination is only indicated for a few laboratory workers ☐

114 Select THREE items about aspirin:

☐ **A** It has been shown to reduce the incidence of cataracts
☐ **B** It reduces mortality if given after a myocardial infarction
☐ **C** In low dose is associated with a risk of retinal haemorrhage
☐ **D** It is effective in the treatment of venous thromboembolism
☐ **E** It has been shown to have a role in the primary prevention of cerebrovascular disease

115 Select FOUR items about proton pump inhibitors:

- ☐ **A** Can cause severe headaches
- ☐ **B** Cause gynaecomastia more commonly than H2 antagonists
- ☐ **C** Are the treatment of choice for stricturing and erosive oesophagitis
- ☐ **D** Can be used with antibiotics to eradicate *H. pylori*
- ☐ **E** Are safe to use in breast feeding
- ☐ **F** Can cause severe diarrhoea

116 Child physical abuse is associated with an increased incidence in which TWO of the following:

- ☐ **A** Females
- ☐ **B** Illegitimate children
- ☐ **C** Those of low birthweight
- ☐ **D** Adolescence

117 Choose TWO of the following about the pre-menstrual syndrome:

- ☐ **A** Caffeine restriction has been shown to decrease symptoms
- ☐ **B** Fertility is not affected
- ☐ **C** Less than 50% of women seek help from their doctor with symptoms related to the condition
- ☐ **D** Suppression of ovulation typically relieves symptoms

118 Choose THREE statements about accidental carbon monoxide poisoning:

- ☐ **A** It is the most common cause of death by poisoning in children
- ☐ **B** Initial symptoms are characterised by headache
- ☐ **C** Mental lethargy is typical
- ☐ **D** Effects are typically reversed about 3 days after removal from the source
- ☐ **E** Cyanosis occurs in the later stages

119 You are investigating a couple for involuntary infertility and the sperm count of the husband is returned showing azoospermia. TWO of the following are true:

- ☐ **A** The condition is strongly related to mumps orchitis
- ☐ **B** If due to Klinefelter's syndrome, FSH levels will be raised
- ☐ **C** In the majority of cases a cause can be detected by full investigation
- ☐ **D** Endocrine treatment will achieve a viable sperm count in more than 29% of cases
- ☐ **E** Intercourse the night prior to collecting the sample has been shown to produce a temporary azoospermia

120 Oral decongestants used for the treatment of common colds are contraindicated in which THREE groups of patients?

- ☐ **A** Taking beta blockers
- ☐ **B** Who discontinued monoamine oxidase inhibitors 1 week previously
- ☐ **C** Who is hypothyroid
- ☐ **D** Who is diabetic
- ☐ **E** Who is taking non-steroidal anti-inflammatory drugs

THEME: THROMBOLYTIC TRIALS

Thrombolytic therapy trials include:
A ISIS-2
B ASSET
C ISIS-3
D ISAM
E GREAT
F GISSI

For which trial is the following true

121 Compared side-effects and efficacy of thrombolytic agents and showed aspirin and streptokinase as probable treatments of choice ☐

122 Compared streptokinase against aspirin, against both, and against neither ☐

123 Compared alteplase against placebo ☐

124 Compared streptokinase plus heparin against placebo ☐

125 Compared streptokinase against placebo ☐

126 Which ONE of the following drugs cannot be administered via a nebuliser?
☐ A Terbutaline
☐ B Sodium cromoglycate
☐ C Theophylline
☐ D Ipratropium bromide
☐ E Beclomethasone

127 Select THREE items about Down's syndrome:
☐ A There is an increased incidence of ischaemic heart disease
☐ B There is a deletion in chromosome 21
☐ C Atrioventricular canal defects are common
☐ D Patent ductus arteriosus is rarely seen
☐ E IQ is usually in the range 80–100
☐ F There is a higher incidence of hypothyroidism than in matched control subjects
☐ G There is a higher incidence of glue ear than in matched control subjcts

128 Select TWO statements about tuberculosis in the United Kingdom:
- ☐ **A** Notifications of the disease are increasing
- ☐ **B** The majority of isolates are now resistant to isoniazid
- ☐ **C** Trials conducted in the British Isles have failed to show the effectiveness of BCG vaccination
- ☐ **D** Is significantly associated with the homeless population
- ☐ **E** About 30% of patients with AIDS will develop tuberculosis

129 Excessive hair loss is not associated with which ONE of the following:
- ☐ **A** Seborrhoeic eczema
- ☐ **B** Tinea capitis
- ☐ **C** Minoxidil treatment
- ☐ **D** Hormone replacement therapy
- ☐ **E** Hirsutism

130 Studies published in the United Kingdom have shown a significant association between low blood pressure and FOUR of the following:
- ☐ **A** Decreased blood glucose levels
- ☐ **B** Increased depressive illness
- ☐ **C** Dizziness
- ☐ **D** Raised serum cholesterol levels
- ☐ **E** A decrease in the patient's perceived feeling of well-being

131 Which of the following statements regarding irritable bowel syndrome are correct? (select THREE)
- ☐ **A** Irritable bowel syndrome is a diagnosis of exclusion
- ☐ **B** It is commoner in females
- ☐ **C** RAST testing for food allergens should be carried out on all patients
- ☐ **D** Rectal bleeding and steatorrhoea are common in IBS
- ☐ **E** May respond to relaxation therapy
- ☐ **F** Treatment with SSRIs may substantially improve symptoms of visceral hyperactivity
- ☐ **G** Is associated with urinary frequency and dyspareunia in some women
- ☐ **H** Referral is recommended for patients with onset in early adulthood

132 Which ONE of the following would indicate a diagnosis of stress incontinence in female patients?
- ☐ **A** Nocturia occurring three times nightly
- ☐ **B** Dribbling after passing water
- ☐ **C** Leaking small amounts of urine
- ☐ **D** Having to 'rush' to get to the toilet on time

133 You receive the following blood results from a fasting sample. The patient is a fit 35-year-old male non-smoker, with no other medical problems and no significant family history.

Total cholesterol   6.2 mmol/l   (<5.2)
HDL cholesterol   2.6 mmol/l   (>1)
LDL cholesterol   3.6 mmol/l   (<4)
Triglycerides   6.0 mmol/l   (<2.5)

From the following statements select the THREE correct answers.

□ **A** This patient is at increased risk of acute pancreatitis
□ **B** The first line treatment of choice is a statin
□ **C** Diet control may cause a decrease in HDL levels
□ **D** This patient is at significantly increased risk of ischaemic heart disease
□ **E** These results may be caused by alcohol abuse
□ **F** Treatment with cholestyramine will reduce the triglycerides

134 A previously well patient is seen in hospital for pre-op anaesthetic assessment before a hernia repair. Bloods show no abnormality other than a non-fasting blood sugar level of 8.9 mmol/l. Regarding future management which ONE of the following statements is true?

□ **A** The patient has diabetes and should be started on metformin immediately
□ **B** 80% of diabetics in the community are undiagnosed
□ **C** The WHO cut off for normal random blood sugar is 7.8 mmol/l
□ **D** The patient should have a fasting blood sugar test
□ **E** The prevalence of type 2 diabetes is falling in the UK

135 A 19-year-old woman comes to see you concerned that she may have contracted Chlamydia. Which of the following statements are true? (select THREE)

□ **A** Chlamydia is a viral infection
□ **B** Chlamydia may cause conjunctivitis
□ **C** There is no effective screening test
□ **D** Chlamydia is a significant cause of infertility
□ **E** May cause dyspareunia
□ **F** Is mainly a problem in the 30–40 age group
□ **G** Can only be detected with endocervical swabs
□ **H** Is treated with doxycycline

THEME: INCOME

GPs derive their income from sources including:
A   Non-medical income
B   Private medical work
C   Practice allowance
D   Capitation fees
E   Reimbursements
F   Item of service payments

Match the following with the appropriate source of income

136   Rural practice payment ☐

137   Temporary resident fee ☐

138   Emergency treatment ☐

139   Immediately necessary treatment ☐

140   Child health surveillance ☐

141   Immunisations ☐

142   Insurance report completion ☐

143   Cremation fee ☐

144   A prescription issued for a controlled drug must comply with TWO of the following:
☐   **A**   It cannot be issued on a computer-generated script
☐   **B**   The address of the doctor must be handwritten
☐   **C**   The script must be marked with C.D. by the issuing doctor
☐   **D**   The total quantity of the drugs must be given in words and figures
☐   **E**   The frequency with which the drug is to be taken must be given in words and figures

145   Select TWO features about dermatofibroma:
☐   **A**   Are more common in women
☐   **B**   Are typically pigmented
☐   **C**   Have malignant potential
☐   **D**   Typically ulcerate centrally
☐   **E**   Have an irregular edge

THEME: CHILDHOOD DEVELOPMENT

Developmental milestones are looked for at various ages in children by parents and health professionals. Consider the following ages and match them with the developmental milestones shown:

A   6 weeks
B   12 weeks
C   6 months
D   12 months
E   18 months
F   2 years
G   3 years
H   4 years
I   5 years

146 Chooses own friends; names 3–4 colours ☐

147 Feeds with spoon; scribbles ☐

148 Feeds with biscuit ☐

149 Turns head to sounds on level with ear ☐

150 Builds tower with 6–7 cubes ☐

151 Knows two colours; goes up stairs one foot per step, down stairs 2 feet per step ☐

152 Builds tower of 3–4 cubes ☐

153 Select TWO items about nitrate tolerance:
☐ **A** Tolerance to the adverse effects, such as headache, bear no relation to the therapeutic effects
☐ **B** It typically takes at least one month to develop
☐ **C** Topical nitrates have been shown not to produce tolerance
☐ **D** Isosorbide mononitrate has been shown not to produce tolerance
☐ **E** Tolerance is rapidly abolished by a nitrate-free period

THEME: LITERATURE

Consultations are discussed in literature which includes:

A *Culture, Health and Illness* by C Helman
B *The Exceptional Potential in Each Primary Care Consultation* by Stott & Davies
C *The Inner Consultation* by R Neighbour
D *Effect of a General Practitioner's Style on Patients' Satisfaction: A Controlled Study* by Savage & Armstrong
E *Games People Play* by E Berne
F *Six Minutes for the Patient* by Balint & Novell
G *Doctors Talking to Patients* by Byrne & Long

Match the statements below with the most appropriate of the titles listed

154 Coined the term 'safety netting' ☐

155 Noted severe time constraints of the consultation on audio tape ☐

156 Described the 'flash' ☐

157 Looked at complex transactions between people, described as pastimes ☐

158 Used the terms 'connecting' and 'summarising' ☐

159 Described a four-part framework of the consultation, one of which is 'opportunistic health promotion' ☐

160 TWO of the following are true about cholesterol:
☐ **A** A raised cholesterol has been shown to be a risk factor for coronary artery disease
☐ **B** Decreasing cholesterol has been shown to decrease overall mortality
☐ **C** A low cholesterol has a significant association with carcinoma
☐ **D** Good dietary control will reduce cholesterol levels by about 30%
☐ **E** Those who smoke should not be screened

161 You read the following statement in the methods section of a paper in the BMJ: "Statistical Analysis. This was done on an intention to treat basis,…" Which ONE of the following correctly describes the method?
☐ **A** Only patients who completed the trial were included in the results
☐ **B** The results are less applicable to clinical practice
☐ **C** All patients who volunteer for the trial are included
☐ **D** Patients who are initially treated in one of the study arms but subsequently drop out are included in the final analysis
☐ **E** This method is most suited to retrospective studies

THEME: MINOR SURGERY

In general practice, minor surgery procedures are usually:
A   Injections
B   Aspirations
C   Excisions
D   Incisions
E   Curette or cryo-cautery

Match the following with the procedure in general practice

162 Thrombosed piles ☐

163 Haemorrhoids ☐

164 Lipomas ☐

165 Verruca ☐

166 Molluscum contagiosum ☐

167 Hydrocoele ☐

THEME: BACK PAIN

Causes of back pain seen in general practice include:
A   Mechanical back pain
B   Disc prolapse at L4/L5 level
C   Disc prolapse at L5/S1 level
D   Depression
E   Ankylosing spondylitis
F   Neoplastic lesions

Choose the most appropriate of these causes for the following scenarios

168 A 38-year-old labourer has recurrent back pain, worse on coughing and sneezing; he has reduced right-sided straight leg raising; further examination shows weakness of dorsiflexion of right foot and sensory disturbance at the dorsum of the foot ☐

169 A 33-year-old mature student complains of low back pain especially worse in the morning when he feels stiff ☐

continues ...

170 A 41-year-old accountant describes pain worse on movement which came on after a weekend gardening; it has improved since going back to work □

171 A 35-year-old roofer has back pain which prevents him working; he has noticed a strange feeling on the outside edge of his left foot; examination reveals that plantar flexion of his left foot is weak and the ankle jerk is absent on the left □

THEME: BOWEL DISORDERS

Change in bowel habit may be caused by a variety of disorders other than carcinoma. These include:
A   Irritable bowel syndrome
B   Diverticular disease
C   Crohn's disease
D   Ulcerative colitis
E   Ischaemic colitis

Match the following clinical scenarios with the most appropriate bowel disorder from the above list

172 A 32-year-old male presents with painless bloody diarrhoea; there is no abdominal tenderness and no masses are felt in the abdomen □

173 A 60-year-old lady presents with abdominal pain and bloody diarrhoea; she is known to have angina; abdominal tenderness is noted at examination □

174 A 43-year-old man has abdominal pain and diarrhoea; there is abdominal tenderness at examination; anal tags are also noted □

175 A 33-year-old teacher complains of wind and diarrhoea with several loose motions passed in the morning and after meals; abdominal pain is often relieved by defaecation; examination reveals tenderness over the sigmoid colon □

176 A 51-year-old laboratory technician complains of pain in the abdomen with alternating diarrhoea and constipation; examination reveals tenderness in the left iliac fossa □

THEME: HYPERTENSION TRIALS

Some important trials in hypertension include:
A   Hypertension Optimal Treatment (HOT) Trial
B   MRC Mild Hypertension Trial
C   Veterans Administration Co-operative Study
D   European Working Party on Hypertension in the Elderly
E   MRC Trial for Hypertension in Older Adults

Link the following statements with ONE of these studies

177 A randomised trial studying calcium channel blockers with other drugs

178 Single-blind trial which recruited over 4000 patients, and used diuretics, beta blockers and placebos

179 Almost 400 men with hypertension took part in this double-blind trial, which had a particular impact on stroke reduction; the average age of participants was 50 years

180 A 15-year trial which involved about 86,000 patient years of observation of almost 200 GPs

181 A single-blind trial using bendrofluazide, propranolol and placebo, but using higher doses of bendrofluazide than used now; one CVA was saved for 850 patient years of treatment

THEME: ECG CHANGES

Option list
A   J waves
B   letter A
C   letter B
D   letter C
E   P waves
F   pathological Q waves
G   R waves
H   U waves
I   reduced amplitude
J   slow rhythm
K   ST elevation

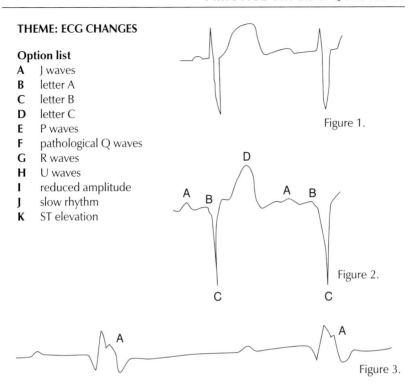

Figure 1.

Figure 2.

Figure 3.

Read the following information about ECG changes. Fill in the spaces with the appropriate word from the option list. Each word may be used once, more than once, or not at all.

Characteristic ECG changes are seen in myocardial infarction. (figure 1 and figure 2) **(182)**_____ is seen in anterior chest leads in an anterior myocardial infarction, but **(183)**_____ result later. This later change is shown in figure 2 as **(184)**_____.

Some ECG changes are not due to cardiac conditions.

The ECG show in figure 3 is from a patient with hypothermia. It shows typical **(185)**_____ at letter A and also shows sinus bradycardia. Myxomedema also gives sinus bardycardia together with **(186)**_____.

THEME: CERTIFICATES

The following certificates are issued in general practice:
A   Med 3
B   Med 4
C   Med 5
D   Med 6
E   DS1500

Which would be the appropriate certificate to issue in the following circumstances?

187 A patient is seen with a chest infection and he is advised to be off work for the next 2 weeks   ☐

188 A patient tells you that she is being assessed under the all work test and has been asked for a certificate from her GP   ☐

189 A patient is terminally ill and wants to claim Attendance Allowance   ☐

190 A patient brings you a hospital discharge letter after an admission of 3 weeks' stay, but he has not had a certificate from the hospital   ☐

191 You issue this certificate to give an accurate diagnosis, when the patient has been given a medical certificate for his employer with a vague diagnosis   ☐

192 A patient has had medical certificates to be off work for the last 9 months, and you are now giving a long term certificate to be off work   ☐

193 **Mrs Brady, a 69-year-old woman who has never taken HRT asks for a bone scan to make sure she is not osteoporotic. Which ONE of the following is an appropriate indication for a bone density scan?**
☐ A   Patients commenced on a bisphosphonate for osteoporosis already, to monitor response to treatment
☐ B   Patients on 5 mg prednisolone a day for the treatment of polymyalgia rheumatica
☐ C   Patients with previous low trauma fracture
☐ D   Patients who have taken the combined oral contraceptive pill for over 10 years
☐ E   Patients who have a body mass index over 30

THEME: INFECTIOUS DISEASES

Option list:
A   Scarlatina
B   Measles
C   Chickenpox
D   Influenza
E   Mumps
F   Parvovirus B19
G   *Haemophilus influenzae* (B)
H   Diphtheria
I   Tuberculosis
J   Herpes simplex

Instruction:
For each scenario described below, select the most appropriate option from those above. Each one may be used once, more than once or not at all.

Items:
194   A prodromal illness followed by itching and a vesicular rash, which appears in crops over several days. Complications include encephalitis, pneumonitis and secondary infection of vesicles. Neonatal infection may be severe

195   Causes a mild self-limiting condition in children with characteristic unilateral facial erythema

196   In under 5s may cause meningitis or epiglottitis

197   Should be considered in children with a chronic cough

198   Initially causes fever, malaise, conjunctival injection, swollen eyelids, and white spots in the mouth. A rash then spreads from the head to the trunk and the legs

199   May cause orchitis, pancreatitis, encephalitis or meningitis

THEME: STATISTICS

Option list:
A   Number needed to treat
B   Number needed to harm
C   Confidence intervals
D   Confounding
E   Number needed to screen
F   P value
G   C value
H   Positive predictive value
I   Negative predictive value
J   Sensitivity
K   Specifity
L   Power
M   Standard deviation of the mean

Instructions:
From the list of statistical definitions below select the most appropriate option from the list above. Each option may be used once, more than once or not at all.

Descriptions:
200 Is the spurious association between two factors under study due to a third factor ☐

201 Is the proportion of true negatives identified by the test ☐

202 Is an estimate of a result telling the reader within a specified probability that the result lies between two values ☐

203 Is the proportion of patients with positive test results who are correctly diagnosed ☐

204 Is the probability of a result occurring by chance ☐

205 Is the reciprocal of the absolute risk reduction ☐

Practice Paper 1

Answers and Teaching Notes

1: A D E
The so-called 'Wilson Criteria' for screening are important to know. The condition must be important, there must be a recognisable latent stage of the disease (when effective treatment is possible) and there must be a policy about screening and treatment. Diagnosis must be by an acceptable method which might or might not involve clinical examination.

2: C
A bilateral progressive sensorineural loss can be induced by noise exposure. Generally there is sparing of low frequencies and also very high frequency sounds. Excessive noise damages the hair cells of the organ of Corti. Recruitment (sudden amplification of the sound) is common as it is in presbyacusis. Hearing aids are particularly effective. The hearing loss is typically insidious progressing over a long period of time.

3:	P	(qualitatively)
4:	C	(comparative)
5:	T	(universally)
6:	I	(heterogeneous)
7:	S	(steroid)
8:	D	(confounders)
9:	O	(proactive)
10:	R	(reactive)
11:	M	(positive)
12:	G	(efficacy)

13: E
The regulations with regard to practice leaflets have to be carefully adhered to. The age does not have to be stated but the sex of the doctor does! The date of first registration of the practice nurse does not but that of the doctor needs to be stated. Fees charged are of no concern to the FHSA. Computerisation is often stated on leaflets but is not a requirement. However, the facilities for the disabled must be stated as must the means by which people may comment on the service available.

Literature
14: D 15: F 16: E 17: A 18: C 19: C
What Sort of Doctor? looked at doctors' accessibility and the premises. *Doctors Talking to Patients* was a study of audio-taped consultations and noted doctor-centred and patient-centred consultations. *The Doctor, his Patient, and the Illness* observed the effects of the doctors as people. *The Inner Consultation* discussed housekeeping. *The Consultation: An Approach to Learning and Teaching* suggested addressing patients' ideas, concerns and expectations.

20: C
Primary herpetic infection in the third trimester carries a 40% risk to the fetus. There is also a risk of premature labour. Post primary infection only carries an approximately 5% risk of fetal infection. Aciclovir is not licensed for use in pregnancy but it has been used extensively with no evidence of harm to the baby. If herpes lesions are apparent at the onset of labour a caesarean section is indicated. In pregnancy there is a decrease in cell mediated immunity and therefore the risk of infection is probably increased.

21: C D
At birth about 4% of foreskins are retractable, at 6 months it is 20%, at one year 50%, and by 3 years it is 90%. If left untreated phimosis may ultimately lead to problems with micturition and sexual function. Inability to clean under the foreskin is associated with stones in the preputial sac and the development of cancer of the penis. Circumcision has a low rate of complications and is reported to be the safest surgical procedure in childhood.

22: B
Eating disorders produce definite symptoms. There are certain features that would suggest an organic disorder. A loss of pubic hair would indicate hypopituitarism. LH levels are typically low in eating disorders. The ESR is normal and cortisol levels are usually high, normal or above normal, possibly related to an associated depression. If the eating disorder has started before puberty gonadotrophin release will be delayed and therefore amenorrhoea will be primary.

23: A C
Although the incidence of chronic bronchitis is falling in men it is rising in women. Great Britain still has the highest incidence in the world reflecting high smoking rates, poor management of industrial waste and a readiness of doctors in this country to make the diagnosis. It accounts for more days away from work than any other illness including back pain and is associated with living in an urban industrial environment.

24: B
It is possible for viral infections to behave in this way. Asthma is the most common missed diagnosis and a trial of bronchodilators is always worthwhile. Pertussis, after five weeks, will probably have started to resolve slowly. It will have been accompanied by malaise and probably vomiting accompanying the cough. Inhaled foreign bodies will produce signs in the chest and be accompanied by tachycardia and malaise by five weeks. Antibiotics are rarely justified, but are often given on a 'blind' basis.

25: C E
Tinnitus is typically associated with sensorineural deafness but conductive deafness can lead to an awareness of sounds generated within the body, such as from a carotid bruit. Treatment is often unrewarding, but treatment for depression by drugs or psychotherapy helps a proportion of patients. Surgical treatment is rarely used and the patient must be aware that the condition can be made worse by the operation.

Hypertension
26: B 27: E 28: C 29: A 30: A
The MRC Mild Hypertension Trial was a single-blind trial between bendrofluazide (in doses larger than now used) propranolol and placebo. The trial showed that ICUA was saved by 850 patients treatment years. The European Working Party on Hypertension in the Elderly was a double-blind trial using hydrochlorothiazide, triamterene and placebo. Only 840 patients were recruited. The Veterans Administration Cooperative Study was a double-blind trial in a highly compliant group. The Systolic Hypertension in the Elderly Program Cooperative Group used low-dose diuretics, beta blockers and reserpine.

31: D
Ten per cent of shiftworkers like nightwork, 20% hate it, and the rest tolerate it. There is no increased cardiovascular mortality but peptic ulceration is much more common due to irregular diet, poor meals, chronic fatigue, excessive smoking and alcohol. Mental symptoms are not increased and the rate of industrial accidents is not increased.

32: D
Closed questions are easy to quantify and analyse, but may give limited information. A combination may be needed. Validity indicates that it measures what it was meant to measure. Reliability indicates patients would give the same answers on another occasion. Comprehensibility shows that patients understood the questionnaire. In a Likert scale, a score is given to a preferred response on a continuum of possible responses.

33: E
About one-third of all subarachnoid haemorrhages occur in those over 65 years. The majority are due to a ruptured cerebral aneurysm, pre-existing hypertension worsens the prognosis. The most common presentation in the elderly is with confusion or coma. The mortality in this age group is greater than 50%.

34: C
Breath-holding attacks tend to occur in children who are easily frustrated. Recovery from an attack is rapid and there are no after effects such as drowsiness which would occur after a fit. Cyanosis is transient and extended tonic posture and shaking or twitching might make the parents think that the child has had a convulsion.

35: C D
The onset of jaundice in cirrhosis is variable, malaise and lethargy are common at the onset. Vague gastrointestinal symptoms and especially pain with tenderness over the liver are common. Spider naevi are frequent along with other symptoms of liver failure such as gynaecomastia, testicular atrophy and a loss of male hair distribution. The prognosis is poor but is dramatically improved if alcohol can be avoided.

36: D
Non-A-non-B hepatitis has an incubation period of 6–8 weeks and is transmitted by blood transfusion, coagulation products and by contaminated water. It is associated with a carrier state unlike hepatitis A in which carrier states do not occur. Acute cholangitis is a medical emergency with a high mortality rate. Failure to eliminate the virus in hepatitis B occurs in 5–10% of people, it has a poorer prognosis especially if associated with the presence of virus D.

37: D
Dithranol has been used for many years and is the mainstay of treatment for psoriasis. Contraindications include rapidly spreading lesions, pustular psoriasis, or the use of potent steroids in the recent past. Prolonged use is not associated with skin malignancy and it can be used in patients with hepatic and renal problems. Short contact therapy of 30 minutes per day is as effective as conventional overnight treatment.

38: A C D
Alzheimer's disease is often missed in the early stages because early symptoms such as preference for routine and mild spatial disorientation are associated with 'forgetfulness' of age. Memory loss is characteristically short term for recent events. In the later stages loss of speech, grand mal seizures and spasticity of limbs add to the worsening mental problems.

39: D
For a list size of 3000, one pneumothorax would be expected per annum, half of these spontaneous and half secondary. The commonest causes of secondary pneumothorax are central venous cannulation and lung biopsy. Patients may fly once their CXR has returned to normal. It is commonest in young males.

40: D
Isolated hyperbilirubinaemia is extremely unlikely to be pathological. Gilbert's is seen in 1–2 % of the population and results in hyperbilirubinaemia at times of stress, e.g. intercurrent illness or starvation. It can be diagnosed from the history or by LFTs before and after a 24 hour fast. Cirrhosis and hepatitis cause derangement in ALT and GGT, pancreatitis a raised amylase.

41: A D E
Eighty per cent of thyrotoxic patients have Graves' disease with positive thyroid antibodies. A raised TSH in a thyrotoxic patient would indicate a rare TSH-secreting tumour of the pituitary. Blocking all thyroid function with antithyroid drugs such as carbimazole and then replacing with thyroid hormone is the treatment of choice for Graves' disease. Thyroid adenoma is best treated surgically. Graves' ophthalmopathy is more common in smokers and people who have had recent radioiodine treatment. Post-partum thyroiditis is common, occurring in 5% of pregnancies, and often requiring no treatment, as it is frequently a minor disturbance.

Dermatology
42: G 43: D 44: F 45: E 46: C 47: B
Scales are horny cells loosened from the skin surface. A macule is a flat spot, usually of a different colour from the surrounding skin; a papule is a raised spot. Nodules are lumps deep in the skin. Vesicles are skin blobs filled with clear fluid; bullae are blisters filled with blood-stained fluid.

48: A E
Basal cell carcinoma is the most common skin malignancy. Although due to exposure to ultra-violet light, it rarely appears on the bald scalp, ears, lower lips, or back of the hands. It typically starts as a small pink or pearly papule. Eventually the centre breaks down forming the ulcer which may become crusted. It is more common in those with freckles, red hair and blue eyes.

49: C D
No study has shown an improvement over placebo with diuretics or pyridoxine. Gamolenic acid produces improvement in over 50% of cases, tamoxifen 10 mg daily improves pain but this is not covered in the product licence. HRT and the combined oral contraceptive make pain worse because of the oestrogenic drive.

50: B C
The only two of these that are so-called 'first rank' symptoms are thought insertion and auditory hallucinations commenting on the patient's appearance or actions. Visual hallucinations and paranoid delusions may occur but are not diagnostic. Ideas of reference can occur in other disorders.

Depression
51: E 52: B 53: F 54: A 55: D 56: C 57: C
Amitriptyline is a tricyclic antidepressant with sedative properties; lofepramine is less sedative. Carbamazepine and lithium are used in bipolar disease. Carbamazepine is also used in epilepsy. Patients on lithium should have thyroid status monitored. Patients taking MAOI are instructed about dietary restrictions. Fluvoxamine is an SSRI.

58: B E
An IUCD is effective for five days after coitus. The morning after pill is only effective for 3 days. There is no teratogenic risk to the fetus and it is not contraindicated when breast feeding. Mastalgia is in fact a side-effect in the non-pregnant woman. Because 50% of the female population is unaware of these methods they have failed to reduce unplanned pregnancies.

59: A D F
Balint observed how doctors' personalities influenced patient care. Pendleton defined communication tasks of defining problems and choosing appropriate action. Neighbour described safety-netting as anticipating what might happen next and

planning; he described house-keeping as dealing with the feelings left over by one consultation. Byrne & Long looked at 'doctor-centred' and 'patient-centred' consultations; Berne looked at a transactional model. Longer consultations improve patient satisfaction especially if there is a major psychological component.

60: A B
Of patients with osteoarthritis 40% have a first-degree relative affected. The knee is the most commonly affected joint and is made worse by obesity. There is little correlation between X-ray appearances and the clinical condition. Activities such as swimming should be encouraged, low impact sporting activities should be gradually increased.

61: B C
Solvent abuse is usually a group activity of boys between 11 and 16 years of age. Surveys show that it is a transient form of experimentation with 75% stopping abuse within 6 months. Acute effects include visual hallucinations, impaired judgement, slurred speech and dizziness. Chronic effects are cerebellar signs with cerebral ventricular enlargement and sometimes peripheral neuropathy. Death is not due to toluene but to freons.

62: D
Chest infection is common, the prognosis is worsened by co-existing heart disease. A very high or a very low white cell count is an adverse indicator of prognosis. Confusion is often the presenting feature of an underlying pneumonic process in an elderly patient who may appear otherwise well and have a minimum of chest signs.

63: A C D
It is virtually impossible to distinguish clinically between gastric and duodenal ulceration. They have many features in common, 10% of gastric and 15% of duodenal ulcers bleed. Night pain is present in both but is more common with duodenal ulcers. *Helicobacter pylori* is found in 90% of duodenal ulcers but the significance of this is controversial at present. A familial tendency is common to both and both have a blood group association. Patients over 40 years of age presenting for the first time with dyspepsia should be investigated because this presentation accounts for about 26% of the total number of cancers detected.

64: A B C
Eighty-five per cent of carcinomas of the bladder present with an episode of haematuria. It is associated with exposure to various industrial carcinogens, the use of phenacetin and cyclophosphamide, and of course cigarette smoking. It is probably because of the latter that the incidence is rising in women. About half the superficial lesions treated with cystodiathermy will reoccur within 2 years.

65: B C
Haemorrhages, especially the more minor ones, are often misdiagnosed as infarcts. This has important implications if aspirin is to be given. A cerebral haemorrhage

typically has an abrupt onset with headache, vomiting and possible neck stiffness. The patient will often remain unconscious after 24 hours and will have a raised diastolic blood pressure at this time.

66: B C D

Ten per cent of all new entrants to the blind register are directly due to chronic glaucoma, they are usually over 65 years of age. Myopic patients are at a greater risk than long sighted patients, who are at a greater risk of acute glaucoma. There is a very strong familial tendency and first-degree relatives of those patients with glaucoma get free eye tests.

67: B D

General Practitioners are responsible for care at any venue of treatment in the practice area, even if this care is delegated to a deputising service or practice nurse. The GP is also responsible for all staff including when their family answers the telephone. If a GP perceives the need for a drug and it is available on a NHS prescription it must be provided. A private prescription cannot be used even if the drug is cheaper to the patient privately. Of course if it is available 'over the counter' without a prescription the patient can be advised of this. The most common reason for a complaint against a GP is failure to visit.

68: A C E

Surveys have shown that 50% of women who complain that their menstrual loss is heavy have an average loss by normal criteria. Dysfunctional uterine bleeding is diagnosed when there is absence of other factors such as fibroids. D&C is usually employed to detect an underlying endometrial carcinoma, the incidence of which in those under 40 years is 1:100,000. Younger patients would probably be better given a vabra curettage or a hysteroscopy. Mefenamic acid has been shown to decrease blood loss by 25% and also to decrease associated pain.

69: A D E

Emergency care is free to all visitors to the UK no matter which country they come from. So is any domiciliary nursing care that is needed. For other care, reciprocal arrangements exist with many countries and their nationals can be treated under the NHS; Australia is one such country. A fee can be charged by the first doctor who attends any person involved in a road traffic accident. The bill is usually paid by the insurance company of the vehicle involved without detriment to the driver's 'no claims bonus'.

70: A D

Constitutional delay is the most common reason and is defined as puberty delayed beyond 16 years in girls and beyond 18 years in boys. It can be regarded as a variation of normal. The bone age corresponds to the stage of development not chronological age. A raised gonadotrophin level would be indicative of perhaps Turner's syndrome, Klinefelter's or primary gonadal failure. There is typically a family history of late puberty, so it is always worth asking the parents.

71: C D E

Breast feeding fails because of inadequate support and poor, inconsistent and antiquated advice from health care workers. Practices that were shown to be incorrect 30 years ago are still being taught. Initial feeds should not be time restricted, they should be for as long as mother and baby feel comfortable. If sore breasts occur it is usually poor positioning of the baby, not excessive sucking. Just feeding from one breast at a particular feed is justifiable. The fat content of the milk has been shown to increase as the feed progresses. The subsequent incidence of breast cancer in breast feeding women is not increased, various studies have shown a decrease.

Studies
72: C 73: D 74: B 75: A 76: E

A descriptive study could indicate the prevalence of a condition in a population. A clinical trial might involve patients with a disease being assigned randomly to treatment or placebo. A case-control study could look at the previous use of a drug in TWO separate cohorts. Correlation would look at the occurrence of a disease compared with another factor to see if there was any link. Meta-analysis combines the results of several investigations.

77: E F

When sampling populations it is essential to decrease bias. Retrospective studies are prone to bias as are subjective studies because the results are based on opinion rather than fact. Standardisation is essential between the control group and the group under investigation. Stratified sampling compartmentalises the groups within a sample allowing less variation. It is better to use random numbers than sampling at regular intervals. The regularity could coincide by chance with some other unforeseen regularity in the material under study.

78: A B C

Suicide in alcoholics is especially prevalent during relapses after a period of abstinence. If episodes of aggression are directed towards themselves they are particularly at risk. The social and psychological isolation engendered by physical illness leaves patients at an immense risk. An urban environment is more associated with suicide than a rural one. The most vulnerable people are male, older age and single, but there has been an increase recently in the incidence in younger males.

79: D E F

There is no specific diagnosis in about 80% of presentations. More than 50% will have recurrent problems, and about 50 million working days are lost each year. About one in five of all new orthopaedic referrals are for back problems.

80: A C D

Hair loss of a diffuse nature is associated with iron deficiency in the elderly. Conversely, scalp ringworm only causes localised loss in children. Warfarin has hair loss as a reported side-effect. Alopecia areata, with the typical exclamation mark hairs typically causes patchy loss but diffuse loss is known. Trichotillomania, in which the patient deliberately pulls the hair out, produces a well defined area of hair loss. The hairs are very short rather than absent.

81: A B
Ectopic pregnancy has increased by 30% in the last 20 years, possibly due to the increase in pelvic inflammatory disease. The death rate has fallen but it still accounts for 10% of maternal mortality. If the pregnancy test is positive with low levels of HCG and the uterus is empty at 6 weeks' gestation then ectopic pregnancy is likely. Ultrasound on its own is unreliable with 5–10% showing an adnexal mass with a gestational sac. Neither the IUCD nor the progestogen only pill are associated with ectopic pregnancy.

82: B E
Pompholyx is an extremely itchy variant of eczema, typically affecting the soles of the feet and the palms of the hands. The epidermal fluid of the eczematous condition is trapped in the thickened stratum and produces a 'sago' like appearance. Strong steroids are often needed in resistant cases. It is not associated with atopy or eczema elsewhere. Mycology should be checked before starting treatment if the condition is severe.

83: B E
Ovarian cancer is much more common in nulliparous women, even a single early spontaneous abortion seems to afford some degree of protection. One year of treatment on the combined pill produces the same protection as a full term pregnancy. If a first degree relative has had the condition the risk is increased by 2–3-fold. The overall survival is 30% rising to 65% if detected at stage 1. Unfortunately, the presentation is often silent, only 15–20% have abnormal bleeding. The most common presentation is abdominal pain either with or without abdominal swelling.

84: B E
Faecal occult blood testing is unacceptable to a lot of people. It has a high false positive rate of approximately 54% in one trial. Sensitivity is of the order of 75% for a three-day test rising to 90% for a five-day test. It is more sensitive for distal tumours. In caecal tumours, haematin released may be broken down in its passage through the remaining colon. Certain foods such as banana, radish, broccoli, parsnip, turnip and cauliflower have peroxidase activity which can lead to false positives.

85: B D
Proliferative retinopathy is seen on the optic disc but background retinopathy is first seen on the temporal side of the macula. The earliest visible changes are micro-aneurysms and haemorrhages. In the UK, diabetes is the most common cause of blind registration between the ages of 20 and 65 years of age.

86: A C
Many antibiotics have been implicated in causing pseudomembranous colitis but systemic clindamycin, amoxicillin, ampicillin and the cephalosporins are the most common. The toxin of the organism *Clostridium difficile* is the causative factor. Vancomycin and metronidazole have been shown to be effective in a patient who is toxic. Blood in the stools is a rare finding usually only with the severe type of infection. The peripheral blood film shows a polymorph leucocytosis and there are leucocytes in the stools.

Lipid-lowering drugs
87: B 88: A 89: E 90: B 91: D 92: A
Cholestyramine is an anion exchange resin which binds bile acids decreasing absorption; it has been used in children. Simvastatin is a HMG CoA reductase inhibitor and has been reported to cause sleep disturbance. Nicotinic acid can cause severe flushing. Cofibrate predisposes to gallstones by increasing biliary excretion of cholesterol.

93: B C D
Dupuytren's contracture is progressive fibrosis of the palmar fascia causing painless flexion. More than one finger is often affected with 65% ring, 55% little, 25% middle, 5% index and 3% thumb. There is also a high incidence in patients with liver disease especially alcoholics. It is said to affect the white race only and is eight times more common in men than women.

94: B D E
Risk factors for congenital dislocation of the hip include female sex, breech delivery, being first born, a family history and oligohydramnios. The left hip is more likely to be affected.

95: A E
Currently in vogue is the term 'heartsink patient', they are difficult to define and are not always frequent attenders. GPs usually have such patients within the practice and do not refer elsewhere. The average doctor has 20–30 such patients and examining their medical record folders reveals a variety of different diagnoses at each consultation. They also have significantly more psychological, social and family problems.

96: A C D
One hundred babies with sickle cell disease are born in the UK each year. Six thousand people in Great Britain have the disease. Priapism can occur in any male after 5 years of age, most commonly in sexually active men and if prolonged can lead to impotence. Fertility is normal in women but pregnancy is associated with potential serious medical and obstetric complications. Stroke occurs in about 7% of patients and can affect any age group from 18 months onwards. It is often precipitated by dehydration or infection. Gallstones occur in 70% of adults.

Hypersplenism occurs in infancy and is gradually replaced by a state of hyposplenism as the patient's spleen becomes more damaged, eventually leading to a state of 'autosplenectomy'.

97: A
Seventy-five per cent of patients have a preceding history of psoriasis, in 15% the onset of the rash is synchronous and in 10% the arthritis precedes the rash. Distal interphalangeal joint involvement is common and is associated with psoriatic nail changes. About 20% develop conjunctivitis and 7% iritis. Only 7% of patients with psoriasis will develop evidence of arthropathy.

Infectious diseases
98: E 99: A 100: B 101: C 102: D
Scarlet fever has a very short incubation period but a long infectivity. Infectious mononucleosis (glandular fever) has a very long incubation period. Most adults are immune to chickenpox, but it can be a serious illness for smokers and pregnant women. Measles is a notifiable disease. Health staff not immune to rubella are immunised.

103: A C E
The symptoms and signs of colorectal cancer vary depending upon the site of the tumour. Right-sided lesions typically are painful with a palpable mass in 70%, rectal bleeding only occurs in 20%. In the left colon pain occurs less frequently but 60% have a change in bowel habit. 40% have a palpable mass. In the rectum, change in bowel habit is the most common symptom, bleeding occurs in 60% and pain in only 5%.

104: B C E
Bereavement is prolonged if it lasts more than six months. Men are affected by post-bereavement mortality more than women, with 20% of widowers dying in the first year of bereavement. Blunted emotion is a common initial reaction.

105: A E
Febrile convulsions are associated with temperatures in the 6 month to 6 year age group and 90% of the fevers are caused by viral infections. The prevalence in one recent study was 2.4%. The fits typically last less than 10 minutes and autonomic behaviour and transient neurological sequelae are not usual. Diazepam can safely be repeated within 20 minutes of the first dose if the fit does not respond or recurs. There is a 50% chance that a first-degree relative has had a febrile convulsion; with idiopathic epilepsy there is only a 10% chance of a family history.

106: E
Cholestyramine, a bile acid sequestrant, is allowed in pregnancy, breast feeding and for use in children. Fenofibrate is allowed for the last group, experience with all the other agents is limited. Sleep disturbances with simvastatin are typically minimal.

The flushing with nicotinic acid may be severe and is also associated with dermatitis. Fibrates and HMG CoA reductase inhibitors adversely affect liver enzymes.

Visual loss
107: B 108: C 109: E 110: D 111: A
Migraine is of course a cause of headache with visual distortion; sudden transient loss of vision can occur. Central retinal vein occlusion can present with a fairly rapidly progressive visual loss; ophthamoscopy reveals the extensive scattered retinal haemorrhages. Senile macular degeneration gives loss of central vision, but a relatively spared peripheral field. Retinal detachment is more common in high myopes. It can result in visual loss like a curtain going across the visual field. Optic neuritis may cause intense pain; peripheral vision will be mainly intact.

Social class
112: B 113: F 114: C 115: D 116: C 117: A
Social Class 1 includes all medical practitioners; Class 2 includes teachers. One-third of the population are in group 3N (including secretaries); electricians are in group 3M. Class 4 contains semi-skilled manual workers. Class 5 includes labourers.

118: B C F
PSA testing causes many false positives and as yet early treatment has not been shown to significantly affect outcome. The PPV depends on the prevalence within the population, hence in populations with different rates of disease the PPV will vary. Studies of women being tested for STDs have shown that feelings of guilt are common, and may significantly affect quality of life. Screening involves testing an apparently healthy population, it does not involve diagnostic testing. The need for repeat screening depends on the disease; genetic disorders e.g. phenylketonuria need be tested for only once, cervical smears on a regular basis to detect new cases.

Mental Health Act
119: A 120: B 121: B 122: D 123: C 124: E
Section 2 is used for the compulsory admission for assessment of patients; it is for a maximum of 28 days. Section 3 is appropriate for compulsory treatment; its maximum duration is 6 months. Section 4 is used in an emergency. Section 7 relates to guardianship. Section 136 is for police use.

Child development
125: D 126: E 127: A 128: C 129: D 130: E
At 6 months, most children have definite person preferences. By 12 months, children can walk with one hand held. By 18 months, they can build 3–4 cube towers and can say 10–12 words. By 24 months, older children playing nearby are tolerated.

Benefits
131: C 132: C 133: B 134: A 135: C
AA and DLA are tax-free, none means-tested benefits payable to people who need help with either personal care or supervision during the day or night. AA is paid to

people claiming over 65 years; DLA is paid to people under 65 years of age, and can be paid to those who are unable to walk or require supervision when walking. SDA is payable when people are unable to work and are 80% or more disabled.

Paraesthesia and weakness
136: B 137: D 138: F 139: G 140: A 141: E

Meralgia paraesthetica is tingling on the outer aspect of the thighs; it occurs on sitting, is worse on standing, but disappears when lying down. Lateral popliteal nerve lesions give numbness of the outer border of the foot with foot drop. Lumbar disc lesions give pain and paraesthesia down the back of the thigh and lateral aspect of the lower leg. Subacute combined degeneration of the cord occurs in B12 deficiency, and gives a standing type sensory loss and an extensor plantar response. MS can give rise to an 'electric shock' feeling when the neck is flexed.

142: B E

Sulphonylureas are associated with an increase in weight, metformin is the drug of choice in the overweight diabetic if dietary measures fail. This increase in weight and the loss of effect the longer they are used is the greatest limitation to the use of sulphonylureas. In the elderly there are probably more important problems than strict control, such as good foot care, associated hypertension and control of eye symptoms. Clinically 20–30% will show retinopathy at the time of diagnosis, but fluorescein angiography shows that the majority have started with retinopathy. The current view on diet is that it should be kept simple with a restriction of fat and encouragement to eat complex carbohydrates.

143: B D

Resting ECGs are of little value, ST segment and T wave changes could reflect LVH, or in inferior leads they can appear with changes in respiration and posture. The amount of ST depression at a given workload and the time this persists after exercise is highly relevant. The normal physiological response to exercise is an increase in heart rate and a rise in systolic blood pressure. If the BP falls this indicates impaired left ventricular function due to myocardial ischaemia. Ambulatory monitoring indicates how easy it is to underestimate the problem of ischaemia. The morbidity of coronary angiography is 1:300 with a mortality rate of 1:2000.

Dyspepsia
144: D 145: C 146: E 147: G 148: B 149: A

Omeprazole can be responsible for photosensitivity, ranitidine can cause confusion. Misoprostol has been associated with post-menopausal bleeding, whilst metoclopramide can cause galactorrhoea and gynaecomastia. Magnesium trisilicate is associated with diarrhoea, but aluminium hydroxide is associated with constipation.

150: A
The management of glue ear is one of the main controversies in general practice/ENT. Early referral leads to unnecessary intervention and subsequent damage to eardrums which would have remained healthy. Conservative management, especially decreasing passive smoking, and possibly treatment with antibiotics has much to recommend it.

Normal distribution
151: B 152: A 153: C 154: C
The mode is the most frequent, whilst the median is the middle number when all are placed in order. The standard deviation is a measure of the distribution around the mean, and is actually the square root of the variance.

155: F H I
The 'Green Book' states that the only contraindications to vaccines in healthy children are personal history of severe local or general reaction to a preceding dose of that vaccine. Children who have a family history of febrile convulsions are at increased risk of these and their parents should be counselled on prevention of pyrexia prior to vaccination. Immunosuppression, including steroid therapy at doses greater than 2 mg/kg/day are contraindications. HIV positive children may receive all vaccines except BCG and yellow fever. Egg allergy is a contraindication only to influenza vaccine and yellow fever.

Screening
156: A 157: G 158: H 159: B 160: J
Sensitivity and specificity are about the test itself. Sensitivity is the portion of positives detected as positive by the test. Specificity is the proportion of negatives detected as negative by the test. The positive predictive value is the proportion of these detected as positive who really are positive.

Anaemia
161: A 162: C 163: B 164: B 165: A 166: C
Microcytic anaemia is found in thalassaemia and non-deficient anaemia. Macrocytosis is found in PA and alcoholism. Chronic renal failure and malignancy will usually result in monocytic anaemia.

Lesions in the mouth
167: A 168: C 169: G 170: E 171: B
Lichen planus gives flat purple papules with wide streaks at the wrist; in the mouth the lesions are hard based and erosive. Koplik spots are diagnostic of measles Syphilitic mouth ulcers resemble snail tracks. Herd foot and mouth disease can give painful oral lesions. Behçet's disease is associated with arthritis, iritis and oral ulceration.

172: **Q** (randomised)
173: **H** (inclusion)
174: **T** (usual care)
175: **J** (intervention)
176: **D** (confidence intervals)
177: **A** (> 0.05)
178: **K** (lack of)
179: **R** (significant)
180: **P** (non-significant)
181: **L** (larger)

Practice Paper 2

Answers and Teaching Notes

1: A D E
Ischaemic ulcers are typically painful presenting for the first time in those over 70 years of age. They are punched out, necrotic and found anywhere on the lower leg or foot. Venous ulcers tend to be painless, pigmented with marked induration and oedema. The surrounding skin may be eczematous.

2: C
In the second trimester of pregnancy cardiac output increases dramatically so that by 20 weeks it reaches a peak output of 40% more than in the non-pregnant state. Enhanced utilisation of dietary iron is one of the arguments used against routine iron supplementation in normal pregnancy. Gastric acid secretion is decreased but there is delay in gastric emptying leading to increased reflux and 'heartburn'. Introversion increases throughout the second trimester and can lead to marital problems.

3:	N	(standardised)
4:	C	(consistency)
5:	L	(recruitment)
6:	F	('Hawthorne effect')
7:	O	(standardisation)
8:	E	(endpoints)
9:	A	(applicability)
10:	M	(recruitment)
11:	H	(intervention)
12:	I	(outcome)

13: E
Intraventricular haemorrhage is more common in premature babies than small for gestational age babies. There is a definite association with convulsions in later life and remaining small. 50% will have mental handicap and learning difficulties. Diabetes tends to be familial and the babies of diabetic mothers tend to be larger than average rather than smaller.

14: A B
The pain of a tension headache is typically bilateral, occipital, biparietal or diffuse, either being described as a weight on top of the head or a band. Tender spots occur because of irritation of the cervical nerve roots. Flushing and pallor are features of vasomotor instability and would suggest migraine. A watery eye is a feature of cluster headache and unilateral pain of migraine.

15: D
Section 3 is for up to 6 months, and is renewable after that. The patient must have been seen within the last 24 hours when signing a Section 4 recommendation. Detention under a Section must be in the interest of the patient's health or safety or for the safety of others. The appropriate forms can be completed in any reasonable location.

16: B
In people over 65 years the most common causes of accidents are falls, road traffic accidents and fire.

Screening
17: H 18: C 19: D 20: G 21: J
Remember that specificity is the proportion of true negatives detected as negative by the test, and sensitivity is the proportion of true positives detected as positive. The positive predictive value is the proportion of those detected a positive who really are positive.

22: A D
Symptoms most correlating with peptic ulcer disease are epigastric pain with a definite food association, night pain, periodicity of symptoms and prompt predictable antacid relief. A positive family history is also important.

23: A
Lasers are being used with greater frequency in the treatment of many conditions. Acute glaucoma is treated either by iridectomy or trabeculoplasty. The distortion of senile macular degeneration caused by leaking areas on the retina is amenable to laser treatment. Radial keratotomy is used for the treatment of myopia and surgical treatment is now being replaced by laser.

24: B
A rare complication but if pulmonary fibrosis occurs it is worth looking at drug therapy as a cause.

25: A
The expenses of running a practice are divided into three main groups. Those directly reimbursed by the FHSA. Those partly reimbursed by the FHSA, e.g. staff salaries. Those which are included in the expenses element of the GP reimbursement and increased annually in line with the Review Body recommendations.

26: A C E
Follow-up studies of opiate users show that after 7 years 25–33% are abstinent but 10–20% have died from drug-related causes. Methadone liquid is used as an aid to withdrawal because it cannot be used intravenously, unlike the tablets which can be crushed and injected. Cocaine and hallucinogens are 'recreational' drugs associated with the more privileged groups in society. Chronic amphetamine abuse is associated with a paranoid psychosis indistinguishable from paranoid schizophrenia.

27: D
Charges can be made for ear piercing because it is a treatment not usually provided by a General Practitioner. Housing letter payments are often dealt with on a local basis. Payment is often made by the local council or housing association.

28: A
Normal pressure hydrocephalus is a reversible cause of the symptoms of dementia. The usual progression of the triad of symptoms is of gait disturbance of which apraxia (forgetting how to walk) is the most common. Following this, most cognitive impairment occurs and then urinary incontinence develops. The symptoms are temporarily reversed by lumbar puncture. Approximately 50% of patients are improved by shunts, but the operative procedure has a high incidence of complications.

29: C
The consent must also state whether the patient wishes to view the report. The patient has the right to provide a statement of his/her views to be attached to the report in the event of disagreement with the doctor over the content. The doctor should keep a copy for 6 months only and the patient has a right to view this. If the patient requests a copy the doctor can charge a reasonable fee for providing one. If there is a problem about divulging a patient's records it may well be prudent to consult your medical defence organisation.

30: A B
Only after employment for one month is a new employee eligible for a minimum period of notice based on the length of service. A written reason for dismissal must be given on request only after 2 years of service. Absence due to maternity is only payable after 26 weeks of employment but paid time off must be given for antenatal care.

31: E
Jet lag is due to an upset in the usual circadian rhythm. It is less marked if travel results in a longer day, i.e. when going towards the USA from the UK. The effects of jet lag on individual performance may last for several days.

32: B
Long term follow-up in hospital does not favour outcome and is probably an inappropriate use of resources. Psychological support is best effected by the primary health care team. Tamoxifen if given for 5 years has been shown to improve survival and decrease the risk of recurrence. Cancer in the opposite breast is six-fold greater in those already having a malignancy, it is especially greatest for those who develop their first tumour under 40 years of age. Hormone manipulation is often used first because of the decreased incidence of side-effects. However, the response rate is only 30% compared to 60% for chemotherapy.

33: A
Only residents of nursing homes, residential homes and other long stay institutions are recommended to have the vaccine. In non-pandemic years health care workers are not included. Patients vulnerable to acute infections because of a variety of chronic diseases should also be immunised.

34: B
Maternity medical fees are payable to all doctors, although those on the obstetric list receive a higher fee. The fees are payable for all pregnancies once the patient has signed the FP 24, if she subsequently decides that she wants a termination then a fee is payable. The GP does not need to attend the confinement. Post-natal visit fees are only payable for visits up to the 14th day.

35: B D F
Kawasaki's disease is seen mainly in children under five. There is an acute febrile illness with a cluster of symptoms; these may include fever, conjunctivitis, swelling of cervical lymph nodes, rash on trunk and extremities, reddening of the palms and soles and changes to the lips and oral cavity.

36: B C
Approximately 60% of patients die in hospital. Most patients with pain have two or more different pains so a careful history needs to be taken as different pains need different methods of control. About 95% of chronic pain can be controlled with drugs. If the patient is able to swallow, intramuscular drugs have no advantage over oral. If they cannot swallow, a syringe driver will last 24 hours before the syringe has to be changed.

37: A C
Seventy-five per cent of patients with Bell's palsy will recover within 3 weeks. Although controversial the use of steroids has been shown to be effective in some trials. Neither taste nor lacrimation is affected in a brainstem lesion. Loss of lacrimation would indicate a lesion between brainstem and geniculate ganglion. Repeat attacks typically are less likely to resolve than the initial attack.

38: A B E
Surveys have shown that 65% of patients develop immunity to the wart virus and they will disappear within 2 years. Salicylic acid preparations are effective if the patient is able to persist with treatment for longer than 3 months. Podophyllum is irritating and teratogenic. It works quickly. It is usually washed off after 6 hours. Liquid nitrogen gives a rapid cure with little or no scarring, it can be painful.

Paraesthesia
39: A 40: C 41: D 42: E 43: B 44: F
Carpal tunnel syndrome (affecting the median nerve) will cause problems in the index and middle fingers. Ulnar nerve lesions will affect the little finger and can cause wasting of the small muscles of the hand. Peripheral neuropathy may give a

'glove and stocking' sensory loss. Cervical spondylosis and multiple sclerosis can both give tingling with neck movements; flexion in MS typically gives an 'electric shock' feeling. Syringomyelia results in loss of pain and temperature sensation

45: E
By 6 months of age children should have settled into a regular day/night pattern of behaviour. Hypnotics should be avoided except in extreme circumstances. Strict adherence to a regular bedtime routine followed by leaving the child in bed will usually rapidly bring about an improvement in the problem. If allowed to continue there is an increased incidence of behavioural problems and an increase in family stress.

46: A C E
The dermatitis following gold injections can be avoided by careful management and good patient co-operation. Azoospermia is a complication of sulphasalazine treatment, which is also associated with thrombocytopenia. Chloroquine produces retinal damage and patients on long term treatment should have regular ophthalmoscopic examination. Methotrexate has been implicated in hepatic fibrosis.

47: A B
Down's syndrome is the most common cause of moderate or severe sub-normality. Only 20% have heart disease at birth. Death in early or middle life is still usual. Aggressive and disruptive behaviour is less common than in other disorders. Hypothyroidism is much more common than in the general population but not that common!

48: C E
Subarachnoid haemorrhage is typically due to rupture of an intracranial saccular aneurysm. Ten per cent die without warning, 45–50% of all patients will die within 3 months. Only 30% of patients will survive without disability and of those coming to surgery about 45% will achieve their previous quality of life. Surgery has an operational mortality of approximately 2% in major centres. Peak age range is 55–60 years of age and there is a familial tendency.

49: A C D
One in 10 mothers get a depressive illness which can be differentiated from 'maternity blues'. It may need no more than support and counselling. Various studies have shown various associations. Obvious things such as hormonal state, social class, parity and legitimacy are NOT associated. Housing needs have been shown to be a factor in one survey. Maternal deprivation as a child, previous psychiatric illness and ambivalence or anxiety about the pregnancy have all appeared as risk factors.

50: A C
Cancer of the cervix can occur at any age from 20 to 90, the majority of cases occur in the 40–55 age group. Risk factors also include high parity, early pregnancy and lack of participation in screening. Fifty-five per cent of patients will survive more than 5 years and 47% more than 10 years.

51: A B D
Flat feet are common especially in children, usually they are asymptomatic. Although more than 50% of 2-year-olds have the condition by the time they reach 10 years it occurs in less than 10%. Surgery is a last resort, physiotherapy and orthotic devices are the treatment of choice.

52: A C
Attico-antral perforations are the dangerous ones and they produce a foul smelling discharge. The perforation is marginal and cholesteatoma may be produced. Even a large central perforation may be repaired after the otorrhoea has resolved. A marginal perforation should be referred without delay.

53: D E
Normal BMI is 20–24.9 BMI is calculated by dividing the weight in kilograms by the square of the height in metres. Weight-watching groups can be successful but there is no evidence that GPs are more successful than other groups. The basal metabolic rate remains elevated for several hours after exercise. Exercise has probably been under-used as a method of weight reduction.

54: C D E F
Aluminium salts cause constipation, magnesium salts diarrhoea. Cisapride does not have dopamine receptor antagonist properties and therefore does not cause the dystonic reactions of metoclopramide. Intermenstrual bleeding with misoprostol occurs because it is a prostaglandin analogue, it can result in menorrhagia, intermenstrual bleeding and postmenopausal bleeding. The raised prolactin induced by metoclopramide can lead to galactorrhoea and gynaecomastia. The confusion induced by H2 receptor antagonists is reversible on stopping the drug, it can also occur in a younger age group. Omeprazole is also associated with severe skin reactions in the absence of photophobia.

55: A E
Air travel is being undertaken by an increasing proportion of the population. Dehydration occurs which thickens secretions and therefore vital capacity can be reduced still further. Epileptics are vulnerable to a mixture of hypoxia, fatigue and stress which will all increase fit frequency. Diabetics on oral agents should take their drugs as per local times. Diabetics on insulin do need to change their dosage regimes and this depends whether the flight is eastbound or westbound. Motion sickness on aircraft decreases with age and with flying experience. Gas trapped in the eye or any internal cavity will expand on increasing altitude therefore patients should not fly until all the gas is absorbed, possibly 6–12 weeks.

56: A

A sore throat is usually an early feature of hand, foot and mouth disease and it is often the main symptom of the illness. Ulcers are painful in the mouth and tender on the limbs, they do not usually itch. Spots on the buttocks are very typical. It has an incubation period of 2–10 days and is caused by an enterovirus, usually Coxsackie.

Literature

57: E 58: F 59: A 60: D 61: C 62: B

Games People Play looked at 'parent, adult and child' type transactional analysis. *Six Minutes for the Patient* described the 'flash'. *Culture, Health and Illness* describes questions patients ask like 'why me, why now?' *The Consultation: An Approach to Learning and Teaching* looked at communication tasks and consultation mapping. *The Inner Consultation* mentions connecting and housekeeping. *The Doctor, His Patient and The Illness* describes the 'apostolic' function of the doctor.

63: B C E

Nocturnal diarrhoea is rare in irritable bowel syndrome. One painless variety of the syndrome is profuse diarrhoea on waking in the morning. Pain is often related to menstrual disorder and the patient may have a lot of gynaecological investigations prior to recognition of the problem. If painful the pain is typically relieved by defaecation.

64: A B

Antenatal care is done in a blind routine fashion by some health care workers. Concepts of care have been handed down from hospital obstetric practice in an unquestioning manner. In one survey only 44% of small for gestational age babies were detected antenatally. Also for every one born with a correct diagnosis 2.5 were given the diagnosis incorrectly.

65: E

Breast lumps occurring in those under 30 years of age are usually fibroadenomata. In those over 30 years they are either a cyst or a carcinoma. Aspiration is an easy technique for a GP; if the lesion is solid or the aspirate blood stained, referral is indicated. There is a 30% chance of a cyst recurring or further cysts developing. Cyclical mastalgia rarely requires treatment, oil of evening primrose is effective, but is expensive.

66: A C

Those persons at high risk of developing diabetes include patients with a positive family history, those with gestational diabetes, obese patients and those who have given birth to babies weighing more than 4.5 kg.

67: C D

Rheumatic fever does not present with atrial fibrillation but rheumatic heart disease does. Thyrotoxicosis and alcoholic causes are relatively common, even American presidents are not exempt.

Mental Health Act
68: A 69: C 70: F 71: D 72: B 73: E
Section 2 is used for compulsory assessment of patient; section 3 is used for compulsory treatment. Section 4 is used in an emergency only requiring the involvement of one medical practitioner. Section 7 is concerned with guardianship. Section 12 contains the details about approval of doctors. Section 136 is for use by the police.

74: A E
Following admission for an act of deliberate self-harm 20% of patients will require admission to a psychiatric unit. Twenty-five per cent of all patients will repeat the episode at least once in the next year. No amount of psychiatric or social help seems to reduce the incidence. 'Help' lines are useful in individual cases but have not reduced the overall incidence. About 2% will successfully commit suicide within the next year.

75: A B D
Polycythaemia vera may well present with a vascular incident secondary to haemodynamic changes. Increased turnover of cells leads to hyperuricaemia and gout may be a presentation. Itching is a common presentation. Approximately 30% terminate as acute leukaemia and the incidence of this is increased by radiotherapy or chlorambucil therapy.

76: A B
Sudden loss of vision in a migrainous episode is associated with complete recovery. Central retinal vein occlusion can lead to an extensive haemorrhage visible at the fundus. The visual loss typically develops over a period of a few hours. Senile macular degeneration produces a gradually progressive loss of central vision with preservation of peripheral vision. Optic neuritis presents with gradual loss in the 20–45 age group with intact peripheral vision. Toxic optic neuropathy may be due to heavy cigarette smoking or alcohol intake, again peripheral vision remains intact.

77: A
The inclusion of child surveillance as a part of general practice was one of the more positive aspects of the 1990 contract. A GP must either undergo further training or have had special experience in order to be included on the list of approved doctors. The child must register separately for inclusion on the child surveillance list. Child clinics are not eligible for a payment as a health promotion clinic and immunisations are subject to target payment regulations. Any suitably trained doctor within the practice can perform the check and some of the tests still remain more the responsibility of the health visitors.

78: A B E
SLE is the most common autoimmune disease in childbearing women. The rate of miscarriage is 70%, some people who miscarry repeatedly develop SLE in later life. High follicular levels of LH correlate with failure to conceive and recurrent miscarriage. An abnormal parental karyotype is present in 5% of those couples who have recurrent miscarriages.

79: A B D
Neonates and older children are little affected by RSV. Stridor is indicative of croup not bronchiolitis. In the UK it has a strict seasonal pattern occurring between December and May. Examination of the throat is a problem in acute epiglottitis which is caused by *Haemophilus influenzae* infection.

Studies
80: A 81: B 82: A 83: A 84: B 85: B 86: A
Cohort studies are population based, requiring long-term follow-up, and are time-consuming. They allow the evidence of a disease to be found. Case-control studies are relatively easy and inexpensive, but have more potential for bias.

87: A C E
Topical steroid absorption is enhanced by urea and by occlusion. This includes nappies and plastic pants. It takes about 4 g of steroid for a single application to the trunk, 1 g to the arm, 2 g to the leg, 1 g to the hand and foot. Local side-effects of prolonged steroid use are thinning of the skin, acne, mild depigmentation and increased hair growth. Ointments are indicated for dry conditions and creams for moist conditions.

88: B D E
The average age of menarche in the UK is 13 years of age. The periods stop at an average age of 50 years. There are a lot of 'old wives' tales' about periods, it is often quoted but untrue that an early menarche begets a late menopause. Estimation of LH and FSH is the most reliable method of determining that symptoms are due to the menopause.

89: A C E
Epiphora often occurs because the irritant effect of having dry eyes causes an overflow of tears. It is associated with sarcoid and also autoimmune diseases such as rheumatoid arthritis. Schirmer's test is diagnostic. Sjögren's syndrome is an autoimmune disease in which dry eyes are but one feature. People with entropion often have epiphora.

90: A B C
The first three questions are the cardinal rules for the treatment of undescended testes. The only other point is that some people think that 2 years is the latest age by which a testes should be placed in the scrotum because this increases fertility even more. A hernial sac is present at most operations, but usually it is asymptomatic.

91: C D
The average practitioner will have 2–3 new patients with gout per year, 20% of patients will have a family history. It is six times more common in males than females. Chronic tophaceous gout is now rare, but that and renal gout with calculi are indications for allopurinol treatment. 25–40% of those with gout will have or will develop hypertension. Triglyceride levels are higher in gout sufferers.

92: C D

About 90% of patients will stop bleeding spontaneously. However, the mortality rate is still about 10% and is not reduced by urgent endoscopy. Drugs such as ranitidine do not stop bleeding but some studies show that they prevent rebleeding. Gastric ulcers are more likely to rebleed than duodenal, also if blood vessels are visible at endoscopy a rebleed is more likely.

93: A B C

Terfenadine is an OTC antihistamine and there have been reports of serious cardiac arrhythmias if given with erythromycin or systemic antifungal agents. Ciprofloxacin causes a potentiation of theophylline levels. Theophylline has a narrow therapeutic window and therefore toxic effects can occur. Cimetidine potentiates the effect of oral anticoagulants including warfarin. There is no significant interaction between allopurinol and captopril, it is included in the manufacturer's list of interactions because of the risk of renal damage in patients with gout.

94: C

In differentiating between depression and dementia, the symptoms develop more rapidly in the former. Complaints of memory loss would suggest that insight is retained, depressive symptoms are worse in the morning. Rather than 'don't know' demented patients tend to reply with near miss or inappropriate replies.

95: B C E

Alcohol abuse can be detected by the use of simple questionnaires of which CAGE and MAST are good examples. Fishermen, along with publicans and barmaids, are at high risk of alcoholism. Single males over 40 years are also at high risk. The incidence of carcinoma of the oesophagus is increased three-fold in patients with alcohol problems.

96: A C E

The DVLA Medical Standards of Fitness to Drive state that diabetics diagnosed since 1/4/91 cannot hold a category 2 licence. Those who were diagnosed prior to this date are dealt with on an individual basis. Following pacemaker insertion, provided no other disqualifying conditions are present, driving may resume after 1 week for category 1 and 6 weeks for category 2 licence holders. Following a first seizure, category 1 licence holders must be fit free for 1 year, for a category 2 licence a 10 year period free of seizures without medication is required. After an MI category 1 holders may drive after 4 weeks and category 2 after 6 weeks as long as they pass an exercise test.

Lipid tests
97: C 98: A 99: D 100: B

The WOSCOPS Trial studied people without coronary heart disease; the 4S trial was of patients with known CHD. ASPIRE and CARE both looked at survivors of myocardial infarction. ASPIRE revealed that many had not had lipids measured; CARE looked at those with mildly elevated cholesterol levels.

101: B E
Temazepam is a controlled drug but is exempt from hand written prescribing requirements. Benzodiazepine withdrawal may develop at any time up to 3 weeks after stopping treatment and symptoms may persist for weeks or months. Zopiclone is not a benzodiazepine but acts on the same receptors. It is not licensed for long term use and may cause dependence.

102: B D F
St John's wort has been shown in studies to be as effective as imipramine with fewer side effects. ECT is an effective treatment for severe depression but is unsuitable for mild depression as a first line treatment. Beta blockers are used for the treatment of anxiety, although there is minimal evidence for their efficacy. Melleril® (thioridazine) is an antipsychotic which may cause life threatening cardiac side effects. There is no good evidence of a difference in efficacy between SSRIs and tricyclic antidepressants, but the side effect profiles are different. Lithium is used for bipolar disorder and recurrent depression, not for first episodes. Carbamazepine is used in bipolar disease.

103: B C F
Phenylketonuria is inherited as an autosomal recessive trait, affecting 1:10,000 infants. Asthma, atherosclerosis and congenital heart disease have multifactorial origin. Ankylosing spondylitis is associated with HLA B27, but the two are not synonymous. Nephrogenic diabetes insipidus is inherited as an X linked dominant trait. Pellagra is caused by dietary niacin deficiency.

104: A
It is now generally accepted that episiotomy has been overused. It does not protect against subsequent prolapse or rectocele. The babies have no decreased incidence of immediate problems after birth. A significant proportion of those who have an episiotomy performed have a double wound due to an associated tear. GPs and community midwives have known for a long time that it is rarely necessary and that the relaxed atmosphere of a well-controlled home delivery reduces the need.

105: B C E
RCTs aim to reduce bias by comparing identical groups, but bias may enter by imperfect randomisation, failure to blind assessors or inclusion bias, i.e. not offering participation to some groups of patients. A good example of potential recall bias in case-control studies is the onset of autism and timing of MMR vaccination. Where confidence intervals are wide or cross the line of no effect this suggests only that this study has not confirmed an effect. Larger studies may give narrower confidence intervals. The validity of meta-analysis depends on strict, validated inclusion criteria.

Epilepsy
106: A 107: E 108: B 109: B 110: D

Primidone is converted to phenobarbitone in the body. Sodium valproate is highly protein-bound, and can lead to a false positive ketonuria test. Carbamazepine and sodium valproate are both sometimes used in recurrent depression, but carbamazepine can give rise to visual disturbances especially double vision.

Coronary Heart Disease
111: F 112: H 113: G 114: B 115: D 116: C 117: A

The Framlingham study looked at a group in the USA and examined all coronary events. The North Karalia Project was set up because of the high mortality rate from coronary events in Finland. The Seven Countries Study looked at differences in consumption of saturated fats in different populations. The British regional heart study linked risk factors with coronary events. The Shaper Score and the Dundee Risk Score are both indicators of the risk of a future heart attack. The Oxcheck Study offered health checks to individuals with selective measurement of cholesterol levels.

Statistics
118: B 119: C 120: D 121: B 122: A

Correlation looks for a link between one variable and another. The predictive value of a test depends on the sensitivity, specificity and prevalence. Incidence is the occurrence of new cases. Studies need to attempt to eliminate any confounding factors.

Prescribing
123: D 124: A 125: C 126: E 127: F

The PACT Scheme produces quarterly reports about a GP's prescribing; The National Medicines Resource Centre produces monthly reports. The Prescribing Unit at Leeds University looks at the range of prescribing. The Prescribing Allocation Group advises on allocation of drug budgets, while the Prescribing Advisor monitors indicative prescribing.

Professions
128: C 129: A 130: D 131: B

Health visitors and community nurses are employed by the health authority. Health visitors have some statutory roles. Practice nurses and practice managers are employed by GPs; the practice manager will be involved with hiring and training of staff.

Misuse of drugs
132: A 133: C 134: D 135: C 136: A

Schedule 1 drugs include diamorphine and cannabis. Schedule 3 contains diethylpropion, and Schedule 4 has in it both diazepam and amylobarbitone.

Benefits
137: C 138: A 139: D 140: E 141: B
Family credit and child benefit are both payable to people with children. Family credit is means tested and payable if on low income; child benefit is tax-free and payable to all with children. Income support is also means tested and payable if on low income. Invalid care allowance is payable if a person does not work because they look after a disabled person. Social fund payments are one off payments.

Developmental milestones
142: C 143: D 144: E 145: A 146: B 147: C 148: D
At 6 months, a child will transfer a cube from one hand to another. By 9 months, most children will crawl. At 12 months, a child will walk with one hand held and say a word with meaning. By 18 months, the child will jump and manage a spoon well. At 24 months, the child can build a tower of 6–7 bricks.

Immunisations
149: E 150: A 151: B 152: C 153: D
Yellow fever immunisation is given 10 yearly (but not given to young children). Tetanus is administered 5–10 yearly. Polio is a live vaccine, and paralysis can result (rarely) following immunisation. It may be worthwhile testing for antibodies in some travellers before giving hepatitis A immunisation. Typhoid is administered 3 yearly.

154: D
Fundholders have their prescribing costs included in their general fund. Savings on the indicative budgets cannot be carried forward. Formularies are not compulsory, they are to be 'encouraged'. If drug spending is found to be excessive without clinical justification the GP can be called before a hearing in front of three doctors and a withholding of remuneration can result from this. If the FHSA is aware of patients whose drug therapy is expensive this can be allowed for in the calculation of the budget.

Swellings in the neck area
155: C 156: E 157: D 158: B 159: A 160: D
Mumps typically causes swollen parotid glands. Brachial cysts are remnants of the 2nd pharyngeal pouch. Devoid cysts often contain hair, whereas a sebaceous cyst contains keratin. Thyroglossal cysts are midline, move on swallowing and with protrusion of the tongue.

161: A
Squamous cell carcinoma appears on the helix, rodent ulcers on the skin behind and below the ear. Tophi appear on the antihelix. Psoriasis affects the external auditory meatus and the skin behind and below the ear. Atopic eczema affects the whole ear. Kerato-acanthoma appear as rapidly growing lesions on the helix. Chilblains of the ear are common, painful and itchy.

162: C (blinded)
163: P (reporting)
164: J (observer)
165: M (placebo controlled)
166: E (control)
167: G (intervention)
168: F (generalisability)
169: Q (secondary)
170: D (confounding)
171: S (validated)

172: D
The main indication of lithium treatment is to prevent the relapses in bipolar affective disorders. It is only available as an oral preparation and is of no value in acute episodes of illness. It does not cause a chronic nephropathy and changes in urea and electrolytes are reversible on stopping the drug. Thyroid enlargement may occur and thyroid function tests should be monitored regularly.

Ear problems
173: F 174: E 175: D 176: C 177: B 178: A
Kerato-acanthoma and squamous cell carcinoma grow on the helix. Tophi appear on the anti-helix. Psoriasis affects behind and below the ears; and affects the entire ear. Chilblains are painful and itchy.

179: C
Phenytoin and carbamazepine both potentiate the effect of alcohol, also an epileptic taking these drugs who drinks alcohol will be at a greater risk of having a fit. Although indomethacin does potentiate alcohol, salicylates do not have this effect. Atenolol does not cross the blood–brain barrier and therefore does not interact, but propranolol has been shown to cause drowsiness, presumably because of its lipid solubility. In susceptible individuals even the newer non-sedating antihistamines can cause some sedation with alcohol. Nearly all antidepressants potentiate the effects of alcohol and affect psychomotor performance.

Practice Paper 3

Answers and Teaching Notes

1: A E
Spacer devices decrease the incidence of oral candidiasis by preventing the deposition in the mouth. Salmeterol is a long-acting beta-antagonist, its action is slow in onset and therefore it should be given regularly rather than p.r.n. The Committee on Safety of Medicines has reported that salbuterol and terbutaline have not been shown to lead to a worsening of mild asthma. In adults an inhaled dosage of steroid of 1500 micrograms daily is associated with adrenal suppression. Sodium cromoglycate is of no value in an acute attack and is only indicated for prophylaxis.

2: C
Squints in children, unlike in adults, are usually caused by reduced acuity in one eye, hence the cortex depresses the image from the abnormal eye and amblyopia results. Covering the good eye should cause the weaker eye to take up fixation. Covering the bad eye has no effect on the other eye. Full assessment of the eye is vital in all cases of squint, to ensure retinal causes are not missed. Patching of the good eye encourages sight to develop in the weaker eye. Surgical treatment after the age of 8 is largely cosmetic as amblyopia after this age cannot be reversed. Excessive patching may cause the good eye to become amblyopic.

3: A B C
Risk factors for osteoporosis can be divided into high, medium and low. Alcoholism is a medium risk factor and cigarette smoking, although a risk factor, carries a lower risk. The others quoted are high risk factors.

4:	**K**	heterogeneous
5:	**R**	randomised
6:	**D**	confounding
7:	**N**	modalities
8:	**O**	outcome
9:	**H**	efficacy
10:	**P**	placebo
11:	**S**	randomised
12:	**B**	blinding
13:	**I**	extrapolated

14: A C
At present less than 50% of mothers breast feed their babies successfully. Whether this government target can be met is a matter of considerable doubt. Mastitis is typically caused by Staphylococcus. Breast feeding does take considerably longer than bottle feeding and this point should be emphasised to reassure mothers. Obesity is rare in breast fed infants but more common in bottle fed infants.

Introduction of cows' milk should not take place until one year of age. The solute load is too great for children until this age. Full cream milk and not semi-skimmed should be used.

Bodies allied to general practice
15: A 16: D 17: C 18: E 19: B

The General Medical Council, GMC, is the national body concerned with standards of care and conduct of doctors; the General Practice Committee, GPC, is a national committee of the BMA representing GPs. The Prescription Prescribing Authority, PPA, is a special health authority concerned with prescriptions and uses a large computer system. The Health Education Council, HEC, has regional status and promotes training and health education. Medical Audit Advisory Groups, MAAGs, are local bodies.

20: E

There are relatively few absolute contraindications to HRT. The main one quoted is oestrogen-dependent tumours, but recent evidence has cast some doubt on this. Diabetes is only a relative contraindication. All routes of treatment are helpful with the symptoms of atrophic vaginitis. Lipid levels are favourably affected by unopposed oestrogen, it is the progestogenic component which appears to cause problems with elevation of lipid levels. If given for 10 years it has been estimated that the incidence of osteoporotic fractures would be halved.

21: E

Blood pressure reduction has not been shown to be helpful and may harm. Thrombolysis reduces the risk of dependency but increases the risk of death. Neither GABA agonists, steroids or anticoagulation have been shown to be helpful.

22: A E

This is a common condition usually occurring in young children under 3 years of age. The mechanism of injury is typically that of a traction injury to the child's arm when it is held in an extended position, such as being pulled onto the feet by the hands or being 'bounced' with the arms above the head. It is more common on the left side. The annular ligament probably slips or has a small tear which allows subluxation of the radial head. X-ray shows no abnormality. Reduction is simply done by forced supination, anaesthesia not being necessary.

23: E

Streptococcus pneumoniae is the commonest isolated pathogen in 36% of cases; viruses are isolated in 11%. Legionella is best detected by antigen detection in urine. Radiological changes may take up to 6 weeks to resolve after cure. CXR is only indicated if there is a suspicion of malignancy, or poor response to antibiotics. Amoxycillin is the first-line treatment of choice in uncomplicated community acquired pneumonia. If the patient is allergic to penicillin, erythromycin or clarithromycin are used.

24: A B E
About 40% of all accidents in children under 14 years are due to road traffic accidents. In the over 65-year-old age group, falls account for about 50% of accidents. Seat belt legislation resulted in a substantial reduction in death or serious accidents in drivers. Drowning is another common cause of accidents in under 14-year-olds, with alcohol being a significant factor in accidents in young people and the elderly.

25: D
Dopamine inhibits prolactin, therefore dopamine agonists such as bromocriptine inhibit prolactin release and are used to treat prolactinomas. Conversely, dopamine blockers, such as metoclopramide, will stimulate prolactin release.

26: A B C
Ototoxicity induced by quinine is usually reversible on stopping the drug but if it is given in the first trimester of pregnancy it may cause hearing loss in the baby. The hearing loss induced by frusemide occurs if the drug is given rapidly intravenously, it is typically transient. However, the loss may be permanent if aminoglycosides are given concurrently. Erythromycin is only ototoxic if given in high doses.

27: A B E
Post-menopausal bleeding is defined as any vaginal bleeding occurring 6 months after the last period. It should always be investigated. Exogenous oestrogens from whatever source can cause bleeding. Polyps can still occur in this age group and urethral caruncles do bleed. If the discharge is profuse and offensive, cervical cancer is a distinct possibility, but senile vaginitis also leads to vaginal infection.

28: C E
Coronary artery bypass is highly successful with an operative mortality of less than 3% in the UK. Patients with improved lifespan after operation are those with triple vessel disease, unstable angina and blockage of the left main coronary artery. The results of grafting are better if an artery rather than a vein is used. Operative mortality is greater in females and in those with unstable angina. The recurrence of angina occurs at a steady rate of about 3–4% per annum.

29: A
Thirty per cent of women and 33% of men smoke. However, in the 11–15 age group 7% of boys and 9% of girls smoke and this is a decreasing incidence in both groups. Male smokers consume an average of 20 cigarettes daily and females 15 daily. Gastrointestinal and psychiatric problems plus accidents account for the increased consultation rate of those with alcohol problems. Heavy drinkers have an increased incidence of cancer of the oral cavity, larynx and oesophagus. There was an increased rate of breast cancer in one survey.

30: A D
Post-viral fatigue syndrome is a complex subject. The overwhelming feature is fatigue and fatiguability that is both physical and mental. Approximately 75% of the patients have a significant psychiatric problem and over 50% have depression of such severity that a trial of antidepressants is worthwhile. Prolonged rest is not advised, patients need to regain control of their illness and need to be encouraged to increase activity.

31: A D E
The onset of schizophrenia is usually between 15 and 45 years with males having an earlier onset by about 5 years. Paranoid delusions are not themselves diagnostic. Negative symptoms of schizophrenia include apathy.

32: B D E
SIDS shows no association with the mode or type of delivery. The risk increases with the parity especially if the pregnancies are closer together. If the mother is addicted to narcotic agents there is a 30-fold increase in risk. Twins are at risk and if one twin suffers a sudden infant death or a 'near miss' the other twin should be monitored very closely. Children are best placed on their side or supine at night.

33: C
Amitryptyline is a treatment for atypical facial pain, sumatriptan a treatment for migraine. Carbamazepine is the first choice treatment at present. Gabapentin has shown promise in neuropathic pain and may become the first-line treatment. Radiofrequency ablation should be reserved for those patients who do not respond to medical therapy.

Stroke management
34: B 35: A 36: C 37: D 38: A 39: B
Warfarin is used in high-risk patients, and this might include patients with previous transient ischaemic attack. Aspirin can be used when risk is relatively low, and this might be in a patient with AF but no family or personal history of stroke. An MRI scan would differentiate infarction from haemorrhage. Carotid endarterectomy might be indicated for carotid stenotic lesions.

40: B D
Hot baths cause vasodilatation which enhances penetration of the drug and increases the risk of CNS toxicity. This toxicity is why the drug is contraindicated in pregnant women. A single application is usually sufficient to eradicate the mite and it decreases the chances of toxicity. Scabies typically does not affect the face, except in one variety that occurs in mentally handicapped patients and is known as Norwegian scabies. Itching may take 4 weeks to resolve after successful eradication of all the mites.

41: E

Some heavy drinkers are not physically dependent but conversely some moderate drinkers develop severe symptoms of withdrawal. Seizures typically occur within 10–60 hours of the last drink. The mortality of delirium tremens is about 10%. Many psychiatric symptoms including confusion, disorientation, paranoia, auditory or visual hallucinations may occur 72 hours or more after the last drink. The typical early withdrawal symptoms are tremor, sweating, anorexia, nausea, insomnia and anxiety.

42: A C

Agoraphobia is a disease which typically affects women. Although they are often highly dependent on their husbands there is no increase in the rate of divorce or separation. Thoughts tend to focus on a fear of losing control, e.g. fainting. Depersonalisation (feeling that one's body is unreal or remote) is a very typical symptom but this can also occur in depression. Programmed behaviour therapy is the psychological treatment that produces the best results.

43: A C E

The most common drugs to cause fixed drug eruptions are NSAIDs, sulphonamides, tetracyclines and quinine. They may take up to 2 hours to develop, a brown discoloration of the skin may last for several months. The acute reaction of an oval inflammatory patch may or may not contain blisters.

44: C D E

Following on from the provisions of the Data Protection Act this provides access to handwritten notes. It applies to all 'employed by the health service body'. Only notes made after November 1991 are included. As in the Data Protection Act the GP has 21 days to comply with request for access and can make a charge to the patient and can also charge for any copies provided.

45: D

After a heart attack, patients are now told to avoid driving for one month. If a pacemaker is fitted, driving is allowed from one month after insertion, provided the pacemaker is checked regularly. Driving is to be avoided for one week following coronary angioplasty. An epileptic can drive when he has been fit-free for one year. Patients with migraine should not drive from the onset of the warning period. Patients should not drive for 24–48 hours after a minor operation requiring general anaesthetic.

46: A C E

Aortic stenosis is now the most common valvular lesion in all adults, usually due to degenerative calcific disease. A soft murmur does not exclude severe aortic stenosis especially if the patient has low output cardiac failure. In contrast mitral stenosis is invariably due to rheumatic heart disease. Mitral regurgitation is most commonly due to the same factors as aortic stenosis. A prolapsing mitral valve is the next most common cause. Seventy per cent of patients over 70 will have a murmur.

47: A C
Drugs that undergo significant first-pass metabolism by the liver must be given with caution to those patients with liver disease, for instance coma may be precipitated in the cirrhotic by the use of analgesics containing opiates. Aciclovir along with many antibiotics is excreted unchanged by the kidney.

48: C
There is good evidence to support the use of ACE inhibitors (HOPE study), spironolactone (RALES study), beta blockers (MERIT-HF study), and digoxin. Calcium channel blockers have no effect on heart failure. Studies of exercise training improves functional capacity, quality of life and reduces cardiac events.

49: B C
The peak incidence of acute suppurative otitis media is at 4–8 years of age. The majority of infections are mild and only 10% of these are bacterial. About 90% of severe cases are bacterial. Only 1% develop chronic suppurative otitis media and of these only a few will get mastoiditis.

50: C D E
Pulmonary embolism is the most common cause of death in the UK associated with pregnancy. Two-thirds occur post-natally. Increasing age and increasing parity are risk factors. Complicated delivery also increases the risk. Women who have had thromboembolism in the past have a 1:10 to 1:20 risk of a further episode and anticoagulation throughout the pregnancy with heparin is usually advised.

51: A B C
Appendicitis is still missed, especially in the young and the old. The incidence in a population is inversely proportional to the amount of dietary fibre consumed by that population. Therefore the incidence in the UK is decreasing. Retrocaecal appendices are associated with atypical symptoms and a high retrocaecal appendicitis may mimic the symptoms of renal tract infection.

52: C D E
Acute lymphoblastic leukaemia (ALL) is the commonest 85% with 14% acute myeloblastic. The average age of onset of the former is 3–5 years and of the latter neonates. The best prognosis is for ALL in boys aged 1–8 years. The overall survival of the disease after completion of 5 years' treatment is 65%. Maintenance cytotoxics are usually continued for 3 years once remission has been achieved.

53: A B C
Familial adenomatous polyposis coli is uncommon. It is inherited as an autosomal dominant gene but accounts for only about 1% of all colonic cancer. Hereditary non-polyposis coli is relatively more common. Familial adenomatous polyposis coli is asymptomatic in teenage years but later causes a change in bowel habit with rectal bleeding and passage of mucus. Faecal occult blood testing is a sensitive test for blood but not sensitive or specific for colonic cancer.

54: B

Impotence due to an organic cause is usually of insidious onset. It is more common in patients with vascular diseases and various neurological abnormalities, e.g. diabetic neuropathy, multiple sclerosis. Papaverine is given by intracavernosal injection and an erection should last for 3 hours maximum. It is usually limited to twice-weekly use. Vacuum condoms are not available on NHS prescriptions.

Breast cancer screening
55: D 56: A 57: B 58: E 59: C

Breast cancer screening has often been controversial. The Health Insurance Plan was an early trial which showed reduction in mortality; The Malmo Trial showed a significant difference in mortality, the Nijmegen Project showed a large reduction. In the UK, the Forrest report led to the introduction of the Breast Screening Program, whilst the UK Trial of Early Detection of Breast Cancer Group discussed breast self-examination.

Diabetes
60: D 61: B 62: A

The Oslo Study showed that diabetic retinopathy showed deterioration with subcutaneous insulin infusion. The Pine Study was a group of whom 50% were diabetic. The Stone Study showed that most worsening in diabetic retinopathy was seen in both with worst and best control.

63: B C E

This condition of extreme self-neglect usually affects people who live alone. The incidence is 0.5 per 1000 population so most GPs will have one patient on their list. Fifty per cent have a normal mental state but the rest have significant psychopathology. Physical illness is very common and often severe leading to a mortality of 50%. Admission to hospital worsens the condition with apathy developing. Patients tend to be of above average intelligence.

64: C

By February 1991, 89% of all 2-year-old children had received MMR vaccine. The vaccine is not contraindicated in those who are HIV positive but it is in those who are immunocompromised, for example those receiving chemotherapy for leukaemia. The rates of laboratory confirmed rubella in pregnancy have fallen from 164 in 1987 to 20 in 1990. Although meningoencephalitis has been reported following exposure to the vaccine it is much less than the rate for mumps prior to introduction of the vaccine.

65: A D

If retinoblastoma is a cause of squint, instead of a red reflex there is the typical white reflex. The majority of squints in children are non-paralytic. If treatment is left until 8 years the eye will be amblyopic and surgery will only be cosmetic. If patching of the good eye is excessive, cases have been reported of it becoming amblyopic. To maximise sight, referral should be made before 6 months of age.

66: A

Anxiety may be triggered by a multitude of factors including physical illness, caffeine ingestion, alcohol withdrawal or the use of drugs such as sympathomimetics or antihistamines. Treatment is directed to both the somatic and psychological aspects. MAOIs are very effective in anxiety especially when there is a phobic element.

Scrotal swellings
67: C 68: A 69: B 70: D

With an inguinal hernia the upper end of the swelling cannot be found. A hydrocele will transilluminate well. An epididymal cyst may transilluminate but the lump will be above the testis; similarly in TB of the epididymis the lump will be above the testis, but here it will be a hard thickening.

71: B C D

Cervical erosion is twice as common in pill users than in a matched population who have not taken the pill. Benign breast diseases are suppressed in long term users of combined oral contraceptives. Endometrial cancer and ovarian cancer rates appear to be reduced by about 50% in those who have had two years or more of continual ovulation suppression with oral contraceptives. Cervical cancer rates are not reduced, some data would suggest an increased incidence but because cervical cancer is so related to sexual activity, it is difficult to work out a relationship.

72: A B

Addison's disease may present insidiously with episodic vomiting and diarrhoea accompanied by weight loss. Abdominal pain is often severe and colicky. Eventually symptoms may lead to an addisonian crisis with a shocked, hypotensive patient. Chronic insufficiency is marked by postural hypotension. The typical blood picture is hyponatraemia, hyperkalaemia and a raised blood urea.

73: A B

Restless legs syndrome has been described for over 100 years. It has been associated with many factors most of them disproved, but it may be the presenting complaint in uraemia. Typically, it is worse in the evening and at night causing insomnia. Benzodiazepines are said to help. There is no association with coffee or tea ingestion.

74: A B E F

At 6 weeks most children are smiling and it is a worrying sign if they are not. At 9 months most children stand with support, and walk with support at 12 months. Also at 12 months they can use about 2–3 words with meaning. By age 3, children are usually dry by day and can go both up and down stairs.

75: A F

Audit is now a contractual obligation on behalf of General Practitioners. There are lots of ways and viewpoints as to how it should be practised. Audit is a process of education through experience, not looking for mistakes. It must be free from blame or guilt if it is to be successful. It should be dynamic with the aim of helping people to do their jobs better. It can illuminate problem areas but it is not solely concerned with problem solving. The boundaries between audit and research are often blurred.

76: B C D

Pyelonephritis is the most common medical emergency in pregnancy occurring in 1% of pregnancies. It typically presents in the second and third trimesters and in about one quarter of cases reoccurs throughout the rest of the pregnancy. There is an increased association with pre-term labour, fetal growth retardation and perinatal death. 4–Quinolone antibiotics are contraindicated in pregnancy because experimental work has shown an association with arthropathy in the fetus.

77: B C E

Severe puerperal psychosis presents in the early puerperium typically by the 10th day following delivery. It may present as psychotic depression or hypomania. Those with hypomania often become depressed at the end of a spell of being 'high'. Some show a fluctuating pattern. ECT has been shown to be of benefit and often produces a rapid remission. With treatment it tends to run a course of about 2–3 months of illness, the risk of infanticide during this time is increased.

78: A B D

Campylobacter often starts as a febrile illness after an incubation period of 3–5 days. If bleeding is present in a Shigella infection this is an indication that antibiotic treatment may be necessary. In Giardia, pain is not a feature but watery diarrhoea is. Salmonella without blood stream invasion is often a relatively mild diarrhoeal episode only lasting a few days.

79: A C E

Hypertrophic obstructive cardiomyopathy is important because it is the most common cause of sudden death in apparently healthy young adults especially athletes. It was found in half of athletes who died during participation in a sporting activity. It is an inherited condition and it occurs at any age from neonate to old age. All family members should be investigated preferably by echocardiography. The commonest presentation is with shortness of breath often accompanied by syncope and angina. The electrocardiograph typically shows changes of left ventricular hypertrophy.

80: D

Dementia is not preventable by social support but depression is reduced. A well-balanced diet helps general health and may reduce cardiovascular disease but does not reduce dementia. Eating beef has not as yet been shown to cause a transmittable form of dementia. Treatment of hypertension over the years decreases atherosclerosis and therefore the incidence of multi-infarct dementia. Over 75 screening by GPs has not yet been shown to decrease dementia or related problems.

81: A B E F
Poor predictive factors include early and insidious onset, low socioeconomic status, a schizoid personality trait, history of perinatal trauma, a family history of schizophrenia, and being in a developed country.

82: B C E
Herpes simplex infection usually heals within 6–10 days with topical aciclovir. Recurrence rate is less than 5% if treatment is commenced promptly. Visual acuity is not affected with peripheral lesions, but is more likely if the central cornea is affected. Referral is indicated because of the potential threat to vision.

83: B D E
In women Chlamydia is usually asymptomatic and causes a cervicitis rather than a vaginitis. A negative MSU with dysuria in a sexually active woman should lead to a search for the organism. If present in pregnancy there is a 50% transmission rate to the neonate with the risk of conjunctivitis and pneumonitis. Treatment should begin before delivery. In men the common presentation is with non-specific urethritis or epididymitis, it is not associated with prostatitis.

84: A C D
There are about one million new cases of back pain per year and the average General Practitioner sees about 50 acute backs per year. Many people do not consult, although 10–15 million working days are lost per year because of back pain. Eighty per cent recover in 3–4 weeks, but in 50% of patients there is a recurrence within the next 5 years. About one-third of patients are referred for specialist opinion but only 1:200 of the original sufferers and 1:60 of those referred undergo surgery. Early mobilisation and continued activity has been shown to be most effective.

85: A B C
Irritable bowel syndrome has been treated by increasing dietary fibre, although some patients find that excess bran makes the symptoms worse. In one study, 70% of patients improved on a bland diet free of wheat and milk. Increased fermentation in the gut is directly implicated as a trigger for the condition. Metronidazole substantially alters the aerobic/anaerobic balance within the bowel and can increase the fermentation rate. Nystatin has been shown to decrease fermentation and improve symptoms. Stress is a well-known trigger factor and hypnosis and relaxation techniques decrease the symptoms and the relapse rate of IBS.

86: A D E
Cramps, especially occurring during the night, are common. However, there are a large number of causes which should be excluded. Drug therapy, especially diuretics and sympathomimetics, even if the latter are inhaled, are frequent causes. Peripheral vascular disease and venous obstruction do not cause cramps, but cramps may coexist. About 80% of those with cirrhosis have nocturnal cramps. Lumbar spine dysfunction especially nerve involvement at the L5/S1 level is a potent cause of nocturnal cramps.

Childhood milestones
87: D 88: E 89: A 90: B 91: F 92: E
At 12 months, most children will say 2 or 3 words with meaning. By 18 months, they can build a 3–4 cube tower. At 3 years they will know age and sex; by 4 years they will know full name and be able to copy a circle. By 5 years of age, they can hop on one foot.

93: C D E
Trials comparing active and physiological management of the third stage of labour have shown that it is reduced from an average of 15 minutes to 5 minutes and that the incidence of primary post-partum haemorrhage is decreased from 18% to 6%. However, one study has shown that there is an increased rate of retained placenta and all studies have shown an increase in maternal vomiting and hypertension.

94: A C D
Hypercalcaemia can result from malignancy, thyrotoxicosis, thiazide diuretics, immobilisation, vitamin D excess and renal failure.

95: A B C
Closure of the ductus arteriosus usually takes place within 48 hours of birth and is brought about by muscular contraction initially and then fibrosis. Delay is associated with maternal rubella and prematurity. Indomethacin therapy does close the duct but in some cases it reopens and surgery is necessary. If untreated, 20% of patients will have died by 30 years of age and 60% by 60 years of age. Bacterial endocarditis is especially common in patients with this condition.

96 : C D F
Ninety per cent of travellers who contract malaria do not become ill until after they return home. An experimental malaria vaccine is being studied in Colombia but at present has not been shown to be effective. Malaria may present in different ways but is usually characterised by fever (which may be swinging), tachycardia, rigors and sweating. Doxycycline may cause photosensitivity which may lead to severe sunburn. Partial immunity may develop in children brought up in endemic areas, but this is lost if they leave the area. 12% of people with malaria follow a severe course, including the development of renal failure or cerebral malaria. The fatality rate is 2–6% in adult travellers.

Chest pain
97: D 98: E 99: A 100: F 101: G 102: B 103: H
Pulmonary embolism may well be associated with severe chest pain, dyspnoea and haemoptysis. Myocardial infarction may cause chest pain, sweating and dyspnoea, with arm pain often being present. Pneumothorax may cause a tight chest pain with dyspnoea. The pain in oesophageal reflux is often 'burning' occurring after bending and heavy meals. Chest pain related to spinal cord problems is likely to be positional in nature. The pain of aortic aneurysm is often a

'tearing' radiating to the back. Cardiac neurosis may give ill defined pain around the chest area and under the nipple.

104: E
Streptokinase is given via an infusion and is therefore unsuitable for community use. Anistreplase is given by i.v. bolus. Aspirin given as a concomitant has been shown to decrease mortality further. Age alone is no reason for limitation of use of these drugs. Streptokinase cannot be repeated within the next 12 months. Anything that may bleed, such as a recent surgical procedure or a recently diagnosed ulcer, is a contraindication to the use of these drugs.

Headaches
105: B 106: D 107: A 108: F 109: C 110: C
Tension headaches may be described as a 'weight' on the head. Cervical nerve root stricture can give hardness of the scalp. Migraine is often throbbing and associated with flushing, pallor and visual problems. Cluster headaches are severe and episodic; they are associated with watering of one or both eyes. The headaches associated with depression may be accompanied by poor appetite and often symptoms relating to the mental state.

111: D
At 7 months 90% can stand with support and 70% can sit without support. 75% can say three words at 12 months. At 30 months the majority will be dry in the day but not at night. At 54 months 75% of girls and 60% of boys can dress themselves.

Income
112: B 113: B 114: D 115: E 116: F 117: C 118: B
Private medical work includes solicitors' reports, work as a school medical officer, and lecturing on courses. Practice allowances include the rural practice allowance, whereas capitation fees include the child health surveillance. Night visit payments are item-of-service payments. Reimbursements can include payment for computers.

Thrombolytic trials
119: D 120: A 121: C 122: B
ISIS-2 compared streptokinase and aspirin use. The GREAT Study compared antistreptase and placebo in a rural study at home or hospital; the European Myocardial Infarct Project also compared these agents in different situations and also showed the benefit of pre-hospital treatment. The British Heart Foundation Group suggested that GPs giving thrombolytics should have a defibrillator.

Mental Health Act
123: D 124: C 125: A 126: B 127: E
Section 2 is for a maximum of 28 days; section 3 is for 6 months but can be renewed – if so there must be an appeal. Section 5 is used in an emergency in hospital. Section 135 and 136 are to remove a patient to a place of safety: section 135 with right of entry, section 136 from a public place.

Benefits
128: C 129: E 130: A 131: B 132: C 133: D
Disability Living Allowance can be made to someone who is virtually unable to walk, and to someone under 65 needing personal care. If the person claims over 65 years of age, they may be entitled to Attendance Allowance. Incapacity Benefit is paid to a person who is unable to work because of medical problems; if they have not paid national insurance contributions they may be eligible for SDA if they are 80% disabled. Statutory Sick Pay is paid by employers.

134: A D E
If the dehydration is significant the eyes are sunken and crying produces few tears, the skin is doughy and there is tachycardia and tachypnoea. The mouth is dry and the fontanelle, if open, is sunken. Weight loss is not reliable; a child with diarrhoea who has been starved but is well hydrated may have lost a visible amount of weight.

Infectious diseases
135: E 136: D 137: B 138: C 139: A
There is a long period between disease onset and rash in typhoid. The interval for measles is shorter (3–5 days), and the interval for scarlet fever is shorter again (1–2 days). There may be no such interval in chickenpox and rubella.

Statistics
140: B 141: E 142: A 143: C 144: D
The mode is the most common, the median is the middle figure, the mean is the average. The standard deviation measure the spread around the average. The correlation coefficient indicates an association.

145: B C D
Acute asthma is often under-diagnosed and under-estimated by both patient and the doctor, and undue reliance placed on bronchodilators. Peak flow levels at this age should be a good predictor of severity whereas the extent of expiratory wheeze is not related. Tachycardia greater than 120 and pulsus paradoxus are good indicators of a severe attack. Young men in their late teens and early twenties are vulnerable to the development of spontaneous pneumothorax.

Screening
146: E 147: L 148: F 149: K 150: B
Sensitivity is the true positives detected as positive; specificity is the true negatives detected as negative by the test. Positive predictive value is the proportion who test positive who really are positive.

151. C
Parkinson's disease has an incidence of 1:1000 in middle life rising to 1:200 in the elderly. In the latter it typically presents with rigidity. Levodopa is effective in reducing symptoms but its effect lasts for 5–8 years. Selegiline is effective both early and late after levodopa has failed to be effective and may delay progression of the disease. Dementia is a common feature of late disease.

Illustrations
152: H 153: A; 154: G; 155: E; 156: C
These are excellent illustrations of conditions that mostly are common in General Practice. Questions may just ask for 'matching' a picture to a diagnosis but they may also give a scenario rather than a diagnosis.

157: B C E
Episcleritis causes slight or no pain with normal vision and usually settles without treatment. Conjunctival haemorrhage should be painless with normal vision. Keratitis causes impairment of vision if the ulcer or opacity is near the visual axis. Acute glaucoma causes severe pain with vomiting and severe visual impairment. Finally iritis could also cause an increase in floaters and the pupil would be small and distorted.

158: A B C
Infected eczema is usually an endogenous eczema with a secondary staphylococcal infection. With scabies look for burrows along the sides of the fingers. Pustular psoriasis will probably also occur on the soles of the feet as well. Ichthyosis causes a scaly dry skin and erythema multiforme has a characteristic rash of a large vesicle with a surrounding red halo.

Rheumatoid arthritis
159: C 160: B 161: A 162: C 163: A 164: B 165: E 166: D
Methotrexate can cause hepatic and pulmonary fibrosis and is also used in severe psoriasis. Chloroquine can cause renal damage and so Amsler tests are used in long-term treatment. Gold can cause exfoliate dermatitis and oral pigmentation. Penicillamine may cause a transient loss of taste. Azoospermia has been reported with sulphasalazine usage.

167: D
There is no definite association with *H. pylori*, and some studies even suggest *H. pylori* eradication may worsen symptoms. Surgery is beneficial for erosive GORD, but is a second line treatment. H2RAs are effective but less so than PPIs. Weight loss and dietary modification are traditional treatments for GORD but there is limited evidence for their effectiveness.

168: B C
Before ovulation the cervix is closed and firm. During ovulation it is fully open admitting a finger tip and is wet due to the production of stringy mucus. Within 48 hours of ovulation the cervix closes and becomes firm again, the mucus becomes rubbery and thick forming a plug. Tests that predict ovulation measure LH secretion. Basal temperature rises during ovulation and stays raised in the luteal phase.

169: B
Doxazosin may cause stress incontinence. Anterior colporrhaphy may be harmful and is ineffective. Intermittent self catheterisation is a treatment for retention, which may be a side-effect of colposuspension. Faradic stimulation is less effective than pelvic floor exercises and may cause adverse effects.

170: **B** (diagnostic)
171: **F** (high)
172: **L** (predictive)
173: **E** (gold standard)
174: **V** (validated)
175: **J** (objective)
176: **A** (blinded)
177: **Q** (standardised)
178: **O** (sensitivity)
179: **P** (specificity)

180: A B D

Congenital abnormalities occur in 7% of babies born to epileptic mothers. Sodium valproate increases the risk of spina bifida to 1–2% (normally 0.023% of all births). The incidence of congenital heart disease in the babies of mothers taking phenytoin is 8%, it is also associated with orofacial cleft deformities. Carbamazepine appears to be relatively safe, it is chloramphenicol which causes bone marrow suppression. Warfarin is associated with CNS defects, heparin is not implicated.

Mouth ulcers
181: A 182: B 183: E 184: D 185: F 186: A

Reiter's syndrome is associated with arthritis, iritis, genital ulcers and lesions on soles and palms. The mouth lesions of primary syphilis are painless and have a hard base; those of a lichen planus are often 'cotton wool' peticles; aphthous ulcers are often painful. Herd, foot and mouth disease is associated with sore throat, and spots on the buttocks are common.

Practice Paper 4

Answers and Teaching Notes

1: **B** (associations)
2: **M** (recruitment)
3: **I** (inclusion)
4: **G** (exclusion)
5: **H** (generalisability)
6: **C** (bias)
7: **K** (observer)
8: **N** (representative)
9: **O** (sampling)
10: **T** (valid)

11: E
Usually cryotherapy cannot be tolerated until 7 years of age. Basal cell carcinomas are often suitable for cryotherapy but one must be sure of the histology. The usual pattern of response is a triple response followed by tissue swelling. Liquid nitrogen does not destroy viruses effectively, therefore instruments should be disposable or be sterilised between treatments.

12: A B E
Amenorrhoea or oligomenorrhoea accompanied by hirsutism is almost certainly due to Stein-Leventhal syndrome. Fertility is reduced and early miscarriage is common in those who do conceive. LH is raised and FSH is depressed but the significance of this is not fully understood. Ultrasound will detect polycystic ovaries.

13: C
Seborrhoeic eczema has a peak onset at 4–12 months, it usually involves the body, face, scalp and hands with erythema and scaliness but it is not itchy. It does resolve spontaneously in the vast majority of children. Emollients are the mainstay of treatment especially as soap substitutes. Atopic eczema involves the flexures, seborrhoeic eczema does not.

Social class
14: B 15: A 16: A 17: F 18: C 19: B
Managing directors, lawyers and doctors are in social class 1. Teachers and shopkeepers are in class 2. Clerical office workers are in social class 3N. Labourers are in social class 5.

Leg ulcers
20: A 21: B 22: A 23: A 24: B
Ischaemic leg ulcers are typically painful, punched out in appearance, and present in those over 70 years of age. Venous ulcers are typically pigmented and the surrounding skin is often affected.

25: A
The classic studies of Murray Parkes showed that bereavement has a definite and high mortality for the remaining partner. Over 55 years of age the death rate for men is 40% in the first year following death of a spouse. Overall the death rate is 20%. Even by the third year the death rate is still greater than for the normal population.

26: A C
In the elderly it is ill health or death of a partner that stops people from having intercourse. Atrophic vaginitis itself is itchy and causes pain and soreness, secondary Candida infection is common, but remember to exclude diabetes. The soreness induced by local oestrogens soon wears off with continued use.

27: A B C
Folic acid is found in liver, nuts and green vegetables. The daily requirement is 100–200 micrograms and it is absorbed in the duodenum and jejunum. Body stores last up to 4 months. The macrocytosis induced by alcoholism is not folic acid dependent and in fact beer contains some folate.

28: A
Under the Children Act 1989 the wishes of the child are paramount and the doctor must treat the child if he feels that the child is mature enough to make a decision about himself.

29: D
The relative risk reduction is the ratio of risk reduction (events in the placebo group-events in treatment group) divided by events in the placebo group, i.e. (12–8)/12, =30%. The absolute risk reduction (AAR) is the difference between placebo rate and treatment rate i.e. 12–8, =4%. The NNT is 1/ARR. The number needed to harm is calculated from the rates for side effects.

30: A C E
Females are affected more than males and the first attack is on average at 30 years of age with a steep fall in incidence after 45 years of age. Eighty per cent of patients will remit after the first attack, with relapses occurring about twice per year. In the 20% that have the progressive form of the disease they usually present at over 40 years of age. In 25% it is relatively benign with no evidence of disability after 10 years. There are no specific tests available, MRI scanning is abnormal in many patients.

31: D
ACE inhibitors must not be started in patients taking coincidental potassium supplements or potassium sparing diuretics. Occult renovascular disease may develop into renal failure when ACE inhibitors are started, particularly in patients with heart failure. Renal function must be monitored. The mean reduction in BP in the HOPE study was 3/2 mmHg.

32: A D E

Cancer of the cervix accounts for less than 5% of all female cancer deaths. A large number of cervical smears are taken each year but there is an increasing death rate in young women from cervical cancer. High-risk groups include those with early age of first pregnancy and those in low socio-economic classes. HPV types 16 and 18 have been found in invasive cervical cancer, and HPV types 6 and 8 have been found in benign lesions. The time taken to progress from CIN I to invasive cancer is uncertain; many women with CIN I and II have treatment and many women with invasive cancer have never had a smear.

33: A D

Because of the availability of efficient pediculicides the overall incidence of head lice is falling. Resistance does emerge and because of this most health authorities operate a three-year rotational policy. Malathion confers a residual protective effect against reinfection which lasts up to 6 weeks. However, frequent washing of the hair or swimming in chlorinated water destroys the effect. Lotions are the treatment of choice as they are more effective. Nit combing is not medically necessary but may be needed for cosmetic reasons.

34: C D

Wood's light is a source of ultraviolet light from which visible light has been excluded. It does not cause eczematous skin to fluoresce.

35: A D

Accidents are preventable, measures such as wearing seat belts decrease death and injury. One-third of all childhood deaths in the UK are due to accidents. Given that 10% of children attend their doctor each year with an accident the scope for opportunistic education is enormous. 40,000 children attend casualty departments annually with suspected poisoning, yet only 20 die, usually aged 1–5 years.

36: B D

After blind registration, a reduced TV licence is payable, SDA is available along with parking concessions and free postage on certain items.

37: A E

Cotton wool spots are retinal infarcts in the nerve fibre layer and are of serious prognostic significance. Once early changes of retinopathy develop they rarely respond to treatment. Retinal haemorrhages only interfere with vision if the macula is involved. Papilloedema due to hypertension is usually accompanied by other signs of hypertensive retinopathy and elevation of the optic disc. In the elderly hypertensive arterio-venous changes are the first discernible retinal change.

38: B

Ten per cent of myeloma are detected as an incidental finding whilst the patient is being investigated for something else. The classic features are of bone pain with osteolytic lesions on X-ray, and renal involvement with eosinophilic hyaline casts and slowly progressive renal failure. Bleeding may occur due to renal failure or thrombocytopenia. Peripheral neuropathy can occur especially if amyloid is associated.

39: A D
Endometriosis is common and ectopic endometrium is very common. It is found in 10% of all gynaecological operations and has been reported as present in 60% of laparoscopies done for infertility. Cyclical pain, dyspareunia and a pelvic mass with lack of uterine mobility are typical signs and symptoms. Medical treatment produces improvement within 2 months both histologically and clinically. However, it fails to produce an improvement if fertility has been affected.

40: A D
The Children Act 1989 came into effect in October 1991. The main feature is making the wishes of the child paramount. Emergency Protection Orders replace Place of Safety Orders, they last for 8 days and any person can apply to a court for the order. Parental access is not precluded. Police protection provisions provide for police protection for up to 72 hours if a child would otherwise suffer harm. Parental responsibility is not transferred to the police. Care orders place the child in the care of the local authority, whereas supervision orders place the child under the supervision of a local authority or probation officer. They cannot exist together.

41: C E
The majority of pacemakers are inserted for sick sinus syndrome. Activity is not restricted by the pacemaker, more by the underlying condition. Primary pacemaker failure is an uncommon cause of death. The average pacemaker lasts over 5 years with some lasting 20 years. If there is a myocardial infarct, ST and T wave changes may not be typical.

42: D E
Cystic fibrosis is the most common lethal genetic disorder in Caucasians. It varies in severity and milder cases are often detected later in life. If a child is affected there is a probability of 1:4 of subsequent children having the disorder. Survival now occurs into the third and fourth decade of life. Boys will be azoospermic but girls have reduced fertility and conception is possible. Fifty per cent of adolescents will develop a degree of glucose intolerance.

Immunisations
43: A 44: B 45: D 46: C 47: D
The DTP course is given at an early age, and DT is given later usually between 3 and 5 years. MMR is given at just over 1 year. BCG is usually given to tuberculous negative children over the age of 10.

48: B D
So-called 'brachial neuritis' is often caused by carpal tunnel syndrome especially if the pain is at night. If bilateral, carpal tunnel is usually worse in the dominant hand.

Local injections and immobilisation are often curative. It is also associated with acromegaly, amyloid, multiple myeloma, rheumatoid arthritis and pregnancy. Thenar wasting is a late feature and is rarely seen.

49: A C
Acute torticollis is a common condition occurring in the 15–30 age group. It starts acutely with a sudden pain and inability to move the head. Active and passive movements are restricted and the head is typically held in a position flexed away from the pain. It is not associated with significant arthritis and there are no neurological symptoms.

Acts
50: A 51: C 52: B 53: D
The NHS and Community Care Act 1990 allows budget control for primary care services. The Access to Health Records Act 1990 allows patients to see their medical records; the Access to Medical Reports Act 1988 allows access to reports. The Data Protection Act 1984 states that information held must be for a specific lawful purpose.

54: A D
Metered-dose inhalers are the most effective way of giving inhaled steroids, nebulisers are very inefficient. Dry powder inhalers are slightly less inefficient than aerosol devices but are more user friendly and are also ozone friendly. Large volume spacer devices increase the intrapulmonary deposition and they are recommended for all patients on more than 1000 micrograms daily. A regular dose of 1500 micrograms in adults has been associated with adrenal suppression. Growth inhibition in children has been reported with doses of 200–800 micrograms daily.

55: C D E
Urinary tract infection is under-diagnosed in young children, approximately 3% of girls and 1% of boys will have an infection by 10 years of age. About 60% have no structural abnormality with 35% having vesico-ureteric reflux. Scarring occurs with missed or inadequately treated infection. A high index of suspicion is needed especially under 2 years of age. It may present with non-specific symptoms such as convulsions, dehydration, diarrhoea, vomiting, failure to thrive, pyrexia of unknown origin or abdominal pain.

Benefits
56: B 57: F 58: A 59: E 60: D
Statutory Sick Pay is paid to employees with short term illness; Incapacity benefit may be paid if the illness continues. Severe Disablement Allowance may be payable if the person is over 80% disabled. DLA can be paid to those unable to walk, and AA (and DLA) can be paid to those needing supervision or care.

61: A C E
Research protocols need to be carefully written and need to adhere to a strict format. If there are excessive financial inducements to a researcher an ethical committee may withhold consent. When involving patients it is very important that a very detailed explanation is given. Retrospective studies do not usually require consent from the patient. The advantage of structured interviews is that they are standardised and they do not need specialised interviewers to conduct them.

62: A B C
Meningococcal vaccine is not available against group B strains. The prevalence is increasing because of recent changes in the cycle of the various strains. Despite the fact that there is decreasing sensitivity to penicillin emerging, benzylpenicillin is still the treatment of choice if the disease is suspected. Rifampicin is the treatment of choice for contacts, resistance to chloramphenicol has emerged. The increased risks for household contacts is over 1000–fold.

Statistics
63: D 64: C 65: E 66: H
The normal distribution curve is altered on the right hand (positive) side if the data is positively skewed. The width of the normal distribution curve indicates the variance.

67: C D E
The majority of people with bulimia are of normal weight. Fluoxetine in particular seems to have a short term beneficial effect but not as much as psychological interventions. If they become pregnant there is an increased risk of cleft lip and palate. One-third of the patients have a history of anorexia nervosa and some have the two diseases together; if this is so the overall prognosis is worse than for bulimia alone. Diuretic abuse, purgative abuse and excessive exercise are all associated.

68: A B C
For years iron supplements have been given routinely in pregnancy. Selecting those that need them is a problem. Estimating the patient's haemoglobin is not an accurate reflection of the iron stores. Serum ferritin is an expensive investigation to employ routinely in all pregnant women but it does reflect accurately the iron stores available. Demands for iron are greatest in the third trimester and maternal iron stores will be at their lowest at this stage of the pregnancy. The fetal iron stores are laid during this trimester.

69: B D E
Second-born children appear at greatest risk of SIDS. Most cases occur at less than 6 months with 70% occurring between October and March. The incidence has been reduced by the 'Back to Bed' campaign. There does not appear to be a relationship with type of delivery.

70: B C D
Classic symptoms of moderately severe depression are early morning waking, a diurnal mood variation feeling worse in the morning and decreased libido. Delusions

of poverty occur in psychotic depression. An abnormal dexamethasone suppression test occurs in some 30% of people with moderate to severe depression.

71: A D E
The changes at puberty are complex but show a similar pattern. The first sign in boys is testicular growth and in girls it is breast development. The major part of weight gain is due to muscle and bone increase not fat. Girls are ahead in all aspects of development. The final height is reached 4 years after the maximum growth spurt in both sexes.

72: D
Seat belt legislation has resulted in an increased use of seat belts and a substantial reduction in deaths and serious injuries for drivers. People can be exempted when carrying out manoeuvres like reversing, and if they have a medical exemption certificate. Few conditions justify exemption and would not include pregnancy or recent surgery. If these patients cannot wear a seat belt they may need to consider if they are fit to drive at that time.

73: A D E
Immersion in water leads to hydrostatic pressure supporting the circulation in the lower body. Sudden removal from the water leads to a pooling of blood in the lower legs and a decreased venous return with the consequence of hypovolaemic shock. At 34°–35° C confusion and disorientation occur. Cardiac arrhythmias start at 33° C. The patient is usually semiconscious at 30°–33° C and loses consciousness below this temperature. Rewarming should never be rapid and the last statement is a practical 'rule of thumb'.

74: C
Sarcoidosis may cause a VIth nerve palsy but would normally cause other symptoms. Mononeuritis multiplex is associated most commonly with diabetes, and by definition involves more than one nerve. Bell's palsy affects the VIIth nerve. Myasthenia gravis characteristically causes fatigability.

75: B C
The density of a cataract does not affect the results of surgery. Retinal detachment incidence is increased but less so after extracapsular lens extraction. Thickening of the posterior capsule is a complication of extracapsular extraction, it can be dealt with by laser capsulectomy as an out-patient procedure. Modern surgical techniques mean that the patient is out of bed on the day of surgery. Intraocular implants are suitable for people with any type of visual defect.

76: B C
Cough occurs in 1:8 patients on ACE inhibitors and only resolves if the drug is withdrawn, usually within one week. ACE inhibitors are both teratogenic and fetotoxic, they are also toxic to neonates. They inhibit the production of aldosterone and therefore cause hyponatraemia in the absence of diuretics. Skin rashes are common and occur in about 4% of patients.

77: B
In childhood cases of Idiopathic Thrombocytopaenic Purpura (ITP), most cases resolve spontaneously. Splenomegaly is not usual. Circulating antibodies may persist even after splenectomy.

78: A C D
Chondromalacia produces pain especially if the patella is pressed distally and the quadriceps muscle is tightened. The pain is worse on descending stairs and also after sitting. Although the X-ray is usually reported as normal it may show some thinning of the cartilage. Hyperextension of the knee joint above 10° suggests hypermobility syndrome.

79: B C E
Even in women who have had three recurrent miscarriages, 60% will have a baby without any intervention. Bacterial vaginosis is associated with mid-trimester miscarriage and warrants treatment. In first miscarriages 70–80% are due to chromosomal abnormalities.

80: A B
Opiate addicts have now become a problem for many GPs. Very few practitioners are licensed by the Home Office. For them methadone or some other opiates are suitable for maintenance treatment or withdrawal regimes. Methadone takes about 36 hours after the last dose before the symptoms of restlessness, insomnia and diarrhoea occur. A withdrawal regime can practically and humanely get an addict free of the drug within 2–4 weeks. Convulsions are more associated with sedative addiction withdrawal.

81: B
Health visitors usually have post-basic training in midwifery and community nursing experience. Their statutory obligation is to continue visiting the baby once the midwife has stopped her visits, usually around the 10th day post-delivery. They are attached staff employed by the health authority but fund-holding practices have been able to purchase their services directly since April 1993. Care of the elderly and over 75 visiting would seem to be a role suited to the skills and training of health visitors.

82: D
Drugs often produce changes in biochemical tests without producing any adverse effects on the patient. However, when an abnormal result is encountered it is important to know whether the patient's medication could be held responsible before subjecting the patient to further investigations.

83: B C
Requests for home births seem to be increasing. A GP is under no obligation to respond positively to these requests. A doctor need not be present at the delivery but a midwife must be. Abnormal deliveries are more common in higher social classes and those who have had fetal monitoring. Only 6% of babies require any form of intervention after birth.

84: B C E

In the last few years this has become the operation of choice for gall bladder disease in many centres. Ninety per cent of cases are suitable for laparoscopic surgery. In America, morbidity is low, day case surgery is common, and patients are up and about on the day of surgery. Operations take longer than conventional surgery. A nasogastric tube has to be passed to decompress the stomach to allow visualisation of the gall bladder.

85: B C E

The first feature to develop in pre-eclampsia is raised blood pressure, late features are proteinuria and a reversed circadian pattern of blood pressure, with it being elevated at night and lower in the day. Oedema is very common in pregnancy but in pre-eclampsia it is severe and generalised in the majority of women. There is no evidence that control of blood pressure arrests the progress of the disease.

Studies
86: C 87: B 88: A 89: D

Quantitative data deal with numbers; qualitative data can be described. Continuous data can have any value, but discrete data have definite values.

Screening
90: G 91: J 92: E 93: H 94: B 95: C

Sensitivity to the proportion of positives detected as positive by the test; specificity is the proportion of negatives detected as negative. The positive predictive value is the proportion of those detected as positive who are actually positive.

96: A D

Rubella has an incubation period of 14–21 days. It is an infectious disease but not transmitted by touching. Symptoms before the onset of the rash are often mild and fleeting, and the rash itself may be transient; the rash is erythematous. Clinical diagnosis is unreliable and the rash is certainly not diagnostic.

97: B C E

Swelling of the cheek is virtually never caused by maxillary sinusitis, it would indicate an infection in the root of a tooth. Once the exit to the maxillary sinus is blocked the pain can become severe and can be felt in the teeth. In acute sinusitis the discharge becomes yellow or green and may be bloodstained.

98: A B E

Chalazia are associated with blepharitis and acne rosacea. Blepharitis is more common in people with eczema and psoriasis. Correction of an entropion is usually a minor procedure done under local anaesthetic. Alkali is especially dangerous to the eye.

Literature
99: A 100: E 101: C 102: B 103: H 104: A 105: C

Michael Balint's *The Doctor, his Patient and the Illness* describes the apostolic function of a doctor, and also coined the phrase 'drug doctor' – meaning the doctor acting as a drug. *Meeting Between Experts* discussed the different priorities that different people give to plans and outcomes. *The Consultation: An Approach to Learning and Teaching* described communication tests and consultation mapping. Byrne & Long's *Doctors Talking to Patients* described doctor-and-patient centred consultations. Eric Berne's *Games People Play* discussed ego status and transactions.

106: B C D

Psychological problems have been shown to constitute one-third of all consultations. Several surveys have shown that many of these problems are missed. Many factors within the patient and within the doctor either decrease or increase the number that are missed.

107: A E

Absorption of drugs from the gut is influenced by many factors. If a drug is fat soluble the absorption will generally be enhanced in the presence of a fatty meal. Water soluble drugs such as digoxin and penicillin are best given with a drink of water one hour before a meal. The other three drugs in this question are all gastric irritants and should be given with food.

108: C E

Vitamin K deficiency is responsible for haemorrhagic disease of the newborn which is sometimes called vitamin K deficiency bleeding. Formula milks are supplemented with vitamin K. The risk of disease is increased if the mother takes anticonvulsants, anticoagulants, or is on medication for TB. If vitamin K is given orally, at least two doses are needed and three are suggested for breast-fed babies. Babies at particular risk are those born prematurely and those with delayed feeding.

109: A C E

Although the mean IQ is 80, it is often average or above. Specific learning difficulties are more common, but speech, language, hearing and visual difficulties are rarely a problem. If a diplegia is present, the early development of spasticity is associated with a better outcome.

110: A B C

Seventy-five per cent of couples will conceive within 12 months and a further 5% within the following year. The most common reason for failure is tubal abnormality (20–30%) with disordered spermatogenesis next (15–20%) and then ovulation problems (10–15%). Reconstructive surgery is associated with at least a 25% chance of a full term pregnancy but an increased risk of ectopic pregnancy. Clomiphene induces ovulation in 70% of women previously anovulatory, but only half of these conceive. *In vitro* techniques do not lead to an increase in the risk of abnormal babies.

111: D
There are still patients who miss out on their free prescriptions and it is up to doctors to advise those so entitled.

112: A D
Forty per cent of throat swabs yield no growth, 30% are streptococcal, 20% viral and 10% other organisms including Haemophilus. The decrease in incidence of rheumatic fever and glomerulonephritis predates the introduction of antibiotics and is ascribed to the raised standards of cleanliness and housing conditions. Tonsillar exudate in an under 15-year-old is more typical of Streptococcus, in an over 15-year-old of glandular fever. However, the appearances and the presence of lymphadenopathy are not characteristic of any specific type of infection.

113: B D
A highly sensitive test will have a low false-negative rate. The prevalence of a disease indicates the total number with that disease; the incidence is the number occurring in a period of time. The predictive value of a test depends on the prevalence when true positives will be higher if the prevalence is higher. The negative predictive value is the proportion of people who screen negative who do not have the disease.

114: B C
The incidence of solar keratoses is increasing especially in fair skinned, fair haired people. About 10–25% of keratoses will develop into squamous cell carcinomas but it is usually a local tumour and they rarely metastasise. Basal cell carcinomas do metastasise but rarely (1:1000) and usually only to local lymph glands. Chronic sun exposure leads to loss of skin elasticity, an increase in telangiectasia and prominent sebaceous glands. Sunburn typically takes 4–8 hours to develop after exposure.

115: B C D
A study in the USA in 1980 showed that owning pets was associated with increased survival following myocardial infarction. An Australian study showed significant differences in blood pressure and lipid levels between pet owners and those without animals. A further study from Cambridge showed a 50% decrease in minor health problems within one month of cat or dog ownership. This reduction was maintained at 10 month follow-up.

Mental Health Act
116: F 117: E 118: C 119: D 120: B
Section 3 is used for compulsory treatments of patients with established diagnoses. Section 4 is used in an emergency in the community; section 5 is used if the patient is already in hospital. Section 7 is used in guardianship. Section 12 concerns the 'approved' doctors.

121: A D F H
A compendium of trial evidence for and against many alternative therapies may be found on the Bandolier website. Randomised controlled trials have found no

evidence for the effectiveness of melatonin or arnica for the conditions described. Acupuncture is effective for the treatment of post-operative nausea and vomiting in adults, but not children. The authors conclude that iridology is no better than guesswork in diagnosis of common conditions.

122: C

Erythema chronicum migrans is a single lesion caused by the tick borne spirochaete. It has an area of expanding erythema. Erysipelas usually presents with a high fever and an unwell patient, there are large blisters with exudate. It is due to group A beta haemolytic streptococcal infection. Erythema nodosum is the most likely diagnosis, crops of lesions on the shins occur with individual ones lasting 7–10 days in crops over 3–6 weeks. Often it is associated with sarcoid, drugs or streptococcal infection. Acanthosis nigricans is increased pigmentation on the body associated with an internal malignancy such as the bowel or stomach. Kaposi's sarcoma are purple/red macules or papules usually on the trunk or back which grow quickly and become nodular or form plaques. It is classically associated with AIDS.

123: D

Heparin and Quinine are most likely to cause thrombocytopaenia. There is a lesser risk with Gold and thiazide diuretics.

Child development
124: E 125: F 126: G 127: F 128: C 129: C 130: B

At 12 months most children can walk holding on to furniture. By 18 months they can say a dozen words with meaning and build a 3–4 cube tower. At 3 years they will play with other children, and are able to balance on one leg. By 4 years they play with imagination, they can copy a circle or cross, know their name and age, and can catch a ball. At 5 years of age they can count to 12.

Polyarthritis
131: A 132: D 133: B 134: G 135: C 136: E 137: F

Rheumatoid arthritis typically gives morning stiffness and symmetrical arthropathy of hand and feet. Osteoarthritis can give swelling at the distal interphalangeal joints (Heberden's nodes). Ankylosing spondylitis would typically give back stiffness and can be associated with iritis. Rheumatic fever gives a flitting arthritis. SLE can be associated with a neck rash. Reiter's syndrome is associated with iritis and lesions on the feet and palms, keratotodena haemorrhagica. In psoriatic arthropathy there may be pitting of the nails and there can be swelling of the dorsal interphalangeal joints.

138: D E

Reactive or stress polycythaemia is a condition in which the red cell mass is normal but the PCV is raised, although, rarely above 0.55. There are strong associations with male sex, smoking, alcoholism and obesity. Alcohol decreases plasma volume by inhibiting the release of antidiuretic hormone. Obesity leads to hypoventilation and oxygen desaturation.

139: A
These results suggest a genuine infection. The risk of ascending infection and renal damage resulting in chronic renal impairment is highest from birth to 6 years. Regular prophylactic trimethoprim or nitrofurantoin has been shown to be beneficial in this situation. All children with proven UTI should be referred to a paediatrician for renal tract imaging.

140: D
Diazepam and trifluoperazine both reduce symptoms but have clinically significant side-effects which limit their usefulness. SSRIs and citalopram in particular are effective with better tolerability. Caffeine may make symptoms worse. Beta blockers, although commonly used, have no firm evidence for their efficacy.

Numbness and paraesthesia
141: G 142: E 143: B 144: A 145: F
Meralgia paraesthetica will give tingling in the lateral aspect of the thigh; it is more common in overweight people. Carpal tunnel syndrome will typically give tingling in the index and middle fingers. Peripheral neuropathy is often associated with a 'glove and stocking' sensory loss. Lumbar disc lesion can given back and leg pain with numbness in the thigh. Multiple sclerosis may give rise to 'shocks' in arms and legs especially on bending the neck.

Hypertension trials
146: C 147: A 148: D 149: B 150: C
The Veterans Administration Cooperation Study was in a largely compliant group. The Multiple Risk Factor Intervention Trial had a low incidence of cerebrovascular incidents in the control group, and no reduction was seen with treatment. The MRC Mild Hypertension Trial used a large dose of bendrofluazide but showed that 1 CUA was prevented by 850 patient years of treatment. The European Working Party on Hypertension in the Elderly was very small in each centre and showed no effect on the incidence of CVA.

151: A B D E
Unfavourable factors in depressive illness include an obsessional personality, previous significant depressive illness, loss of any parent but especially the mother prior to the age of 12 years, bereavement in later life, no sympathetic close relationship, poor social circumstances, being house-bound or tied to the house by an ill relative. Conversely, favourable factors include a secure childhood, support from a friend or relative and an active social life with outside activities.

152: A D E

Infective endocarditis occurs on valves that are deformed such as a bicuspid aortic valve or a prolapsed mitral valve. Only 25% of patients have an obvious source of the infection. Even if treated the mortality is of the order of 20%. Plasma viscosity is replacing ESR in most laboratories.

153: A B D

Penicillamine stains nails yellow and chloroquine stains them blue-grey. White nail streaks are due to minor trauma and occur in most people. Familial leuconychia stains the whole of the nail white and is inherited as an autosomal dominant trait. Tinea causes white or yellow areas and thickening of the nail. It also slows the rate of growth. Yellow nail syndrome is due to disturbance of lymphatics, the nail becomes curved longitudinally and transversely and the rate of growth slows. It is associated with lymphoedema.

154: A C D

Grief reactions show an initial stage of non-reaction for a few hours or days, up to 2 weeks. Delay until 4 weeks is pathological. Hostility to somebody or something is normal, only if it is extreme does it become pathological. Some degree of social isolation may occur but if extreme and prolonged may indicate atypical grief. Most patients return to work within 2 weeks. Suicidal ideas are common, they are atypical when they are strong and well formulated.

155: D

Progestogen-only pills cause little or no change in clotting mechanisms and do not affect lipid levels. They need not be stopped prior to surgery. They are not secreted in breast milk. If started on the first day of the cycle they provide immediate protection. If started after a combined oral contraceptive has been given they should be commenced immediately after the last combined pill has been taken and not at the end of the 7 pill free days.

Eye problems
156: C 157: D 158: A 159: B 160: A

Conjunctivitis often presents as a red eye which may be gritty or sticky. Iritis usually presents with a red eye and intense pain; the pupil is small. In glaucoma, the pupil will be large. In episcleritis there may be some visual disturbance and effuse redness of eye with some pain.

161: A B D

Two separate studies on weight loss in the elderly have produced similar results. Weight loss of 5% in 6 months should not be ignored, 75–80% will have some pathology to account for the loss. Malignancy accounts for 20%, depression 10%, GI tract disease 15%. The reason is usually obvious at the initial examination or with simple tests. If not immediately apparent extensive tests are not helpful. Of those without an obvious reason for the loss 80% will regain some or all of the lost weight within one year.

162: A D

If the diagnosis of vitamin B12 deficiency is in doubt it is still possible to confirm the diagnosis by using the Schilling test even after replacement therapy has been established. Dietary deficiency is very uncommon except in very strict vegetarians. Vitamin B12 is now given every 3 months by injection and this appears to be adequate. However, patients may become psychologically dependent and demand it more frequently. It is cheap and excess is excreted in the urine once stores are saturated. There are no clinical problems associated with more frequent injections.

Abdominal pain
163: B 164: E 165: C 166: A 167: D 168: F

The pain of biliary colic is intermittent and vague in location; the abdomen may be tender in the right upper quadrant. Peptic ulcer might be accompanied by flatulence and may wake the patient at night – the so called 'hunger pain'. Appendicitis is classically associated with vomiting, pyrexia and right iliac fossa tenderness. Diverticulitis often gives tenderness in the left iliac fossa if there is a long history of constipation. Renal colic may give back pain and abdominal pain perhaps with vomiting. Pancreatitis gives severe abdominal pain radiating to the back.

Thyroid disease
169: A 170: B 171: C 172: B

Anaplastic thyroid cancers are the most common in the elderly. In the young, papillary cancers are most common, and these have the best prognosis. Follicular thyroid cancers particularly metastasise to the bone.

Heart problems
173: F 174: D 175: A 176: E

Anxiety can cause palpitations often with a dull ache and a feeling that deep breathing is necessary. Thyrotoxicosis will cause tachycardia and weight loss. Phaeochromocytoma causes palpitations and sweating in intermittent attacks when the patient may be noted to be pale. Carcinoid syndrome causes diarrhoea and episodic flushing and wheezing.

Cancers
177: C 178: B 179: E 180: F 181: A 182: D

A typical GP will see a new case of bronchial cancer every 6 months, and a new case of breast cancer every year. It will be 2 years before the doctor sees a new case of stomach cancer, and 5 years before an ovarian cancer. A malignant brain tumour will be seen every 10 years, and a thyroid cancer every 25 years on average.

Lesions
183: D 184: B 185: A 186: C 187: F

These are all at least fairly common conditions encountered in General Practice. It is worth studying the pictures in some detail with the correct answers.

ECGs

188: **I** (P wave)
189: **A** (A)
190: **K** (PR interval)
191: **I** (P wave)
192: **M** (QRS complex)
193: **M** (QRS complex)
194: **B** (B)
195: **N** (R wave)
196: **O** (T wave)

ECGs are used in the investigation and diagnosis of cardiac disorders. The ECG is recording on special paper, which moves through the ECG machine at 25 mm/sec. The special paper is divided into large squares each measuring 5mm wide. The electrical activity is converted into various waveforms of the type shown in figure 1. The individual components of the waveform have standard names. The P wave is produced by atrial depoloarisation beginning in the SA node, and is show as letter A in figure 1. The PR interval is the time between the onset of atrial depolarisation and the onset of ventricular depolarisation. It is measured from the beginning of the P wave to the first deflection of the QRS Complex. The QRS complex represents septal and vetricular depolarisation. This is shown as letter B in figure 1. The first positive deflection of ventricular depolarisations is called the R wave. The T wave is produced by ventricular repolarisation.

Practice Paper 5

Answers and Teaching Notes

1: D
Reye's syndrome is rare but important as early diagnosis and treatment improves prognosis. It is associated with a previous infection which is probably showing signs of resolution. Vomiting is typically profuse and the child becomes overactive, combative and irritable before becoming lethargic and then comatose with signs of cerebral irritation. Liver function is always disturbed although jaundice is rare. The peak incidence is 2 years. The association with aspirin ingestion has led to a decrease in the paediatric use of this drug and a consequential fall in incidence of the syndrome.

2: B D E
Blood glucose levels have been shown to rise with age and 10% of the elderly are diabetic or have impaired glucose tolerance. Most people with glycosuria have diabetes but not all diabetics have glycosuria. Glucose tolerance testing is rarely needed and a raised fasting glucose is usually diagnostic. Fluorescein angiography shows the presence of early retinal changes in the majority of diabetics.

3: A C D
There are many different models of the consultation, one of the most practical and easy to remember is the one quoted in this question which is a more doctor-centred approach. Four areas of the consultation are considered, the presenting problem, other problems, modifying health seeking behaviour and finally prevention. The candidate is also advised to compare this with other models such as the one proposed by Pendleton *et al*.

4: B
The causes of agitation in the elderly are legion. The GP should be wary of all drug therapy especially if recently introduced but also if used for many years. Depressive illness may be the cause of agitation and it could be worsened by benzodiazepines. Silent infarcts are common and vigilance is needed if they are to be detected. A withdrawn patient may not drink and in warm weather can soon become dehydrated leading to agitation.

Study types
5: B 6: A 7: E 8: F 9: G 10: D 11: I
Quantitative studies involves counting; qualitative studies explore attitudes or beliefs. Descriptive studies would be suitable for looking at patient satisfaction. A retrospective study would look at a previous time period; a prospective study looks at what will happen as the study progresses. Case-control studies compare two groups, and an intervention study looks at the effect of an added factor.

12: A
The statement of fees and allowances is negotiated by the GMSC and government, there needs to be no legislative change to amend this under the NHS regulations.

13: C D E
An HGV driver should not drive for at least 3 months after a myocardial infarct and then, only if certain criteria are met, may he resume. The criteria for driving after fits are strict; an HGV driver needs to be fit-free for 10 years and off medication. He may then apply to hold an HGV licence. HGV driving has to be discontinued if the driver has insulin-dependent diabetes and an unrepaired aortic aneurysm. Any driver should avoid driving from the onset of a migraine attack.

14: A D
Allergic conjunctivitis produces a discharge that is typically clear; mucopurulent discharge would indicate infection, visual acuity should not be affected and photophobia only occurs in very severe cases with involvement of the cornea. Epiphora and itching are the main symptoms. If the patient can tolerate contact lenses they are allowed.

15: **D** (compare)
16: **N** (numerator)
17: **F** (denominator)
18: **C** (cohort)
19: **P** (standardised)
20: **K** (inclusion)
21: **B** (classification)
22: **J** (included)
23: **T** (type 2)
24: **R** (subjective)

Drugs used in hypertension
25: C 26: A 27: C 28: A 29: C
Thiazide diuretics should not be used in patients with gout or glucose intolerance. Beta blockers should be avoided in patients with asthma, COPD, and heart failure.

30: A D
Alcohol problems in women have increased over the last 20 years. Both cerebral and hepatic damage seems to be more prevalent in women. However, the incidence of cirrhosis has not yet reached the same level as for alcohol-dependent men. Women are far more likely to have an associated depressive illness than men. Alcohol Intoxication is achieved with lower intake of alcohol during the premenstrual phase of the cycle. Women tend to start drinking at a later age than men and consequently become problem drinkers at a later age also.

31: C D F
The sensitivity of cervical smears is fairly high at about 80% and the specificity is very high at over 98%, hence false positives rarely occur. The false-negative rate will be about 20% and can be dependent on the smear taker. CIN is really a histological term; dysplasia and dyskaryosis are seen by cytologists.

32: A E F
Psoriasis has a world-wide incidence of 2%. It does not scar and the lesions are rarely itchy. It can occur at any age but the peak incidence is in young adults. The rash is typically symmetrical, red and scaly with clearly defined borders. Although dithranol is the treatment of choice for plaque psoriasis it cannot be used on the face.

33: A C E
The care of epileptics still leaves a lot to be desired. All patients should be referred for assessment after their first fit. Idiopathic epilepsy is a dangerous diagnosis in those having a first convulsion after 25 years of age. Epilepsy is not an inherited condition in the majority of cases. Most GPs do not know all their epileptic patients and they do not conduct annual checks on them as a matter of routine.

34: A
Immunisation with both types of hepatitis B vaccine is specific for that virus. The preferred site of injection is the deltoid by deep i.m. route, injection into the buttocks may lead to depositing the vaccine in fatty tissue and consequently low absorption. The level of sero-conversion in children is virtually 100% with a decreased level in older patients. Systemic reactions are few with hypersensitivity being rare. Local reactions have been reported in 15% of vaccinations.

35: A B C
A high index of suspicion is needed with anybody who has travelled further than Western Europe, especially if they have lived 'rough'. Diarrhoeal illness must be thoroughly investigated, as for instance treating 'ulcerative colitis' with steroids can be fatal if it is really amoebiasis. Lassa fever presents as a sore throat and fever, malaria with a non-specific 'flu-like' illness in the early stages.

Statistics
36: H (6) 37: B (1) 38: G (5)
Remember that the mean is the arithmetic average, the mode is the most frequent, and the median is the number in the middle when placed in order.

39: A C D
In one survey 1% of the population had suffered symptoms of post-traumatic stress disorder. They occur soon after the event and can be helped by early expression of feelings with a professional care worker. Individuals respond in different ways with a mixture of fears of annihilation, emotional problems and reactions provoked by a challenge to control. About 20–25% of those involved in a major disaster go on to develop a chronic disorder.

40: B D

Episcleritis is usually a localised area of inflammation and is a self-limiting condition. Visual disorder in ophthalmic herpes may indicate corneal scarring. Corneal ulcers need referral or sight may be lost. Corneal abrasions are usually dealt with in general practice. Blocked tear ducts in children can be left until 9 months of age and referral then is not urgent.

41: B D E

Only 15% of GPs have direct access to community hospitals. The average age of patients within these hospitals has risen because of a decrease in maternity work. Care is cheaper in community hospitals. The workload of doctors in these hospitals is greater but so is the job satisfaction.

42: A C D

Now replacing hysterectomy in many centres, this procedure is suitable for most patients except for those with malignant or pre-malignant conditions of the endometrium or those with active pelvic infection. The endometrium needs to be thinned pre-operatively with danazol. Day case surgery is increasing and at the most it requires an overnight stay. The ideal result is to cause complete amenorrhoea but a scanty loss is deemed acceptable.

43: A B C

Achilles tendon problems are a common source of injuries in sports enthusiasts. Common factors precipitating tendonitis are a high heel tab, a low heel, running on a hard surface or a sudden change of running surface. Local steroid injections are traditionally associated with an increased incidence of rupture. Rupture is best treated by repair rather than by immobilisation. Tendonitis is best treated initially by a heel raise and ultrasound combined with rest from the precipitating activity.

44: C D E

Innocent murmurs are typically systolic, sitting or deep inspiration makes an innocent murmur quieter. An innocent murmur is soft and there is no thrill, the ECG and chest X-ray are normal.

45: A E

Exposure to asbestos leads to an increase in lung cancer in both non-smokers and smokers, asbestosis does not have to be present. Compounds formed in the manufacture of aniline dyes are associated with bladder cancer. Exposure to radon gas in miners was the first described occupational association with lung cancer.

46: D

Tinnitus is often the first symptom of Ménière's disease and may occur episodically long before the first full attack. The feeling of fullness in the ear often accompanies tinnitus in the acute attack and may become intense. Hearing tends to decrease with each attack. Nystagmus only occurs during the acute attack. If rombergism is present it would indicate either other pathology or an emotional overlay.

47: C D E
Splenomegaly occurs in glandular fever but the spleen is soft and friable and not easily palpable. Carcinomatosis rarely causes an enlarged spleen, a nodular, enlarged liver is a more common finding. Massive splenomegaly is most commonly due to chronic myeloid leukaemia or myelofibrosis.

48: B C
Pompholyx affecting the soles and palms will be very itchy. Keratoderma blenorrhagica is the specific lesion seen in Reiter's syndrome. Pustular psoriasis can affect the hands and feet. Lichen planus characteristically affects the mouth with erosive lesions or 'cotton wool' patches.

49: C D E
The incidence of carcinoma of the oesophagus is rising, possibly due to the increased ingestion of nitrosamines and alcohol. The prognosis is poor and especially worse for adenocarcinoma. The most common presenting symptoms are dysphagia for solids only and weight loss.

50: B
Propranolol and nifedipine both have negative inotropic actions and therefore may precipitate heart failure. The hypoglycaemic effect of glibenclamide is antagonised by thiazide diuretics. Spironolactone is a potassium conserving diuretic and frusemide causes loss of potassium from the body. NSAIDs all reduce platelet adhesiveness and potentiate the anticoagulation achieved with warfarin. Alcohol and antihistamines are both CNS depressants.

51: F
Ten per cent of elderly people have a positive rheumatoid factor with no evidence of an inflammatory joint disease. Morning stiffness takes more than 30 minutes to wear off; the metacarpophalangeal joints are usually involved symmetrically. The feet are also involved. Many patients with early rheumatoid arthritis will have a negative rheumatoid factor. Regular use of NSAIDs has no effect on disease progression; this requires a disease modifying drug.

52: A D
Psychological factors are of great importance in the management of chronic pain. It is important that the general practitioner appreciates that fear, anxiety and social and physical isolation increase the perception of pain. Also the patients personality type affects the overall comprehension of the pain. Placebo affects are great and this needs to be taken into account when gauging the response to therapy.

53: A B E
Diverticular disease is common and often asymptomatic. Rectal bleeding is a frequent presentation and does not usually indicate underlying malignancy. The best treatment is non-fermentable fibre of which coarse wheat bran is the most effective. Fistula can occur and may cause pneumaturia if connecting with the bladder.

Mental Health Act
54: E 55: B 56: C 57: G 58: D

Section 3 is for compulsory treatment of a mental health problem. Section 4 is used in an emergency, and there is no right of appeal; similarly section 5 is used as an emergency for in-patients. Section 7 concerns guardianship. Section 136 is used by the police.

59: C

HIV-positive patients run a variable period before symptoms of the disease manifest themselves. The earliest sign is generalised lymphadenopathy which heralds the commencement of AIDS-related complex. This may produce weight loss, night sweats, diarrhoea and fatigue. The diagnosis of 'full blown' AIDS proper depends upon the presence of opportunistic infection or neoplasm such as non-Hodgkin's lymphoma, Kaposi's sarcoma or Pneumocystis infection.

60: D E

Testicular torsion has a peak incidence at 12–18 years, not epididymitis. Iliac fossa pain is again typical of testicular torsion. In epididymitis the scrotal contents rapidly swell due to enlargement of epididymal structures. High-frequency B mode ultrasound is able to differentiate between torsion and epididymitis. Chlamydial infection is associated with non-specific urethritis.

61: E F

Cholera immunisation is no longer indicated for travellers to any country. Yellow fever immunisation lasts for 10 years. Rabies vaccine is given into the deltoid muscle usually; the antibody response is reduced if given into the gluteal muscle. Gamma globulin interferes with responses to live vaccines and is normally given shortly before travel. Reactions to the typhoid vaccine are more common after the age of 35 years when it should be avoided if possible.

62: A B E

'Frozen shoulder' is a generic term encompassing a variety of conditions that are not always clinically distinguishable. It usually runs a chronic course of about 2 years then recovers completely. Local tenderness over the various muscles, e.g. supraspinatus, infraspinatus or biceps tendon reflects the site of the lesion accurately. Immobilisation may lead to permanent restriction of movement and exercise should be encouraged. The condition may be precipitated by unusual exertion such as home decorating and the pain is often worse at night.

63: D

Pain due to cervical arthritic change is typically worse at night. Carcinoma of the pyriform fossa causes pain in the ear via referred pain along the Xth cranial nerve. The upper molar teeth, temperomandibular joint or the parotid gland can all cause referred pain. Trigeminal neuralgia does not cause otalgia, but glossopharyngeal neuralgia can produce a severe lancinating pain in the ear or throat. Tonsillitis causes pain from the oropharynx via the IXth cranial nerve.

64: B C D

In the UK, sarcoid is the most common cause of hilar lymphadenopathy in patients over 15 years of age. In lymphoma the glands may be mediastinal rather than hilar. Hilar glands due to tubercle are commoner in children but the incidence is increasing in adults especially in large cities.

The red eye
65: A 66: G 67: B 68: F 69: H

Acute glaucoma is typically seen in middle age. Patients often have shallow anterior chambers. Treatment is with topical pilocarpine, oral acetazolamide and analgesia. Purulent conjunctivitis in young people, particularly in association with genitourinary symptoms may be due to chlamydia. Arc eye is seen in welders or people using sun beds without adequate eye protection, treated symptomatically with analgesia.

70: C D

Atypia is often due to human papilloma virus, but a single abnormal smear does not correlate well with the presence of CIN. However, if two or three smears show atypia, colposcopy should be performed. If there is evidence of genital warts a smear should be taken annually until negative smears have occurred on five successive occasions. Cervical erosions may bleed on touch during taking the smear but they do not show any typical abnormality. Carcinoma of the cervix is usually diagnosed on clinical history and appearance of the cervix.

71: A E

Irritant contact dermatitis as contrasted with allergic contact dermatitis does not require the patient to have been exposed previously. The rash typically develops within 24 hours as opposed to 2–4 days for allergy. The severity of the rash depends on the amount of irritant used, whereas in allergic conjunctivitis only a small quantity can produce a severe reaction. Reactivation at other sites does not occur in irritant conjunctivitis.

72: A C E

Toddler diarrhoea is common, the child passes several loose stools per day with undigested food (typically carrots and peas) in the stools. There is never failure to thrive unless other pathology is present. If it occurs, further investigation is necessary. Sometimes, it occurs after an acute infective illness and especially in these patients a milk free diet is helpful. Loperamide is of some use in cases which are proving to be intractable and in which there is no other cause.

73: B C E

Only about one-third of patients on benzodiazepines will become dependent on their drug. The first sign of dependency is often rebound sleep disturbance which has been shown to occur after one week in some people. The loss of appetite which occurs can often be severe enough to cause weight loss. More severe symptoms include auditory and visual hallucinations. Beta blockers have been shown to help some patients who are having problems with stopping their drugs.

74: C D E

Scientific and medical papers quote a lot of statistics and it is a good idea to have a rudimentary knowledge of some of the concepts. The null hypothesis is concerned with results that could occur by chance. Student's t test is of use in small groups of data. Spearman's rank correlation is used when comparing rank correlated groups of data.

Benefits

75: D 76: H 77: B 78: A 79: C 80: E

Income Support is for people on low income and is means tested. Family credit is for people bringing up children on low wages. Child benefit is for anyone with a child. Incapacity Benefit is paid to people incapable of work. Invalid Care Allowance is for people who look after disabled people; Attendance Allowance is for older people needing help with personal care.

Screening

81: G 82: A 83: J 84: K 85: B 86: H

Specificity is the proportion of negatives detected as negative by a test; sensitivity is the proportion of positives detected as positive by the test. Positive predictive value is the proportion of those detected as positive who are actually positive.

87: B D

The cap, contraceptive diaphragm, should be left *in situ* for 6 hours after intercourse to be truly effective. Variations in size of the patient can make it ineffective because of poor fitting, similarly if a prolapse is present the seal will not be adequate. The frequency of replacement depends upon usage, but they should be changed annually because the rubber may perish. All available caps quoted in the drug tariff are made from rubber.

88: C

There is a 'pecking' order of relatives from husband or wife down to nephews and nieces. The majority of admissions are under Section 2. Section 4 should rarely be used except for extreme emergencies. Only a relative or an approved social worker can make an application for admission. Sexual deviancy, alcoholism and drug abuse are not in themselves grounds for admission. Section 139 protects doctors employing the Act from legal retribution if they are over-enthusiastic.

89: A C D

Hyoscine (Scopoderm TTS®) is available as a transdermal patch, the effect of which lasts for 72 hours. Domperidone is available as syrup, tablets and suppositories; the injection was withdrawn because of an association with cardiac arrhthymias. Cinnarizine (Stugeron®) is available over the counter from the pharmacist and is effective for travel sickness. Prochlorperazine is associated with parkinsonian side-effects, hypotension and occasionally acute dystonic reactions. Finally, chlorpromazine has a very weak anti-emetic effect and should not be used for this purpose.

90: A D E

Febrile convulsions typically occur between 6 months and 6 years of age. There is no social class difference and there is no difference in the sex incidence. Prolonged fits are associated with residual neurological deficit. There is a 15% chance of a child having febrile convulsions if a first-degree relative has had them. In the normal population the risk is quoted as 7%.

91: A C D

Sclerotherapy gives good short term results but high saphenous ligation with multiple avulsions is the mainstay of treatment. After treatment, compression is only needed for about 1 week and walking should commence on the day of surgery. The majority of patients only need one week away from work.

92: A E

In pregnancy about one-third of patients will show an increase in fit frequency. Seventy per cent of those with migraine have been shown to improve. Multiple sclerosis is rarely affected by the pregnancy but relapses are common in the puerperium. Asthma appears to be unaffected. Sickle cell disease has a high mortality and needs skilled management.

93: A C E

Before replacing soft lenses in an eye which has been stained with fluorescein it must be thoroughly irrigated with saline. Pilocarpine characteristically causes tight constriction of the pupils. Oxybuprocaine is a local anaesthetic, tropicamide is a short acting drug which dilates the pupils and is useful in diabetic clinics. The local irritation caused by adrenaline is avoided by giving it as a pro-drug.

Voluntary bodies
94: G 95: F 96: E 97: A 98: B 99: C 100: H

Child abuse would be dealt with by the NSPCC. The Marie Curie Foundation deals with problems associated with cancer. Turning Point deals with concerns about drug abuse, and the Terrence Higgins Trust deals with AIDS and related problems. ASH deals with smoking problems. Relate is appropriate for marriage guidance issues, and Cruse for bereavement in widowed people.

101: A D E

The syndrome of acute inflammatory polyneuropathy is an acute peripheral demyelinating condition which has a rapid onset. Motor symptoms predominate and paralysis may be profound requiring assisted ventilation. The majority of cases make a satisfactory recovery and usually remain free of problems.

102: A C E

Good control of diabetes pre-conceptually and during the first trimester will decrease the incidence of congenital abnormalities. Pre-term labour is more common and babies born early are at a greater risk of respiratory distress syndrome than babies of equivalent gestation born to non-diabetic mothers. There is an unexplained incidence of fetal death after 40 weeks' gestation and pregnancies are usually induced no later than term.

103: C
Tuberculosis is possible but is more common at a younger age. Perthes' disease has a peak incidence at 6–8 years and is more common in boys than in girls. Slipped upper femoral epiphysis is typically pre-pubertal. Septic arthritis would be accompanied by pyrexia and malaise. Non-accidental injury is possible but is more common in those under 3 years old.

Prostate problems
104: B 105: C 106: A
Finasteride is a 5α-reductase inhibitor. Prazosin is a selective X-blocker, and tamsulosin appears to be a α1A-blocker.

107: C E
With erythema multiforme, there is usually a precipitating cause, either a viral infection, bacterial infection or drug eruption. The rash is characteristic with round papules or blisters made up of rings of different colours (target or iris lesions). If mucous membranes are involved this is known as the Stevens–Johnson syndrome and carries a significant mortality. Recurrent episodes are common especially if it follows a herpes simplex infection.

Infectious diseases
108: A 109: E 110: D 111: E 112: B 113: C
Immunisation against *Haemophilus influenza* type B is now given to children. Smallpox has been eradicated and so no routine vaccination is given. Most adults are immune to chickenpox despite no immunisation for this. Subacute sclerosing parencephalitis is a rare complication of measles. Influenza virus demonstrates antigenic shift and drift.

114: A B C
Low-dose aspirin is now very widely prescribed but it is not without side-effects both in the short term and the long term. After a myocardial infarction studies have shown a significant decrease in long term mortality if given at a dose of 150 mg for one month. In the treatment of venous thrombosis it does not appear to have a role, although it may have a place in prevention of thrombosis. It has no role in the primary prevention of cerebrovascular disease and may even increase the risk of cerebral haemorrhage.

115: A C D F
Proton pump inhibitors can cause severe headache and diarrhoea. Gynaecomastia can result but is less common than after H2–antagonist treatment. It is best to avoid proton pump inhibitors in pregnancy and breast feeding.

116: B C
The diagnosis of child abuse is fraught with difficulties, but there are certain pointers, such as an implausible explanation for the injuries, previous abuse or abuse in siblings. The children are usually less than 3 years of age (contrasting with sexual abuse which may well continue into adolescence).

117: B C
There is no evidence that restriction of tea, coffee or cola decreases symptoms of PMS. An hourly starch diet may relieve symptoms in some patients. Fertility is not affected. About 20–40% of women consult their doctor at least once with symptoms of the condition. Approximately 150 different symptoms have been attributed to PMS. Suppression of ovulation by using either high dose oestrogen patches or the oral contraceptive does give a small reduction in symptoms in some patients but conversely some women report a worsening of symptoms.

118: A B C
Carbon monoxide poisoning accounts for about 1000 deaths per year in England and Wales. Faulty appliances and blocked vents are the usual cause. The initial symptom is often a dull pounding headache very like a hangover. Mental apathy, nausea and dizziness are also typical symptoms. If the exposure continues, convulsions, coma and respiratory distress follow. The skin typically becomes pink and cyanosis does not occur. The toxic effects are usually reversed within 12 hours of removal from the source of the carbon monoxide.

119: B C
Azoospermia or oligospermia can be caused by the inadvertent use of spermicides but once simple causes have been excluded little hope can be given that a treatable cause will be found. If FSH levels are raised in a patient with small firm testicles further investigation is necessary especially to exclude a chromosomal abnormality such as Klinefelter's syndrome. By careful investigation a cause for the condition can be identified in about two-thirds of cases but only in a very few cases can a treatment be instituted which will lead to a successful outcome.

120: A B D
Oral decongestants are taken usually as over-the-counter remedies and may contain one or all of the following, paracetamol, phenylpropanolamine, phenylephrine, pseudoephedrine, antihistamine. They need to be used with caution in a variety of conditions. They can induce a hypertensive crisis especially in people taking non-selective beta blockers. They stimulate the heart and cause an increase in oxygen demand and therefore should not be used in patients with ischaemic heart disease and hypertension. They can induce arrhythmias especially in hyperthyroidism and can induce a rise in blood glucose and should not be used in diabetics.

Thrombolytic trials
121: C 122: A 123: B 124: D 125: F
ASSOT studied alteplase. ISIS-2 compared streptokinase against aspirin against both and neither. ISIS-3 showed aspirin and streptokinase to be treatments of choice. ISAM studied streptokinase plus heparin; GISSI studied streptokinase against placebo.

126: C
Beta-sympathomimetics, anticholinergics and sodium cromoglycate all have proven efficacy when given via a nebuliser. Beclomethasone is available but efficacy is not proven. Theophyllines are oral or injectable preparations.

127: C F G
There is a decreased incidence of ischaemic heart disease in Down's syndrome; the syndrome is due to trisomy 21. Heart defects are commonly seen, especially atrioventricular canal defects and patent ductus arteriosus. Hypothyroidism and glue ear with hearing impairment are more commonly seen than in the general population.

128: A D
In 1992 notifications increased for the first time for many years, but there is still a significant under-reporting of the disease which has been estimated as about 25%. In the USA new cases have increased dramatically. Drug-resistant strains do occur but 95% of isolates are sensitive to all standard drugs (isoniazid, rifampicin, ethambutol, and streptomycin). Although trials in some parts of the world have shown BCG to be ineffective, in Great Britain there is overwhelming evidence for its efficacy. The homeless are significantly at risk as are patients with AIDS, but in Great Britain the number of such patients developing tuberculosis is approximately 5%.

129: C
Baldness is usually physiological, but it may be associated with local disease of the scalp such as seborrhoeic eczema, tinea capitis, or simply hair pulling (trichotillomania). Minoxidil topically applied twice daily is effective in some people in treating male pattern baldness. However, hair regrowth stops and reverses within 3 months of cessation of therapy. Endocrine causes such as pituitary or adrenal tumours can cause hirsutism and hair loss. Hormone replacement treatment is associated with excessive hair loss in some patients.

130: A B C E
In Great Britain and Scandinavia chronic low blood pressure has been dismissed as of no consequence. Conversely in other European countries, especially France and Germany, it is often treated more seriously than raised blood pressure. Studies, some published in the BMJ, have highlighted the fact that patients with the condition do have a significant morbidity and a perceived feeling of being unwell. The studies do not show if elevation of the blood pressure causes the symptoms described to disappear.

131: B E G

The Rome and Manning criteria may be used to diagnose IBS in conjunction with the exclusion of more significant pathology. Food intolerance has been found in 33–66% of IBS patients. However, true food allergy is rare and RAST testing is unnecessary. Rectal bleeding and steatorrhoea warrant further investigation. Tricyclics are effective, not SSRIs. The British Society of Gastroenterology recommends referral of those patients presenting for the first time in later life.

132: C

Stress and urgency incontinence require different treatments and are often confused. Stress incontinence is typically associated with leaking of urine on coughing, sneezing or laughter, leaking on playing sport or sudden movement. Urgency incontinence or detrusor instability is more likely with a history of frequency of six or more times per day and three or more times at night, leaking at night and having to rush to the toilet. Dribbling is a symptom of overflow incontinence.

133: A C E

The correct treatment for hypertriglyceridaemia is reduction in alcohol (if appropriate), dietary management to achieve a BMI <25 and a reduction in saturated fat intake. Severe hypertriglyceridaemia requires treatment with fibrates to prevent acute pancreatitis. Cholestyramine may cause increases in triglycerides.

134: D

The currently recommended WHO criteria based on the American Diabetes Association criteria require fasting glucose >7 mmol/l or random >11.1 mmol/l. Approximately 50% of diabetics are undiagnosed. The prevalence of all types of diabetes is rising.

135: B E H

Chlamydia are protozoa. Suspect chlamydia in young patients with chronic bilateral symptoms, particularly if they have genital symptoms. Studies have confirmed the efficacy and acceptability of postal screening of urine samples. Pelvic inflammatory disease may result in tubal occlusion and subsequent infertility or ectopic pregnancy. The infection is most common in 16–24 year olds. It may be diagnosed by LCR testing of urine.

Income
136: C 137: D 138: F 139: F 140: D 141: F 142: B 143 : B

Completion of insurance reports and cremation forms are part of a GP's private medical work. Rural practice payments can be part of a practice allowance. Temporary residence fees and child health surveillance fees are capitation related. Fees for emergency treatment, immediately necessary treatment, and immunisations are items of service payments.

144: A D

Controlled drug prescriptions must be handwritten by the prescriber. The address of the doctor is pre-printed on all prescriptions. The drug is marked C.D. in the BNF to denote that it is a controlled drug. The prescription does not need to be marked with this.

145: A B

Dermatofibromata are hard raised lesions which typically occur on the legs of young women, 20% of the female population develop one or more. They are usually brown and grow slowly over many years, the edges are smooth and they do not ulcerate. An irregular edge would indicate a malignant growth and if ulcerated this would be more in keeping with a pigmented rodent ulcer.

Childhood development
146: I 147: E 148: C 149: B 150: F 151: G 152: E

At 12 weeks a baby will turn the head to sounds, and by 6 months will feed with a biscuit. By 18 months, the child will be scribbling and building a tower of 3–4 cubes; by 2 years the tower will be 6–7 cubes. At 3 years, the child knows 2 colours, and goes up stairs 1 foot at a time. By 5 years the child chooses friends and can name 3 or 4 colours.

153: A E

There is no relationship between the tolerance to adverse and to therapeutic effects. Tolerance may develop in less than 48 hours after the initiation of treatment, but is rapidly abolished once there is a nitrate-free period. There is no difference between the various preparations quoted in the question, what is important is the length of time above the therapeutic level likely to cause tolerance in any one particular patient.

Literature
154: C 155: G 156: F 157: E 158: C 159: B

The Exceptional Potential of Each Primary Care Consultation described four parts of the consultation to include health promotion. Roger Neighbour's *The Inner Consultation* used the terms connecting, summarising, and safety netting. Eric Bene's *Games People Play* looked at people's 'transactions' describing them as pastimes. Enid Balint and Jack Norell described the flash in *Six Minutes for the Patient*. Byrne and Long examined audio tapes of consultations in *Doctors Talking to Patients*, and related severe time constraints in the consultations.

160: A C

The MRFIT study in North America established that cholesterol was a risk factor and other studies have shown that decreasing serum cholesterol by 10% decreases cardiovascular mortality. However, no study has shown a decrease in overall mortality. One study showed that a very low cholesterol was associated with an increased risk of malignancy especially carcinoma of the colon. Good dietary control following counselling will decrease the level of cholesterol on average by 10–15%.

The various risk factors are additive and therefore people who smoke and/or have a raised blood pressure are probably more in need of screening.

161: D
Intention to treat analysis is most useful for prospective clinical trials. All patients who pass initial assessment and are randomised are included, and this allows a more valid representation of what happens in practice: when you see a patient in surgery and decide to start treatment, it is on an intention to treat basis.

Minor surgery
162: D 163: A 164: C 165: E 166: E 167: B
The treatment of haemorrhoids in minor surgery would be by injection. A hydrocele would be aspirated. Lipomes would be excised; thrombosed piles would be incised. Verruca and molluscum contagiosum would be treated by curette or cryocautery.

Back pain
168: B 169: E 170: A 171: C
Mechanical back pain is likely to be worse on movement, but to gradually improve with activity and time. The pain of AS is likely to be worse early morning and may well be accompanied by non-specific malaise and constitutional symptoms. A disc lesion at L4/L5 will give reduced dorsiflexion power and a sensory disturbance on the dorsum of the foot. A lesion at L5/S1 will give reduced power of plantar flexion and reduced/absent ankle reflex; there may be paraesthesia of the lateral aspect of the foot.

Bowel disorders
172: D 173: E 174: C 175: A 176: B
Irritable bowel syndrome will usually result in abdominal pain, flatulence, loose motions; the pain is relieved by defecation. In diverticular disease, there is attending diarrhoea and constipation. The pain of Crohn's disease is often associated with diarrhoea and examination shows abdominal tenderness and axal taps. Ulcerative colitis gives painless bloody diarrhoea. Ischaemic colitis occurs usually in an older age group, and there may be other features of general ischaemic disease.

Hypertension trials
177: A 178: E 179: C 180: B 181: B
The Hot Trial used calcium channel blockers. The MRC Mild Hypertension Trial was carried out over 15 years, involved over 85,000 patient years, and about 200 GPs. It was a single blind trial, using bendrofluazide, propranolol and placebo. The study demonstrated that 1 CVA was saved by 850 patient treatment years. The Veterans Administration Co-operative Study was double blind, involved men of average age 50 years, and demonstrated the possibility of stroke reduction. The MRC Trial for Hypertension in Older Adults was a single blind trial involving about 4,000 patients, and (like the MRC Mild Hypertension Trial) used diuretic, beta blocker and placebo.

ECG changes
182: K ST elevation
183: F pathological Q waves
184: D letter C
185: A J waves
186: I reduced amplitude

Characteristic ECG changes are seen in myocardial infarction. ST elevation is seen in anterior chest leads in an anterior myocardial infarction, but pathological Q waves result later. This later change is shown in figure 2 as letter C. Some ECG changes are not due to cardiac conditions. The ECG shown in figure 3 is from a patient with hypothermia. It shows typical J waves at letter A and also shows sinus bradycardia. Myxoedema also gives sinus bradycardia together with reduced amplitude.

Certificates
187: A 188: B 189: E 190: C 191: D 192: A

A Med 3 is used when the patient has been seen, and is not fit for work. It is initially used for short periods of time (up to 6 months) but can then be used for an indefinite period of sickness. A Med 5 is used when the doctor is relying on written evidence or has not seen the patient at the time of signature. A Med 4 forms part of the assessment for Incapacity Benefit. A Med 6 is used if an accurate diagnosis was not given on another medical certificate e.g. a Med 3 or Med 5.

193: C
The Department of Health recommends screening those with previous low trauma fractures, a strong family history, steroids >7.5 mg a day, or women with a premature menopause who are unsure about taking HRT. There is no place for follow-up scans once treatment has been initiated.

Infectious diseases
194: C 195: F 196: G 197: I 198: B 199: E

Neonatal and antenatal chickenpox may be life threatening for the baby and neonatal chickenpox should be treated with aciclovir. In adults pneumonitis may be particularly severe with a mortality of 1%. Slapped cheek syndrome is common in children. If contracted before 24 weeks in susceptible pregnant women, the fetus may suffer an aplastic crisis. Vaccination at 2, 3 and 4 months has virtually eliminated the threat of Haemophilus in children, but it may still be seen in unvaccinated patients. Recent outbreaks of TB in schools in areas with large migrant populations have reinforced the need to consider TB in patients with chronic cough. Orchitis is seen in approximately 20% of adult males with mumps, while lymphocytic meningitis is seen in about 5% patients with mumps parotitis. Pancreatitis is rarely severe and encephalitis is rare.

Statistics
200: D 201: K 202: C 203: H 204: F 205: A

A good example of confounding would be the suggestion that eating ice cream causes skin cancer. Clearly the association between these two is due to the fact that in sunny climes people eat ice cream and sunbathe. By convention, a result is deemed significant if the P value is less than 0.05 i.e. a 1:20 chance of the result occurring by chance. The NNT $=1/$ARR and gives a clinical perspective on statistical results, i.e. how many of my patients would I have to treat with this new drug to prevent one event.

Index

abdominal pain 122, 219
Access to Health Records Act 71, 103, 194, 209
Access to Medical Reports Act 39, 103, 178, 209
accidents 37, 68, 100, 177, 192, 207
ACE inhibitors 100, 107, 206, 211
Achilles tendon injuries 135, 224
Addison's disease 76, 197
adolescence 106, 165, 211
    see also puberty
agitation, in elderly people 127, 221
agoraphobia 71, 194
air travel 44, 181
alcohol
    abuse/dependency 7, 50, 132, 163, 185, 222
    potentiation of effects 62, 189
    use in UK 69, 192
    withdrawal syndrome 71, 194
allergic conjunctivitis 129, 222
Alzheimer's disease 8, 49, 164, 185
anaemia 26, 174
antenatal care see maternity medical services
antibiotics 113, 170, 215
anxiety 75, 117, 197, 217
appendicitis 73, 195
asbestos exposure 135, 224
aspirin 146, 230
asthma 37, 63, 88, 190, 202
atrial fibrillation 45, 182
audit 77, 197–198

back pain 15, 79, 154–155, 168, 199, 235
basal cell carcinoma 9, 165
behaviour, disturbed 10, 165
Bell's palsy 40, 179
benefits 22, 56, 86, 104, 141, 172–173, 188, 202, 209, 228

benzodiazepines, dependence 140, 227
bereavement 18, 51, 99, 120, 171, 206, 218
bladder, carcinoma 12, 166
blindness see vision, loss/impairment
bone density scan 158, 236
bowel disorders 155, 235
    see also diarrhoea; irritable bowel syndrome
breast
    cancer 39, 74, 178, 196
    lumps 45, 182
    pain 10, 165
breastfeeding 13, 66, 168, 190–191
breath-holding attack 7, 163
bronchiolitis 47, 184
bronchitis 5, 162
bronchus, carcinoma 135, 224
bulimia nervosa 105

cancer/carcinoma
    bladder 12, 166
    breast 39, 74, 178, 196
    bronchus 135, 224
    cervix 43, 100, 181, 207
    colorectal 18, 73, 171, 195
    oesophagus 136, 225
    ovarian 15, 169
    skin 9, 165
    types 124, 219
carbon monoxide poisoning 147, 231
cardiac see heart
carpal tunnel syndrome 102, 179, 208–209
cataract surgery 107, 211
cerebral haemorrhage vs cerebral infarct 12, 166–167
cerebral palsy 112, 214
certificates, issuing 158, 236
cervical cancer 43, 100, 181, 207

cervical smears 132, 140, 223, 227
chest infection, elderly patients 11, 166
chest pain 82, 200–201
childbirth 80, 200
    see also maternity medical services
children
    accidents 100, 192, 207
    breath-holding attack 7, 163
    cough 6, 162
    development 21, 56–57, 77, 80, 84,
        115–116, 152, 172, 188, 197,
        200, 201, 216, 234
    diarrhoea 86, 140, 202, 227
    eczema 97
    heart problems 135, 224
    hip pain 145, 230
    immunisations 102, 208
    leukaemia 73, 195
    patent ductus arteriosus 81
    physical abuse 147, 231
    pulled elbow 68, 191
    sleep problems 42, 180
    small for gestational age 36, 176
    surveillance in general practice 47,
        183
    treating 99, 206
    urinary tract infections 103, 117,
        209, 217
    vaccination 174
Children Act 1989 99, 101, 208
chlamydia 78, 150, 199, 233
cholesterol 99, 150, 153, 206, 232, 234
chondromalacia patellae 107, 212
chronic obstructive pulmonary disease
    (COPD) 1–4
circumcision 5, 162
cirrhosis 7, 163
colon, cancer 18, 73, 171, 195
community hospitals 135, 224
complementary therapies 115,
    215–216
confounding 237
confusion, in elderly patients 166
consultation, theoretical model 127,
    221
contraception/contraceptives

diaphragm 142, 228
    emergency 11
    oral 76, 197
    progestogen-only 120, 218
corneal ulcers 78, 199
coronary artery bypass grafting 69, 192
coronary heart disease, studies 53, 187
corticosteroids, inhaled 103, 209
cough 6, 162
cramps, nocturnal 79, 199
cryotherapy 97, 205
cystic fibrosis 102, 208

Data Protection Act 103, 209
decongestants, oral 147, 231
dementia 49, 78, 185, 198
    see also Alzheimer's disease
depressive illness 10, 42, 51, 106, 119,
    165, 180, 185, 186, 210, 217
dermatitis 140, 227
    see also skin conditions
dermatofibroma 151, 234
dermatology see skin conditions
diabetes
    diagnosis 127, 150, 221, 233
    high-risk groups 45, 182
    non-insulin dependent 23,
        173
    in pregnancy 145, 229–230
diabetic retinopathy 16, 74, 196
diarrhoea 86, 133, 140, 182, 202, 223,
    227
diphtheria, pertussis and tetanus (DTP),
    combined vaccine 25
dithranol 8, 164
diverticular disease 137, 225
dog ownership 114, 215
double vision 107, 211
Downs' syndrome 42, 148, 180, 232
driving 50, 71, 129, 185, 194, 222
drugs
    absorption 112, 214
    abuse/misuse 38, 108, 177, 187, 212
    eruptions 71, 194
    first-pass metabolism 72, 195
    interactions 49, 136, 185, 225

Misuse of Drugs Regulations 55
nebuliser delivery 148, 232
ototoxicity 68, 192
teratogenicity 94, 204
ductus arteriosus, patent 81, 200
Dupuytren's contracture 17, 170
dyspepsia 24, 37, 43, 173, 177, 181
dyspnoea 139

ear
    lesions 58, 62, 188, 189
    pain 138, 226
eardrum, perforated 43, 181
eating disorders 5, 162
ECGs 126, 157, 173, 220, 236
eczema 97, 205
    see also skin conditions
elbow, pulled 68, 191
elderly people
    accidents 37, 177
    agitation 127, 221
    chest infection 11, 166
    confusion 166
    heart disease 72, 194
    subarachnoid haemorrhage 7, 163
    weight loss 121, 218
employment rights 39, 178
endometriosis 101, 208
epididymitis 138, 226
epilepsy 52, 133, 187, 223
episiotomy 51, 186
erythema multiforme 146, 230
erythema nodosum 115, 216
erythrocyte sedimentation rate (ESR),
    high 101, 207–208, 212
expenses, reimbursement 38
eye drops 144, 229
eye problems 49, 90, 111, 121, 134,
    139, 184, 203, 213, 218, 222,
    225, 227

facial palsy 107, 211
    see also Bell's palsy
faecal occult blood testing 16, 169
febrile convulsions 19, 143, 171, 229
feet

flat (pes planus) 43, 181
    skin lesions 136
fibrinolytic drugs 83, 201
folic acid 99, 206

gastric/duodenal ulcers 12, 166
gastro-oesophageal reflux 91, 203
gastrointestinal bleeding 49, 185
gastrointestinal infections 77, 198
general practice
    allied bodies 67, 191
    associated professions 55
    child surveillance 47, 183
    literature 4–5, 11, 44, 110, 111, 153,
        161, 182, 214, 234
    quality of care 33–36
    research 104, 210
    staff employment rights 39, 178
    types of studies 48, 184
general practitioners
    income, fees and allowances 38, 84,
        151, 178, 201, 222, 233
    legislation relating to 103
    reimbursement of expenses 38, 177
    responsibilities 12, 167
    treatment of children 99, 206
genital herpes 5, 162
Gilbert's syndrome 8, 164
glaucoma 12, 167
glue ear 24, 174
gout 49, 184
Graves' disease 9, 164
Guillain–Barré syndrome 145, 229

haemorrhagic disease of the newborn
    112, 214
hair loss 15, 149, 168–169, 232
hand, foot and mouth disease 44, 182
hands, rash 90, 203
head lice 100, 207
headache 36, 83, 176, 201
health visitors 108, 212
hearing loss 1, 161
heart disease 24, 53, 72, 83, 99, 173,
    187, 194, 201
heart failure 72, 195

heart murmurs 135, 224
heart problems 123, 219
heartsink patients 17, 170
hepatitis 8, 164
hepatitis B vaccine 133, 223
herpes simplex 78, 199
HGV drivers 129, 222
hip
    congenital dislocation 17, 170
    pain 145, 230
HIV/AIDS 138, 226
hormone replacement therapy 67, 191
hydrocephalus 39, 178
hypercalcaemia 80, 200
hypertension 6, 100, 119, 132, 156,
        163, 217, 222, 235
hypertensive retinopathy 101, 207
hyperthyroidism 9, 164
hypertriglyceridaemia 150, 233
hypertrophic cardiomyopathy 78, 198
hypotension 149, 232
hypothermia 106, 211
hysteroscopic endometrial ablation 135,
    224
immunisations 57, 102, 138, 188, 208,
    226
    see also vaccinations
impotence 73, 196
infectious diseases 18, 87, 146, 159,
        171, 202, 230, 236
infective endocarditis 119, 218
infertility 113, 147, 214, 231
influenza, vaccination 40, 179
inhaler devices 63, 190
iron supplements 106, 210
irritable bowel syndrome 45, 79, 149,
        182, 199, 233

jaundiced patients 8, 164
jet lag 39, 178

Kawasaki's disease 40, 179

laparoscopic cholecystectomy 109, 213
laser treatment 38, 58–61, 177
leg ulcers 33, 98, 176, 205

leukaemia, childhood 73, 195
lipid-lowering drugs 16, 17, 19,
        171–172
lipids, trials 50, 185
literature, general practice 4–5, 11, 44,
        111, 153, 161, 182, 214, 234
lithium carbonate 61, 189
liver function tests 8, 164
lymphadenopathy 139, 227

malaria 81, 200
massage 58–61
maternity medical services 40, 179
    antenatal care 45, 182
        home confinement 108, 212–213
    see also antenatal care
measles, mumps, rubella (MMR)
        vaccine 75, 196
medical research, studies 52, 186
Ménière's disease 136, 224
meningococcal meningitis 104, 210
Mental Health Act 20–21, 36, 46, 85,
        114, 137, 143, 172, 177, 183,
        201, 215, 226, 228
migraine 36
    see also headache
miscarriage 47, 108, 183, 212
Misuse of Drugs Regulations 55, 187
mouth, lesions 27, 94, 174, 204
multiple sclerosis 100, 206
myeloma 101, 107, 207–208, 212
myocardial infarction, drug treatment
        83, 201

nails, discoloured 120, 218
neck, swellings 58, 188
NHS and Community Care Act 103,
    209
nitrate tolerance 152, 234
normal distribution 25, 174
numbness 118, 217
oesophageal cancer 136, 225
ophthalmology see eye problems
opiate addiction see drug abuse
osteoarthritis 11, 166
osteoporosis 63, 158, 190, 236

otitis media 72, 195
ovarian cancer 15, 169
overseas travel 57, 81, 133, 188, 200, 223, 226
ovulation 91, 203

pacemakers 102, 208
pain 40, 137, 179, 225
paraesthenia 23, 118
paraesthesia 41, 173, 179–180, 217
Parkinson's disease 88, 202
periods 13, 48, 167, 184
    see also vaginal bleeding
pernicious anaemia 121, 219
phimosis 5, 162
pneumonia 68, 191
pneumothorax, spontaneous 8, 164
polyarthritis 116, 216–217
polycystic ovary syndrome 97, 205
polycythaemia 47, 117, 183, 216
pompholyx 15, 169, 225
post-traumatic stress disorder 134, 223
post-viral fatigue syndrome 69, 193
practice leaflets 4, 161
pre-eclampsia 109, 213
pregnancy
    chronic diseases 143, 229
    diabetes 145, 229–230
    ectopic 15, 169
    genital herpes 5, 162
    iron supplements 106, 210
    pulmonary embolism 72, 195
    pyelonephritis 77, 198
    second trimester 33, 176
premenstrual syndrome 147, 231
prescribing/prescriptions 54, 57, 113, 151, 187, 188, 215, 234
prolactin, raised 68, 192
prostate problems 145, 230
proton pump inhibitors 147, 230
pseudomembranous colitis 16, 170
psoriasis 8, 133, 164, 171, 223
psoriatic arthropathy 17, 171
psychological problems 112, 214
psychosis, puerperal 77, 198

puberty, delay 13, 167
pulmonary embolism 72, 195
pulmonary fibrosis 38, 177

questionnaire design 7, 163

'Red Book' 128, 222
restless legs 77, 197
Reyes' syndrome 127, 221
rheumatoid arthritis 42, 90, 136, 180, 203, 225
risk reduction 99, 206
rubella 110, 213
    see also infectious diseases

scabies 71, 193
schizophrenia 10, 69, 78, 165, 193, 199
screening
    asthma 37
    breast cancer 74, 196
    criteria 1, 16, 20, 161, 172
    statistics/terminology 26, 88, 110, 113, 142, 172, 174, 177, 202, 213, 215
scrotum, swelling 76, 197
seatbelts 106, 211
self-harm 46, 183
senile squalor syndrome (Diogenes' syndrome) 75, 196
serum alkaline phosphatase 108, 115, 212, 216
shiftwork 7, 163
shoulder, frozen 138, 226
sickle cell disease 17, 170–171
single gene traits 51, 186
sinusitis 110, 213
skin conditions 9, 89, 90, 125, 136, 165, 203, 218
sleep problems, children 42, 180
sleeping tablets 51, 186
smoking 69, 192
social class 20, 98, 172, 205
solvent abuse 11, 166
spleen, palpable 136, 225
squint 63, 75, 190, 196

statistics
  averages 134
  bias 14, 168
  data types 109, 213
  normal distribution 25, 174
  screening 26, 88, 110, 142, 174,
      177, 202, 213
  terminology 54, 87, 105, 140, 160,
      187, 202, 210, 223, 228
steroids, topical 48, 184
stress incontinence 91, 149, 203, 233
stroke 67, 70, 191, 193
studies/trials
  cholesterol reduction 99, 206
  coronary heart disease 53, 187
  diabetic retinopathy 196
  general practice 48
  hypertension 6, 119, 156, 163, 217,
      235
  intention to treat 153, 234
  statistics 140
  thrombolytics 85, 148, 201, 232
  types 14, 52, 128, 168, 184, 186,
      221
subarachnoid haemorrhage 7, 42, 163,
    180
sudden infant death syndrome (SIDS)
    70, 106, 193, 210
suicide risk 14, 168
summary completion questions
  acupuncture 58–61
  antidepressant drugs and generic
      counselling 63–66
  blood pressure control 95–97
  excess mortality in diabetes 129–131
  NT-proBNP in heart failure diagnosis
      91–93
  pulmonary rehabilitation in primary
      care 1–4

quality of care 33–36
specialist nurse intervention in heart
    failure 27–31
sun, exposure 113, 215
surgery, minor procedures 154, 235

tachycardia 123, 219
terminal care 40, 179
testes, undescended 49, 184
thrombolytic trials 85, 148, 201, 232
thyroid disease 123, 219
tinnitus 6, 162
torticollis 103, 209
trigeminal neuralgia 70, 193
tuberculosis 149, 232

urinary tract infections 103, 117, 209,
    217

vaccination 25, 40, 75, 133, 174, 179,
    196, 223
  see also immunisation
vaginal bleeding 69, 192
vaginitis 99, 206
varicose veins 143, 229
vision, loss/impairment 19, 47, 90, 101,
    172, 183, 207
visitors to the UK 13, 167
vitamin B12 deficiency 121, 219
vitamin K deficiency 112, 214
voluntary bodies 144, 229
vomiting 76, 143, 197, 228

warts 41, 179
weakness 23, 173
weight, loss 43, 121, 181, 218
Wilson's criteria 16, 161
Wood's light 100, 207

PASTEST REVISION BOOKS

Hot Topics for MRCGP and General Practitioners 3rd Edition
Louise Newson and Ash Patel   **1 904627 18 8**

- Keep informed of clinical and non-clinical issues in General Practice with 17 chapters of Hot Topics brought fully up-to-date in this third edition
- This book is structured around key subject areas for easy access to relevant information
- It is fully referenced to journals and recent studies, with useful email addresses
- Presented in punchy note form with paper summaries and easy to memorise lists
- Includes updates and new material on the National Service Framework for older people, The New Contract and expanded information on the Consultation

Practice Papers for the MRCGP Written Paper
R Daniels et al   **1 901198 16 2**

- Contains six Practice Papers each consisting of 12 questions for the Written Paper (Paper 1 Exam)
- Features MEQs, Current Awareness and Critical Appraisal type questions to be answered in 3.5 hours
- All question formats are present in the Practice Papers and include the reproduction of journal articles relating to certain questions
- Each question will be accompanied by a set of suggested answers

MRCGP Modular Approach: Second Edition
Louise Newson and John Sandars   **1 901198 91 X**

- Thoroughly revised and updated edition
- Written specifically for the modular exam format
- New Paper 2 section featuring EMQs, SBAs and MBAs, with answers and teaching notes
- Advice on the Consulting Skills video component
- New section on Membership by Assessment
- Written by a team of Royal College examiners and recent successful exam candidates
- Also relevant for candidates taking Summative Assessment

MRCGP: Multiple Choice Revision Book
P Ellis   **1 901198 55 3**

- Over 1500 multiple choice items in EMQ, SBA and MBA formats
- Answers and detailed teaching notes
- Subject-based book enables doctors to focus on specific subject areas
- Expert advice on successful examination technique
- Comprehensive revision index for easy reference to specific topics
- Invaluable intensive practice material for all MRCGP candidates